GASOLINEGATE

WHAT'S IN OUR GASOLINE IS KILLING US

BURL HAIGWOOD AND DOUG DURANTE

NEW DEGREE PRESS

COPYRIGHT © 2022 BURL HAIGWOOD AND DOUG DURANTE

All rights reserved.

GASOLINEGATE

What's in Our Gasoline Is Killing Us

ISBN 979-8-88926-692-1 *Paperback*
      979-8-88926-693-8 *Ebook*

Dedication

This book is dedicated to Bill Holmberg, the friend, mentor, and warrior we learned from and miss daily.

Bill Holmberg. *Photo by Anne Ruthling.*

This book is also dedicated to those who have passed but inspired us to write this story. They worked with us in the trenches for decades and played an essential role in the success of our movement.

Fred Potter, Former President, Information Resources, Inc.

Harry Griffiths, Former Chairman, Clean Fuels Development Coalition

Jim Glancey, Former Chairman, Clean Fuels Development Coalition

Jim Peeples, Former Legislative Director, Information Resources, Inc.

Dr. Max Shauck, Former Professor and Head of the Renewable Aviation Fuels Development Center, Baylor University

Orrie Swayze, Former Fighter Pilot and Ethanol Champion Extraordinaire

Dr. Roger Conway, Former Director, Office of Energy, US Department of Agriculture

Ron Sykes, Former Senior Washington Representative, General Motors Corporation

In gratitude and in memory of those buried in Arlington Cemetery's Section 60, whose life stories were cut short fighting to protect the world's access to crude oil.

Arlington Cemetery Section 60. *Photo by Burl Haigwood.*

A Special Thanks

We thank the subject matter experts who shared their time, insights, and expertise to help us tell this story.

The Honorable Thomas A. Daschle, Former US Senate Majority Leader and US Senator from South Dakota

The Honorable E. Benjamin Nelson, Former US Senator and Governor of Nebraska, Chair, Governors' Biofuels Coalition

The Honorable Boyden Gray, Former Counsel to President George H. W. Bush and Ambassador to the European Union

Ron C. Alverson, Former Farmer, Current Dakota Ethanol Company Board Member

Reid Detchon, Senior Advisor for Climate Solutions, United Nations Foundation, Former Executive Director of the Energy Future Coalition

William (Bill) Kovarik, PhD, Professor, Coauthor of *The Forbidden Fuel: A History of Power Alcohol*

David E. Hallberg, President, Dakota AG Energy, LLC, Founder and Former CEO, Renewable Fuels Association

Seth Harder, General Manager, Husker Ag

Robert Harris, Former Director Nebraska Energy Office and Bioenergy Coordinator, EERE, US Department of Energy

Jim Lane, Editor and Publisher, *The Daily Digest*

Philip Madson, President, KATZEN Associates

Reginald Modlin, Biofuels Consultant, Former Director of Regulatory Affairs, Chrysler Corporation

Plinio Nastari, President, DATAGRO Group & IBIO Brazilian Institute of Bioenergy & Bioeconomy

Edwin Rothschild, Former Public Affairs and Energy Director, Citizen Action

Loran Schmidt, Former State Senator, Nebraska

Jim Seurer, Chief Executive Officer, Glacial Lakes Energy, LLC

Ernie Shea, Founder, Natural Resource Solutions, LLC, Former Assistant Secretary of Agriculture, Maryland

Scott Sklar, President, The Stella Group, Ltd & Adjunct Professor; George Washington University, and Coauthor of *The Forbidden Fuel: A History of Power Alcohol*

Todd C. Sneller, Biofuels Consultant; Former Administrator, Nebraska Ethanol Board

Doug Sombke, President, South Dakota Farmers Union

Marc J. Rauch, Author, *The Ethanol Papers* and *Yes, Tin Lizzie Was an Alcoholic*, Co-Publisher The Auto Channel

Terry A. Ruse, Operations Manager, Benchmark Renewable Energy, Former Petroleum and Ethanol Marketer

David Vander Griend, President and CEO, ICM, Inc.

Steve Vander Griend, Former Technical Director, Urban Air Initiative

Eric Washburn, Former Legislative Director, Senator Tom Daschle

Carol Werner, Director Emerita, Environmental & Energy Study Institute

Contents

FOREWORD — 15
AUTHORS' NOTES — 21
    Burl Haigwood — 21
    Doug Durante — 27

PART 1 — 35

CHAPTER 1. A HISTORY OF ILLUSION AND COLLUSION — 37
The Evolution of Our Benzene Revolution

CHAPTER 2. THE TRUE COST OF GASOLINE — 55
Consumers Pay the Ultimate Price

CHAPTER 3. THE ANTI-ETHANOL WAR — 71
Duped, Hoodwinked, Bamboozled—Gaslit

CHAPTER 4. TALES FROM THE BATTLEFIELD — 91
The Fight for States' Cleaner Gasoline Rights

CHAPTER 5. ETHANOL MYTH BUSTERS — 107
Combating Disinformation Campaigns

PART 2 — 135

CHAPTER 6. A SACRED OATH — 137
EPA Circumvents Energy and Environment Laws, Regulations, and Its Mission

CHAPTER 7. EPA'S ACTIONS OBSTRUCT ENVIRONMENTAL AND ALTERNATIVE ENERGY PROGRESS — 159
A History of Missed Opportunities, Noncompliance, and Creating Regulatory Hurdles

CHAPTER 8.	THE SMOKING GUN AND THE POISON SQUAD	179
	We Are What We Eat	
CHAPTER 9.	2018–2021: IT'S DÉJÀ VU ALL OVER AGAIN	193
	Should'a, Could'a, Would'a, Ought'a, and Didn't	
CHAPTER 10.	ENVIRONMENTAL JUSTICE	201
	Death by Breath	
CHAPTER 11.	ENVIRONMENTAL INJUSTICE	213
	Can We Get an Amen?	
CHAPTER 12.	THE PEOPLE VERSUS BIG OIL, CONGRESS, AND EPA	227
	Preserving Power and Wealth at Any Cost	

PART 3		**249**
CHAPTER 13.	REALITY EV	251
	The Gaslight Is On, but Nobody's Home	
CHAPTER 14.	MOVING FORWARD	275
	To Follow Suit	
CHAPTER 15.	MISSING IN ACTION	293
	Where Have All the Champions Gone?	
CHAPTER 16.	BACK TO THE FUEL FUTURE	315
	Now You Know What We Know	

AFTERWORD.	WHY I SAY YES TO RENEWABLE FUELS	335
	Jim Lane, Publisher, Biofuels	335

ACKNOWLEDGMENTS	345
APPENDIX	351

Foreword

BY CAROL WERNER
Director Emerita, Environmental and Energy Study Institute

Gasolinegate tells a story that involves geopolitics, national security, public health, the environment, food security, energy and transportation, economic development (power and profits), and now the existential threat of climate change that is urgently confronting our global societies today. Yes, these are all elements of the story of biofuels, especially ethanol and oil, and that story continues to unfold to this very day.

Burl Haigwood and Doug Durante have been my respected colleagues for more than thirty years. They are both steeped in history and the facts of this important issue. They are well-equipped to give readers a solid, factual understanding of the background of ethanol and other biofuels, why it is important, and why we should care, particularly if we want to protect public health for us *and* our children.

My interest in biofuels stems from my long tenure working on environmental and energy issues in the public interest and nonprofit world. It did not take long for me to understand that our use of fossil fuels and their presence in our everyday lives is the source of most of our environmental problems, including public health and environmental justice. I sought to instill in staff the lesson that so much in our world is inextricably intertwined. Therefore, it is extremely important to consider issues as part of systems and to understand their interconnections; otherwise, you can inadvertently create or exacerbate another problem. After all, failure to consider the whole results in important conflicts slipping through the cracks unsolved. Our environment bears the scars of such unsolved problems. The mantra we should learn is "do no harm."

A good example of the impact of unsustainable fuel sources is the auto industry. As fuel economy standards for automobiles and light trucks have increased, the auto industry has needed better fuels to help them achieve the standards. For example, improved engine efficiency requires higher-octane fuels to achieve those fuel economy goals. But where does that octane come from? Does it come from the oil industry's preferred choice of aromatics compounds comprised of the highly toxic, polluting, and greenhouse gas-intensive aromatic/BTEX compounds (benzene/toluene/xylene) or does it come from ethanol, a high-performing, clean, renewable source? Don't forget you can *drink* straight ethanol, but it has been denatured for commercial sale for blending with gasoline. In fact, ethanol is so nontoxic that should we experience an ethanol spill, we would not cause nearly the same amount of damage as we do with any oil spill. So why have we not been using it to its full potential?

The fossil fuel industry, especially the oil and gas industry, has long sought to exercise its enormous power to suppress the use of ethanol as a substitute for gasoline. They have invested billions of dollars and decades of time to relentless misinformation campaigns to sow doubt in the mind of the public about the potential of ethanol.

These campaigns have been very successful. A December 16, 2022, article in *The Washington Post* reported that, between 2008–2017, the American Petroleum Institute (API) spent $663 million on communications alone. That same article stated that in 2021, five large oil/gas companies—ExxonMobil, Shell, BP, Chevron, and Total Energies—spent a total of $750 million on communications (Farhi 2022). Think of the impact of seeing the same misinformation over and over, misinformation designed to sow doubt and to raise opposition toward renewable fuels, in this case, the Renewable Fuel Standard (RFS). The RFS is a federal law that requires transportation fuel sold in the United States to contain a minimum volume of renewable fuels. Regardless, the highly profitable petroleum industry still enjoys billions of dollars in annual public subsidies, as it has for more than a century. This continues even though we now know how dangerous the use of fossil fuels is to our health and to our air, water, land, and oceans.

Despite the facts, many in the environmental community have been influenced by these disingenuous efforts and have opposed the use of biofuels—especially ethanol—even as they talk about the imperative to transition away from fossil fuels. Why is this? The unfortunate truth is that a mythology has developed around topics such as food versus fuel, land-use change, and the emissions and carbon footprint of biofuels. Those who claim that growing corn, currently the predominant feedstock of ethanol, is displacing food production generally do not understand that when ethanol is produced in a biorefinery, one gets numerous products: From a corn kernel is produced not only vegetable oil but also high protein animal feed in addition to the starch that makes the fuel. The ethanol molecules can be used to produce a myriad of renewable chemical building blocks. This is very important as our society needs to wean itself away from its dependence on highly toxic and polluting petrochemical products, which we use with great abandon throughout our daily lives. Those products have brought us much of the ease of modern life, but we now know they are creating enormous waste and health problems, such as toxic air and water pollution, and produce many greenhouse emissions.

In the United States, the biggest issue threatening land-use change, which is the impact human activity has on shaping our environment, is development. Development brings carbon-intensive construction, including cement for buildings, roads, and other infrastructure, as well as greater use of transportation fuels to support sprawl. It is important to keep as much land as possible open for forestry, grasslands, and agriculture.

Another conflict in the ongoing competition between biofuels versus ethanol and gasoline versus oil is the use of old and inaccurate data. The oil industry and others, including the Environmental Protection Agency, have failed to use the most up-to-date data and analysis. Because crop yields have gotten better and better, inputs have decreased, and the biorefinery production process continues to become ever more efficient, the greenhouse emissions associated with the growth of the feedstock and the ethanol production process, called the carbon footprint, continues to get smaller and smaller. Ongoing improvement and sustainability practices need to be expressed through current and accurate data.

While policy actions are being taken and auto manufacturers are gradually becoming more committed to eventually fueling transportation solely by electricity, liquid fuels will remain a necessity during this transition. Much has yet to evolve, but as long as liquid fuels are a part of the picture, should we not choose the low-carbon, clean, renewable option? As our global societies make choices, it is incumbent that we also choose to stay informed, make our goals clear, understand the interconnections of the systems we depend upon, and do no harm.

ABOUT CAROL WERNER

Carol has fought for clean energy, environmental protection, and climate change for thirty-five years. As the Executive Director of the Energy and Environmental Institute for over twenty-one years, she organized hundreds of Congressional briefings and built numerous broad coalitions.

Carol serves on the boards of the National Center for Appropriate Technology, the National Association of State Energy Officials Institute, the Ukrainian/American Environmental Association, Morningside University (her alma mater), and the Advisory Board of Planet Forward at George Washington University.

Carol was the founder and long-time Steering Committee member of the Sustainable Energy Coalition and co-founder of the US Climate Action Network and the Surface Transportation Policy Project. She previously served on the Advisory Board of the President's Climate Action Project (PCAP), the steering committee for the peer review of the Department of Energy's Bioenergy R&D Program, the Environmental Advisory Committee of the Business Council for Sustainable Energy, the Policy Committee of the American Solar Energy Society, and the editorial board of *BioCycle Magazine*.

Authors' Notes

WHY US AND WHY NOW

BURL HAIGWOOD

Hardly a day goes by when the news does not cover a crisis about energy. The war in Ukraine, healthcare costs, climate change, the battle to create new jobs, and the goal to shine back on Middle America's growing Rust Belt are connected to the gasoline you use daily. And nearly every one of those days for forty-five years, I have thought about how cleaner fuels could positively impact each of those issues. Since 1979, I have had the great fortune to work on this crusade as a professional, volunteer, or advisor. The fight for alternative fuels ignites my entrepreneurial spirit, passion for advocacy, intellectual curiosity, and love for my country.

In 1985, I helped start Information Resources, Inc. (IRI). IRI was a publishing and consulting firm focused on alternative transportation fuels. While at IRI, I supported the start-up of the Renewable Fuels Association, the Clean Fuels Development Coalition, and the Clean Fuels Foundation. During that time, I also worked with the National Ethanol Vehicle Coalition and served as a member of the Sustainable Energy Coalition. Some previously written works include being coauthor of *Homegrown Defense: Biofuels & National*

Security, the *Fuel Ethanol Fact Book*, dozens of articles and white papers, including *What's in Your Gasoline Is Killing You* and *The True Cost of Oil*.

I created public education campaigns and special events like the Flex Fuel Vehicle Club of America and the Environmental Inaugural Ball. I also created special characters such as Hexxon Blowbull and Jack, the fuel test dummy you will meet in this book. If you search YouTube for "Gasolinegate," you will meet our friend Jack.

Writing *Gasolinegate* was our next right thing. I am grateful for meeting my coauthor, Doug Durante, who founded the Clean Fuels Development Coalition. Doug and I will introduce you to a host of champions who still share the same dedication, passion, enthusiasm, and unbridled commitment to help our country. This book is a shared story of hundreds of others we have collaborated with over the past several decades. You can find their names in the acknowledgments section.

For me, it all started in the summer of 1972. My father and I occasionally skipped church when my mother declared she wasn't going. We would go to his favorite pub for beer, orange soda, and peanut butter crackers. My father retired as a Senior Master Sergeant after twenty-two years in the Air Force and was a prisoner of war (POW) for three and a half years in Japan. He rarely talked about prison camp unless he'd had a few beers with his brother, who was also a POW at the same time.

This was the first time I tried to get him to talk about it. I asked, "What did you and your POW friends do for fun? Was it like the TV show *Hogan's Heroes*?" He looked a bit puzzled, frowned, and said no. I pressed him again. "You had to have done something fun."

He said, "We used to drink the fuel out of the Japanese trucks that brought supplies into the camp."

I gasped, "You can't drink gasoline! It will kill you!"

My father proceeded to tell the rest of his story.

In 1942, the US was the largest oil producer in the world. The US government threatened the Japanese with an oil embargo if they sided with Germany. Their response was to bomb Pearl Harbor. Without crude oil and refined petroleum products from the US, the Japanese had to save their limited aviation fuel and gasoline supplies for their war machine. They turned their sake makers into motor fuel producers to make up the difference. They increased the proof of the ethanol high enough to burn in vehicles. He said, "And that's why I'm here; I didn't drink gasoline. I drank high-proof sake, which turned hell into a little bit of fun for a brief moment or two."

A couple of years after we talked about his prison camp experience, the US suffered its first oil embargo in October 1973. Later the following year, I got my driver's license and my mom's second-hand car. Gasoline had gone from twenty-five cents to a dollar a gallon. The memory of what happened after an oil embargo weighed heavy on my mind. I had long hair, a faint mustache, and my older brother's hand-me-down bell-bottom jeans. Raised in an Air Force family and frequently experiencing life on a military base, I considered myself a country-loving, God-fearing patriot. I admit there were times when I was more afraid of war than God. As a child, I had nightmares about nuclear war and toxic orange skies from Ozone Alert days in Washington, DC. I would get chills reading the *Book of Revelation* about what I thought would be World War III in the Middle East over oil. It was clear to me that if we were willing to fight communism in Vietnam, we would fight for our jobs, low-interest rates to keep our homes, and the right to drive as fast and far as we wanted on any given Sunday.

I was driving home from college one Friday night during my freshman year. I was not thinking about how to chase my dreams; I was thinking about how to avoid my nightmares. While driving over the Chesapeake Bay Bridge, an idea came to me like Saul meeting the angel in the Bible. I saw the light. The country could take all the poop they were dumping in the Potomac River just upstream from our swimming area in Fort Washington, Maryland, and turn it into *ethanol*. Instead of buying bullets, boots, and bombs, the government could pay people a little money to convert their cars to run on the ethanol produced from the newly renovated poop plants. Surely if the Japanese could do this in 1943 and the United States figured out how to land on the moon in 1969, American ingenuity could end the oil crisis.

That night, I ran into the house yelling, "Dad, Dad, the president's gonna love me, the car companies are gonna love me, and the oil companies are gonna love me too. We don't have to go to war over oil in the Middle East. We can make booze out of poop and convert cars to run on high-proof alcohol just like the Japanese did when you were a POW."

My father looked puzzled and said, "I think we should have some ethanol and a talk." He told me, "The car and oil companies sit on each other's board of directors. One makes the fuel and the other burns it. They both spend lots of money getting the president and people in Congress elected. The public has no choice in what fuel they buy, and I can assure you those folks won't love you or help you."

I was devastated. I asked a few more questions, but the air in the room and hope in my heart rapidly escaped. I went to bed confused about the past and future.

At breakfast, my father could see the smile return and asked, "What do you think of your idea today?"

I said, "I am going to spend the rest of my life either proving you wrong or proving you right."

I started searching for the truth by working for a company selling ethanol to independent gasoline marketers. After the second oil embargo cut their supplies from refiners, they needed more fuel. I soon realized the free market was not so free, and my father was right. He told me, "If you can't get companies to do the right thing, go to Capitol Hill and make them."

The following year, I met Dave Hallberg. Dave left his job in the US Senate to start the Renewable Fuels Association. His goal was to unite companies interested in creating and protecting government incentives to produce and use fuel ethanol. I met Doug Durante a few years later when he started the Clean Fuels Development Coalition. He built a coalition of diverse like-minded companies that included ethanol producers, automakers, chemical companies, technology developers, and agriculture groups.

We knew the road ahead needed to be paved with bipartisan common ground. We would need to appeal to the most extensive base of constituents required to influence Congress. It worked, but the mission is only 10 percent complete. The nation is desperately looking for a cleaner-burning, lower-carbon, lower-cost, higher-octane, better performing, job-creating, food-producing, farmer-protecting, non-OPEC, non-terrorist funding, renewable, and safer fuel for cars. We believe we have found the answer, so we are compelled to do the next right thing and share our story.

I often remember my father saying, "Do the right thing, and the right things will happen." My father, Joseph Burleson Haigwood, died on January 20, 1985, and is buried in Arlington Cemetery, Section 60. In the same section in Arlington Cemetery rest too many soldiers who lost their lives fighting in the Middle East over oil.

My passion and compassion are refueled daily by:

- My family for never doubting me, especially my father, who shared his story, which gave me the idea and courage to challenge our leaders and try to change the status quo.
- My coauthor, Doug Durante, who, after four decades of working together, continues to return my emails and

share in my never-wavering passion for finding and defending the truth.
- All the families with loved ones buried near my father in Section 60. Their stories were cut short fighting wars in the Middle East to protect the supply of crude oil to the United States and its allies.
- The amazing cast of characters who supported our mission and shared our dream to build a better future for our children and country.

DOUG DURANTE

After four decades of working to have a positive impact on people's lives, the temptation to write a book and capture those decades in print is natural. But like many people who dream of being an author, I found a lot of reasons and excuses not to—until now.

The genesis of this book is a research project we launched several years ago after finally reaching our limit of frustration while watching the US Environmental Protection Agency, the petroleum industry, narrow-minded environmental special interests, and pseudo-academics doom us to a lifetime of oil dependence.

That research yielded a mountain of evidence that reveals decades-long failures to clean up our fuels and develop alternatives. You can draw your own conclusions as to who is to blame, but certainly, you will come away agreeing we should do better.

As a minor cog in the wheel, I am humbled and proud to have been part of something much bigger than me, and something I was just flat-out lucky to be part of. Growing up in the Washington, DC, suburbs so close you could throw a rock over the District line, the importance of government and specifically energy was ingrained in me. My dad was a nuclear engineer with Westinghouse, and the dinner table conversations often included tales of Washington energy policy and how important a stable energy sector is to our lives. We learned that importance firsthand in the 1970s with the first Iranian oil embargo that sent our day-to-day lives into a tailspin.

My senior year of college, I ran an elevator—yes, the old-fashioned crank wheel elevators—in the US Capitol and got to know some folks who helped me land my first job on Capitol Hill studying transportation policy. When the second oil embargo hit in the late 1970s, a great angst over the lack of developed alternative fuels and ethanol—the fuel Henry Ford originally designed his cars to run on—flooded Congress. The fact that it created new demand for US agricultural products when the farm economy was teetering was a bonus, giving ethanol the one-two punch of energy security and rural economic stimulus.

The environmental benefits of a cleaner burning fuel became more appreciated over time, giving ethanol quite an attractive résumé. As Congress struggled to capture these benefits, I was able to land a position on the National Transportation Policy Commission, where it became obvious that one could not set transportation policy without understanding what powered it. As ethanol continued to emerge as a possibility,

I was able to move to another Commission. This one was specifically charged with making recommendations on how we could develop an alcohol fuel policy. I eventually became the director of public affairs for the National Alcohol Fuels Commission and had the fortune to work with many members of Congress, including some of the biggest names in the Senate and the House. This gave me a chance to meet some of the true pioneers, like my first boss at the Fuels Commission, Mike Stratton, and Scott Sklar, who worked for several senators and was on the cutting edge of biofuels and solar. Dave Hallberg, who worked then for an Iowa Congressman, would go on to form the Renewable Fuels Association to ensure ethanol had a voice in the many policy debates that were taking place.

Then there were legendary guys like Bill Holmberg, Orrie Swayze, Al Mavis, the Vander Griend brothers, Raphael Katzen and Phil Madson, and others who were putting steel in the ground or working the grassroots while we were developing policies to open the market for ethanol.

That period during the run of the Alcohol Fuels Commission was nothing short of incredible. People did not like gasoline shortages. They did not like odd-even days to get gas or paying prices they had never seen before. A nationwide uproar occurred, and nowhere more so than in rural America. Corn prices dipped to two dollars and fifty cents per bushel, which was less than the cost of production. Turning that surplus feed corn into ethanol created *excitement* in farm country. This movement was spearheaded by the Tractorcade protests in 1978 and 1979 when farmers descended on Washington, DC, to demand the government open new markets for their grains, including ethanol. It was a flag-waving, all-American response to the realization the United States was, and still is, at the mercy of the Organization of the Petroleum Exporting Countries (OPEC, now OPEC+), and something needed to be done. The Commission participated in conferences, Congressional hearings, and briefings for all those interested parties across the US.

I later moved over to the Department Energy's Office of Alcohol Fuels, which further exposed me to talented people. That then led to working with a crew led by Fred Potter at Information Resources that included my coauthor, Burl Haigwood, and an incredible cast of characters who used Fred's offices on South Capitol Street as a landing spot that became ethanol central. With the support of Todd Sneller of the Nebraska Ethanol Board, after leaving the Department of Energy (DOE), we formed the Clean Fuels Development Coalition (CFDC) in an effort to broaden the appeal of ethanol.

Unlike the Renewable Fuels Association, which was a trade group for fuel ethanol producers, our vision was to create a bigger market and tent of stakeholders interested in finding common ground with the two partners ethanol needed to succeed: automakers and the petroleum industry.

It may seem inconsistent to write a book about the forty-year obstructionist efforts of the oil industry and say they were part of our movement in the early days. But the oil industry is not monolithic. Texaco owned one of the early ethanol plants and worked with us, as did Sunoco, which candidly told us they were fine with ethanol, they made money off it, and it was just one more of the thousand chemical compounds that make up gasoline. It was only in the later years when ethanol production increased to the point where it was displacing their product that many of them changed their positions. And even after turning against us, Texaco, for example, had no problem using American icon Bob Hope in televised commercials to say their gas was superior because it contained ethanol! (See "Chapter 5: Ethanol Myth Busters.")

The auto industry quickly realized they were the ones responsible for emission controls, and the cleaner the fuel was, the less they had to do on their end. We succeeded in getting General Motors, and later the others, to honor warrantees for the use of ethanol blends, thus slaying one of the dragons the oil companies used to demean ethanol. GM, Ford, and Chrysler were all dues-paying members of CFDC, something I remain proud of to this day.

Over the next twenty years, we worked on many energy and environmental legislative efforts at both the federal and state level. Every time there was a price hike or shortage that caused gasoline prices to go up, Congress and the public would wring their hands and lament that we did not have a hedge against OPEC. I recall going to New York after getting invited to speak before the United Nations Sustainability Council as they discussed a multination effort to develop biofuels. But the price of oil went down and the idea was abandoned.

But the turning point was the 1990 Clean Air Act Amendments (CAAA). In short, it created clean fuel requirements that opened the door for ethanol. During that period, many leaders in Congress took the time to study and understand these issues. Going back and rereading the Congressional Record and floor debates, these members had an incredible grasp of highly technical issues. The effort of a first-term senator from South Dakota named Tom Daschle, who would later rocket to the head of the class as majority leader, was the driving force to pull many of these senators together to pass key provisions. This was a formula established by Congress that the petroleum industry decried as "government gas" but was a proven recipe to reduce carbon monoxide in the winter and smog in the summer.

Keep in mind, this was back when the two parties worked together without the bitter polarization we see today. Democrat Daschle worked with Republican leader Bob Dole to get the provisions through, a scenario hard to envision today.

A decade later, Daschle worked with another heroic Republican, Richard Lugar of Indiana, to morph those programs into the Renewable Fuel Standard (RFS), which we were directly involved with and helped pass. That program has been incredibly successful despite constant attacks from the oil industry and less-than-helpful action by the US Environmental Protection Agency (EPA).

Throughout these past four decades, gasoline quality has improved some, but not nearly enough. EPA has always viewed ethanol as a glass half empty. They have dragged their heels or outright ignored opportunities and requirements to clean up gasoline, and the revolving door of EPA employees going to work for the oil industry has had a negative influence on EPA public policy.

We wrote this book to share our story and challenge readers to demand that our nation does better.

WHY NOW

The world will use trillions of gallons of gasoline while waiting for the electric vehicle market to develop. The US continues to look for a single answer instead of a balanced portfolio of energy sources that will benefit the public, agriculture sector, auto industry, and yes, the oil industry.

Like tobacco, the public needs to know the truth about the total societal impact of gasoline, especially on our children. For one hundred years, oil interests and their cronies have protected the market for gasoline at all costs, and the public pays the ultimate price (See "Chapter 2: The True Cost of Gasoline.")

Despite the failure of multiple administrations and more than a dozen Congressional sessions, we still have a chance to change our fuel future. An educated consumer and their courageous elected officials can create a bright fuel future (See "Chapter 16: Back to the Fuel Future.")

WHY YOU

We hope you are inspired to read this book because you refuse to be duped and are committed to doing the right thing. No single group, product, or silver bullet will be the solution. Like every significant positive change in our society, it will be up to each of us to do our part.

We will donate a portion of the proceeds from book sales to the William C. Holmberg Award Scholarship Fund, organizations that support Gulf War Veterans, and other organizations that championed the development of alternative transportation fuels.

PART 1

CHAPTER 1
A History of Illusion and Collusion

The Evolution of Our Benzene Revolution

Thursday, November 15, 1990, was an unseasonably warm sixty-seven degrees in Washington, DC, the kind of fall day that made you briefly forget about the winter months that were coming. It brightened the mood of an already upbeat group of guests filing into the East Room of the White House. Without long lines to check overcoats, people were seated quickly. Just moments after 3:00 p.m., President George Bush strode to the podium and welcomed a broad mix of administration officials, members of Congress, health and environmental organizations, and others.

The occasion? The signing of amendments to the Clean Air Act, the first time the nation's air quality problems had been addressed in more than twenty years. It was a day that should have ushered in a new era of environmental stewardship and cleaner air, and in some respects, it did. However, thirty two years later, it has fallen short of its full potential.

That a Republican president was in fact the driving force behind the legislation, having presented it to Congress the previous June, sounds like a tale from a galaxy far, far away. In fact, in dramatic contrast to the disconnected political world we live in today, the president genuinely acknowledged the Democrats in working with the opposing party and his Republican Administration. Everyone smiled and high-fived all around. The president summed it up when he said,

> *The result of this new Clean Air Act will be that cancer risk, respiratory disease, heart ailments, and reproductive disorders will be reduced; damage to lakes, streams, parks, crops, and forests will greatly be lessened; and visibility will be notably improved. As an added benefit, energy security will on balance be enhanced as utilities and automobiles switch to cleaner burning alternative fuels (C-SPAN 1990).*

At the heart of this legislation was Title II, the mobile source provisions that established those cleaner burning alternative fuels by defining a formula that had a proven track record in various state and local programs. Decried by the petroleum industry during a bitter period of lobbying acrimony, the formula required oxygenates, which are fuel additives that increase combustion and result in fewer tailpipe emissions. These oxygenates were alcohol based and represented, for the first time, a threat to the monopoly the oil industry had on the fuel market, and they didn't like it.

If grumpy faces had been in the audience that day at the White House, they would have belonged to oil executives, who had waged a bitter war against what they termed "government gas." They were roundly defeated, but at least for the purposes of appearance, liked to pretend they were all for it. It's the old joke where a fire and brimstone preacher is railing against Satan, and when a devil actually appears, he says, "I was really with you all along."

As the president noted, the energy security co-benefit of the legislation was a huge piece of the puzzle, and the clear and present danger of our thirst for crude oil meant we needed to use less.

According to the study "Public Health Impacts of Secondary Particulate Formation from Aromatic Hydrocarbons in Gasoline," published in *Environmental Health*, about 3,800 people likely die prematurely in the United States from aromatic hydrocarbons in gasoline at a total social cost of $28.2 billion in 2006 dollars (von Stackelberg 2013). The methodology in the study was endorsed by a US Environmental Protection Science Advisory Board Panel. Other studies have estimates as high as 130,000 premature deaths (Fann et al. 2012).

There is a lot of pain, sickness, disease, and cost on the journey to premature death.

ALTERNATIVE FUELS WERE NOT REALLY ALTERNATIVES

The nation's love affair with the automobile started with clean-burning renewable fuels. While political influence and misinformation allowed gasoline to quickly replace ethanol as the "chosen" fuel of the future, that would not have been the case had health impacts been even partially understood.

According to Jamie Kitman's *Motortrend* article, "The War Against Ethanol, Part II, A History of the Fuel,"

> In 1920, the *Scientific Journal* reported, "It is a universal assumption that [ethyl] alcohol in some form will be a constituent of the motor fuel of the future." In October 1921, less than two months before General Motors' research laboratory hatched the idea of adding lead to gasoline, Charles Kettering's deputy drove a high-compression Chevrolet from Dayton, Ohio, to a meeting of the Society of Automotive Engineers in Indianapolis, powered by a blend of 70 percent gasoline and 30 percent ethanol. It's equally ironic and sad given Charles Kettering has long been dubbed as the inventor of tetraethyl lead as a gasoline additive. In the beginning, we were told we urgently needed to save fuel, and our corporate leaders told us untruthfully, as it turned out, that lead was the only way. (Kitman 2016).

At that same time, nine million vehicles powered by gasoline were on the road, and service stations selling gasoline were opening around the country. In 1925, Henry Ford's Model T could burn any combination of gasoline and alcohol, but the world clearly did not pan out according to his vision (US Department of Energy 2021).

In the mid-1920s, a coalition of scientists, farm leaders, and industrialists started promoting a "carbohydrate economy," which means rural America could produce the food, feed, and fuel urban cities would need as they experienced explosive growth.

In 1926, the *Dearborn Independent* published the article "Farming Must Become a Chemical Industry" by William Hale. Hale was a renowned organic chemist and husband of the daughter of the founder of Dow Chemical. Hale stated, "The prohibition plague set this country back fourteen years in organic technical progress; it is absolutely impossible for us to advance in organic chemical operations without low-priced basic organic compounds such as alcohol" (Morris 1992).

In our interview with Marc Rauch, author of *The Ethanol Papers*, he told us, "By then, ethanol was blended into gasoline in nearly every industrialized nation. The world was no longer flat, and ethanol was the fuel of the future. What happened? Opposition to alternative fuels almost always stems from the oil industry, the controlling caste of the global energy world. The reason, needless to say, is financial" (Rauch 2017).

All warfare is based on deception.
—SUN TZU, *The Art of War* (TZU 2010).

THEN THE NATION "NEEDED" PROHIBITION AND GASOLINE

During our interview with Professor Bill Kovarik, who is regarded throughout the ethanol industry as a respected author and historian, we learned that while many people believe John D. Rockefeller and Standard Oil used Prohibition of alcohol beverages (1920–1932) to sidetrack ethanol fuel, the reality was complicated. Many agrarian leaders like Henry Ford agreed with Rockefeller about the social benefits of Prohibition and wanted to turn breweries into fuel factories. However, many auto and oil company executives disliked Prohibition and worked to overturn it.

Kovarik explained that marketing ethanol fuel was nearly impossible during Prohibition in the 1920s, but Prohibition was a broad social movement and not just a competition over fuel markets. While Prohibition was supposed to free up alcohol for fuel as Ford hoped, it in fact created a bitter national debate over the illegal diversion of industrial alcohol, which is rendered undrinkable by adding "denaturants," many of which were quite poisonous. In 1925, some 4,154 people died after having consumed this deadly alcohol. There was also concern in the 1920s about using benzene in gasoline with or without lead. Professor Kovarik told us:

> "The market for alcohol fuel began to disappear around 1923 when the oil industry stopped buying *Alcogas* from US Industrial Alcohol (USIA) of Baltimore, Maryland and turned to lead additives for blending with gasoline. USIA was a company that pioneered anhydrous blending and university-level fuel research. In 1927, the Rockefellers staged a hostile takeover and renamed the company US Industrial Chemical. By then, the idea that a new kind of fuel could compete against the oil industry was long forgotten.

Unfortunately for millions of people in the US and billions worldwide, John D. Rockefeller's competitive desire allowed him to kill his competition and eventually his customers. While Mr. Rockefeller failed to keep his oil company monopoly, he did create a monopoly for gasoline which until the 1980s accounted for about 99 percent of motor fuel consumption."

By 1944, the US was producing about 600 million gallons of alcohol a year. About half was used for making synthetic rubber, and the rest was used for aviation, submarine fuels, and medicines. The federal rubber director, William Jeffers, declared at the time that without alcohol produced from grain, "the invasion of France could not have been accomplished at the time it was" (Morris 1992).

THEN GASOLINE NEEDED LEAD
Automakers were searching for a chemical that would reduce engine knock because their engines were growing bigger and needed more power. In 1921, automotive engineers working for General Motors discovered that tetraethyl lead provided octane to gasoline, preventing engine knock. While ethanol was also a known source of octane at the time, lead was the preferred choice because of its lower cost.

As cited prior, early in its use as a fuel additive, public health advocates raised concerns about the use of lead in gasoline. In 1924, fifteen refinery workers in New Jersey and Ohio died of suspected lead poisoning. As a result, the Surgeon General temporarily suspended the production of leaded gasoline and convened a panel to investigate the potential dangers of lead use in gasoline. While the panel found insufficient evidence of lead poisoning over a brief time period, the panel warned that longer exposure to lead could result in chronic degenerative diseases of a less obvious character.

Despite these warnings, the Surgeon General set a voluntary standard of lead content, which the refining industry successfully met for decades. It was not until the 1960s, following extensive health research, that the devastating health impacts of low-level lead exposure were established. Children's developing bodies are particularly sensitive to low-level, ambient exposures to lead. Negative health impacts of lead exposure in children include anemia, behavioral disorders, low IQ, reading and learning disabilities, and nerve damage. In adults, lead exposure is associated with hypertension and cardiovascular disease. Before the lead phaseout in gasoline, the total amount of lead used in gasoline was over 200,000 tons per year (Stolark 2016).

Deemed as low cost, lead was eventually demonized because the true cost was millions of lives lost worldwide that suffered from diseases and then died prematurely. Lead was out, but auto companies still needed a source of octane for their engines. As the health dangers of lead became undeniable, refiners needed to develop an alternative.

THEN GASOLINE NEEDED BENZENE TO REPLACE LEAD TO INCREASE OCTANE

Gasoline is a complex mixture of hundreds of complex hydrocarbons. Hydrocarbons include butane, pentane, isopentane, and aromatics. The aromatic portion of gasoline includes *benzene*, toluene/methyl*benzene*, m-xylene/1,3-dimethyl*benzene*, ethyl*benzene*, propyl *benzene*, and isopropyl *benzene*, commonly referred to as BTEX (Ophardt 2003). Note the *benzene* portion of the aromatic compounds are emphasized. Our emphasis is due to EPA historically focusing on restricting the benzene but not the total aromatic content of gasoline, which obviously leaves benzene. The aromatics in gasoline create benzene emissions either through evaporation or tailpipe emission. The terms aromatics and BTEX are interchangeable and therefore we connect them in the book as aromatics/BTEX.

EPA's Tier 3 regulations set the national standard for emissions and fuel. Mercedes Benz commented with regards to Tier 3 that "Octane is the single most important property of gasoline when determining engine design" (Mercedes Benz 2013). Octane is a challenge, but benzene is not the answer; it is the problem. Benzene is a Class A Category 1 proven carcinogen to humans (US Center for Disease Control 2022).

For the nontechnical folks, octane for gasoline is like the proof of booze.

Most gasoline stations carry three grades of gasoline based on octane ratings. In most cases Regular Unleaded 87 Octane (beer), Mid-Grade Unleaded 88 Octane (wine), and Premium Unleaded 91-93 Octane (liquor/grain alcohol). The booze comparison fits very well with our story. Gasoline refiners and retailers use fuel ethanol to increase the octane of gasoline. The ethanol is two-hundred-proof alcohol (contains no water) and denatured with gasoline immediately after production and before it is shipped.

Ethanol has an octane rating of 113. The Department of Energy states that "Higher octane fuels are often required or recommended for engines that use a higher compression ratio and supercharging or turbocharging to force more air into the engine. Increasing pressure in the cylinder allows an engine to extract more mechanical energy from a given air/fuel mixture but requires higher-octane fuel to keep the mixture from pre-detonating. In these engines, high-octane fuel will improve performance and fuel economy" (Minnesota Biofuels Association 2016).

You have likely noticed the higher the octane, the higher the price, much of which is pure profit to the oil industry.

For over a hundred years, automakers have searched for affordable, effective, and environmentally safe octane-boosting compounds. Today benzene-based "aromatics" and renewable ethanol are the only two commercially viable and legal contenders. About 20 to 30 percent of a gallon of gasoline contains toxic, carcinogenic aromatics/BTEX (Hallberg 2014).

If EPA standardized a higher-octane level for all gasoline, it would allow automakers to design engines with higher compression ratios, turbocharging, and downsizing/down speeding. The result would be increased vehicle efficiency—miles per gallon of gasoline consumed—and lower greenhouse gases and toxic pollution through decreased crude oil and petroleum product consumption. Reducing crude oil consumption lowers its price, and thus the price of almost every other product because all products need to be transported to market. As a bonus, it can reduce the cost of making cars compared to other technologies.

The media, Congress, public health advocates, and the public must not allow the history of tobacco and leaded gasoline to be repeated by not allowing unnecessarily high levels of aromatics/BTEX in gasoline.

EMISSIONS FROM GASOLINE

Understanding the pollution from burning gasoline in your car is like looking at a bowl of alphabet soup. It's a pool of toxic acronyms that make no sense to most people, including many of those advocating on your behalf.

Here are some elementary things to take into consideration as you read.

Air pollution is not equal. Some elements are more toxic and potent, or are smaller and travel further. There are stationary sources (e.g., electricity and manufacturing) and mobile sources (e.g., trains, planes, and automobiles). The amount is about even, depending on where you live, whether closer to a factory, utility plant, or road. The two primary culprits are ultrafine particulates (UFP) and particulate matter (PM).

Everyone has had an opportunity to get the message about cigarettes, marijuana, and asthma medicine. Like medicine in an inhaler or smoke from tobacco or marijuana, the drug is delivered into your lungs and bloodstream. Why would anyone think air pollution is any different? Lack of public education and awareness. Why has the government or environmental organizations not championed filling a noticeable gap? Just like when we learned about drugs as children, it's time to "Say No to BTEX."

The aromatics/BTEX in gasoline increase toxic carcinogenic emissions from vehicles and cause statistically significant increases in non-methane hydrocarbon (NMHC), particulate matter (PM), ultrafine particle matter (UFP), and black carbon emissions (Karavalakis 2015).

Low-carbon high-octane ethanol displaces the aromatics/BTEX content in gasoline. Therefore, ethanol reduces the need to add aromatics/BTEX by simple displacement or dilution. In this case, less aromatics is more ethanol. Adding ethanol to gasoline is like adding filet mignon to your hamburger. Except in this case, the replacement is less expensive, and we know it is better.

HOW MUCH BENZENE IS SAFE?
While there are different data points about how much benzene is in gasoline, there is consensus about the amount that is safe.

The consequence of phasing out lead was the increase of aromatics/BTEX in gasoline. The refining industry invested in producing aromatics/BTEX and other technologies to replace lead because they were compounds in the oil barrel. As a result, the volume of those compounds in gasoline increased from 22 to about 33 percent by 1990. The amount of aromatics/BTEX in premium was as high as 50 percent.

Because Congress was mandating cleaner gasoline through reformulated gasoline and other programs, the oil industry was forced to reduce the volume of aromatics/BTEX to between 25–28 percent. However, some health professionals question the safety of even these levels (Stolark 2016).

How could that be possible if the American Petroleum Institute (API) stated as early as 1948 that "it is generally considered that *the only absolutely safe concentration for benzene is zero*" (American Petroleum Institute 1948)?

The US National Institute of Health Center for Disease Control validated the zero threshold.

> "There is no safe exposure level to benzene; even tiny amounts can cause harm. The US Department of Health and Human Services (DHHS) classifies benzene as a human carcinogen. Long-term exposure to excessive levels of benzene in the air causes leukemia, a potentially fatal cancer of the blood-forming organs. In particular, acute myeloid leukemia or acute nonlymphocytic leukemia (AML & ANLL) is not disputed to be caused by benzene. IARC rated benzene as "known to be carcinogenic to humans" (Group 1). As benzene is ubiquitous in gasoline and hydrocarbon fuels are in use everywhere, human exposure to benzene is a global health problem. Benzene targets liver, kidney, lung, heart and the brain and can cause DNA strand breaks, chromosomal damage, etc. Left unquestioned, unconfronted and unregulated, aromatics will continue to contribute to birth defects, life-long illnesses, cancers, lung disease, heart disease, brain disorders—and the growing healthcare bill of individuals and federal and state governments" (US Center for Disease Control 2022).

The negative health impacts of aromatics have been understood for decades by many in the medical community. As far back as 1989, renowned physician Samuel Epstein penned an editorial in the *Los Angeles Times* with the headline "Health Requires We Replace Gasoline." Dr. Epstein notes in his article, "Gasoline is more dangerous than ever—benzene is formed by combustion of aromatic hydrocarbons even in benzene free gasoline." Dr. Epstein also notes high rates of leukemia, brain and other cancers in refinery workers and neighboring communities (Epstein 1989).

THE NATION NEEDS ETHANOL AGAIN

In 1978, the US government discovered fuel ethanol again. The Energy Policy Act of 1978 was the first federal legislative ethanol subsidy to support farmers and stimulate the rural economies. The legislation created a forty cents per gallon tax exemption, making ethanol cheaper than gasoline. By chance, it also helped refiners replace the high octane they needed after having lost lead. Ironically, the tax exemption flowed to the petroleum industry because they were the taxpayers. They got the financial and practical benefit in 1978, but they knew the smart move was to kill ethanol in the cradle before it began to truly take away market share. Consequently, in many ways against their own interests, the petroleum industry tried to repeal the tax exemption at every turn.

In 2005, Congress passed the Renewable Fuel Standard (RFS) as part of the Energy Policy Act of 2005 (EPAct). Congress created the RFS to reduce greenhouse gas emissions and expand the nation's renewable fuels sector while reducing reliance on imported oil (US Environmental Protection Agency 2022). The RFS required the US transportation fuel pool to contain a minimum volume of *renewable fuel* each year (P.L. 109-58; EPAct05). The RFS required the addition of five billion gallons of renewable fuel. The RFS does not specify ethanol or corn as a feedstock.

In 2007, the RFS was expanded by the Energy Independence and Security Act (P.L.110-140; EISA). Like the transition to unleaded, this was a significant change in motor fuel composition. The new standard would phase in the addition of thirty-six billion gallons by 2022. Congress gave EPA the statutory authority to determine the annual volume requirements after 2022 (Congressional Research Service 2022).

What ethanol detractors did not count on was the resiliency and innovation of the ethanol industry to constantly improve efficiencies to the point where it did not need a subsidy. Ethanol has been less expensive than gasoline ever since. Unlike oil and refined petroleum products from OPEC, fuel ethanol is made in America, creates jobs, supports agriculture, and most importantly, replaces benzene and the family of toxic, carcinogenic benzene derivatives—aromatics/BTEX.

Now that we have plenty of ethanol and are armed with a significantly better understanding of the health impacts, more of it should be in gasoline. So why isn't it?

The "ethanol blend wall" is a term used to describe the upper limit of ethanol that can be blended into US gasoline. This suggests higher blends are negative to performance. Thus far, the largest volume being met under the RFS is for the implied conventional biofuel segment of the mandate, met mainly with corn starch ethanol blended into gasoline. Because of a variety of factors like automaker warranties and fueling station infrastructure, the percent of ethanol in gasoline is regulatory limited to 10 or 15 percent. With a relatively fixed supply of gasoline, the amount of ethanol that can be supplied this way is also limited (Congressional Research Service 2022).

TAKEAWAYS

- The revolution to get cheaper, faster-to-market, and safer fuel has been waged since the Henry Ford Model T, which could run on any combination of ethanol and gasoline. However, according to a 2022 Renewable Fuels Association analysis, Ford is the only company still producing FFVs and making them available for public purchase.

- Corporations without your best interest in mind replaced fuel ethanol with lead.

- It took over seventy years for public health and environmental protection revolutionaries to get the lead out of gasoline.

- Refiners needed octane and replaced lead with aromatics/ BTEX, swapping a poison with a toxic carcinogen.

- The first calvary of revolutionaries was joined by a new wave of national security, entrepreneurial, agricultural, and "Made in the USA" advocates. They worked together to legislatively stimulate ethanol production to force imported oil and aromatics/BTEX out of gasoline.

- Oil interests are not happy with ethanol's growing market share and have been trying to thwart its use ever since the 1920s.

WHAT'S NEXT
- Why is an ethanol blend wall obstructing the growth of fuel ethanol?

- Chapters 2, 3, 4, and 5 will help you form your opinion about gasoline, aromatics/BTEX, and fuel ethanol. We will help you understand:
  - the true cost of your gasoline,
  - what the oil industry and its advocates have done to obstruct the growth of fuel ethanol, and
  - how to combat disinformation campaigns by understanding the myths used to drive fear and doubt into the public's minds.

CHAPTER 2

The True Cost of Gasoline

Consumers Pay the Ultimate Price

The price of gasoline at the pump, as troubling as it is, does not reflect its real and total cost. When including the total societal impact (TSI) costs of gasoline, you are already paying over fifteen dollars per gallon (National Defense Council Foundation 2003). That cost is hidden in your taxes, road fees, and federal subsidies for fossil fuels. Filling your car with twenty gallons of gasoline would be like paying a $300 toll to leave the gas station. The good news is because of biofuels, you are already beginning to pay less.

TSI costs are now part of conventional discussion and are calculated into many products. TSI is often used to evaluate a company's impact on climate change. You can easily find additional examples with a Google search.

TSI is like *the total cost of ownership*. For example:

- The showroom sticker price on a car when compared to how much is paid over the life of the loan. Like TSI, the total cost of ownership includes tags, title, insurance, maintenance, and refueling.

- The listing price on a house is much higher compared to the total cost. We all understand the added costs of realtor fees, insurance, utilities, and maintenance.

- Cigarettes have a similar TSI cost when compared to gasoline. Tobacco companies eventually paid the TSI of their customer's cigarettes when some states sued. The tobacco companies paid back to the states the cost of health care for a tobacco smoker's premature death. As a result, everyone pays more taxes and higher healthcare premiums.

- TSI applies to the ultimate price German automaker Volkswagen AG paid for their Dieselgate scandal. In two related settlements, both with the United States and the state of California and with the US Federal Trade Commission (FTC), Volkswagen AG and related entities agreed to spend up to $14.7 billion after being found guilty of cheating emissions tests and deceiving customers. The companies will spend $4.7 billion to mitigate the pollution from these cars and invest in green vehicle technologies (Department of Justice 2016).

Gasoline's total cost of ownership and TSI must include the direct and indirect cost of public and private health care from air pollution—like tobacco smoke—climate change, national defense spending to protect oil supplies from the Middle East, and government subsidies for fossil fuels.

As noted in the following studies, when the US and other countries subsidize fossil fuels, they provide corporate welfare that protects markets and makes investing in or using alternative fuels less attractive. That is why OPEC drops the price of oil every time the US starts investing in alternative fuels or moves toward policies to reduce climate change or pollution. During our interview with Terry Ruse, a veteran of the ethanol industry who has done everything from marketing fuel ethanol to developing and managing production facilities, he said, "The investment bankers hate the fact there is no true free market or natural control over the price of oil. For example, when the price of oil goes up, gasoline increases with it, so there is no risk to the oil company."

Consumers are held hostage to gasoline's monopoly. This monopoly is a double-edged economic sword. One edge cuts into your wallet with added costs related to pollution, health care, defense, and federal subsidies. The other edge cuts into lost economic opportunity, like the loss of new jobs driven by new technologies (see "Chapter 16: Back to the Fuel Future").

Consider the growing consensus that the TSI cost of gasoline is higher than what appears on the pump. The naysayers and professional gaslighters representing oil interests can argue over the math and support the multitude of studies in the examples cited below. Still, in the end, it all comes down to dollars and common sense.

The current international consensus is that air pollution is expensive. How expensive? We consider death or premature death "the ultimate price." So where does this deadly air pollution come from? Depending on where you live, about 50 percent of air pollution comes from stationary sources such as power plants and manufacturing. The other 50 percent comes from mobile sources, which are primarily transportation fuels (US Department of Justice 2022).

With regards to transportation, light-duty vehicles—including passenger cars and light-duty trucks—are by far the largest contributors of greenhouse gases (GHG) at 57 percent. Medium and heavy-duty trucks are second at 26 percent (US Environmental Protection Agency 2022). It is easy math. Even if you cut global air pollution in half, the numbers are still huge.

Therefore, mobile source pollution, Mobile Source Air Toxics (MSAT), and aromatic/BTEX are synonymous because the benzene emissions from these components are equally toxic and carcinogenic. We explain these relationships and health impacts in more detail in "Chapter 6: A Sacred Oath." Please keep these simple definitions in mind to give context to the alarming statistics below and other references in *Gasolinegate*.

CALCULATING GASOLINE'S TOTAL SOCIETAL IMPACT

The following three studies exemplify the TSI consensus.

According to a press release by the Natural Resources Defense Council, a report commissioned by the United Nations Environment Program, poisoning from leaded gasoline was one of the world's most serious environmental health problems. Gasoline was responsible for 90 percent or more of human lead exposure. The report estimates the benefits of the global elimination of leaded gasoline at over 1.2 million premature deaths avoided per year, of which 125,000 would have been children. The global economic benefit of eliminating lead in gasoline is $2.45 trillion annually (Natural Resources Defense Council 2011). We grew up thinking the problem was from lead paint. The rule was simple: don't eat paint. Peter Lehner, executive director of NRDC, stated,

> "But today's announcement marks the triumph in one battle, not the entire war. We must continue the fight to make cleaner fuels available, and boost fuel efficiency around the world. And as we rid the world of one unnecessarily harmful fuel additive, we look to generate global momentum to clean up harmful diesel pollution that still shrouds many cities worldwide. NRDC will continue the fight for safer, cleaner fuels across the board and around the world (Natural Resources Defense Council 2011)."

The Center for Investigative Reporting estimates the TSI for gasoline at fifteen dollars per gallon and healthcare cost of $1.7 trillion. They produced a unique and informative video that follows the TSI path of a gallon of gasoline refined and consumed in California. The video explains energy use, pollution, and national defense-related costs associated with gasoline production and use (Clendaniel 2011). The video can be accessed in the citation in the appendix for this chapter.

According to their website, "The Fuel Freedom Foundation is a nonpartisan organization dedicated to ending US dependence on oil—and all the terrible trappings that come with it—by opening the market to cheaper, cleaner, American-made alternatives" (Taft 2017). The organization obviously understands and agrees with our assessment regarding the myriad of problems associated with reliance on crude oil and gasoline. Fuel Freedom Foundation's TSI estimate to determine the true cost of gasoline was six dollars and thirteen cents in 2017. The report cites that in 2017, the retail price of gasoline was two dollars and twenty-five cents per gallon. Part 3 of *Gasolinegate* describes how EPA has restricted the market for cheaper, cleaner, American-made alternatives that can partially replace gasoline and make it safer, which exacerbates the cost.

FOSSIL FUEL SUBSIDIES: BOMBS, BULLETS, OR BIOFUELS

We were honored to work with General Lee Butler, former Air Force, and James Woolsey, former CIA director, in their capacity as advisors to the Clean Fuels Foundation. Other notable military biofuels supporters include General Wesley Clark and National Security Advisor Bud McFarlane.

We captured many of the concerns of Lee Butler and James Woolsey when we wrote a chapter in *Homegrown Defense: Biofuels and National Security* titled "Is the War over Oil?" We found the quote below from General Butler to be very transparent and profound for its time, considering the United States would not invade Iraq for several more years.

> *The lure and the illusion of low gasoline prices have lulled us into placing our economic security in jeopardy, our military*

forces at risk and our leadership in question. —Former Strategic Air Command, General Lee Butler, Commander in Chief of the Strategic Air Command of the US Air Force. Former Chairman, Clean Fuels Foundation (Clean Fuels Development Coalition 2019).

Military support to protect Middle East oil started in World War II and continued to escalate beginning in the 1970s. October 19, 1973, right after President Nixon asked Congress for $2.2 billion in emergency aid to Israel for the Yom Kippur War, the Organization of Arab Petroleum Exporting Countries (OAPEC, then OPEC, and now referred to as OPEC+) enforced the first of two oil embargoes on the United States. The onset of the embargo contributed to an upward spiral in oil prices with global economic implications. The price of oil per barrel first doubled, then quadrupled, imposing skyrocketing costs on consumers and structural challenges to the stability of whole national economies (US Department of State 2022). The price of oil has an impact on the price of everything; even the air you breathe is no longer free.

Thirty years later, on October 30, 2003, Milton Copulos, president of the National Defense Council Foundation (NDCF), published "The Hidden Cost of Imported Oil." According to NDCF's report, the economic penalties of America's oil dependence totaled $297.2 to $304.9 billion annually. The report was one of the first to expose crude oil's "hidden costs" or TSI. Their data show the price of gasoline to be five dollars and twenty-eight cents, which equates to an extra one dollar and seventeen cents per gallon compared to retail prices (National Defense Council Foundation 2003).

This geopolitical nightmare came to fruition again in 2022 when Russia invaded Ukraine. World crude oil prices skyrocketed, and the US lost roughly 7 percent of its total oil supply that had been coming from Russia. The reduction in supply was about the same amount during the first oil embargo which resulted in the price of oil increasing by 300 percent.

The NDCF report was one of the first to account for the economic opportunity loss, the other side of the double-edged TSI sword. It listed:

- The loss of 828,400 jobs in the US economy.
- The loss of $159.9 billion in GNP annually.
- The loss of $13.4 billion in federal and state revenues annually.
- The periodic oil shocks over three decades were $2.2 trillion to almost $2.5 trillion from the US economy.

We explain the economic co-benefits of ethanol production in "Chapter 5: Ethanol Myth Busters."

The NFDC citation in the appendix provides links to Copulos's testimony before the Senate Committee on Foreign Relations and two related studies:

- International Center for Technology Assessment (CTA): The Real Price of Gas
- Oil Imports: An Overview and Update of Economic and Security Effects

James Woolsey summed up the nation's grave oil dependence predicament in his testimony before the Senate Finance Committee, April 19, 2007, while he was a member of the National Energy Commission on Energy Policy. At that time, Congress was considering changing the national gasoline standard to include a renewable fuel requirement (e.g., the RFS). It would be an injustice to paraphrase Woolsey's statement in his testimony.

> *But in the interests of our national security, our climate, and our pocketbooks, we should now move together as a nation—indeed as a community of oil importer nations—to destroy, not oil of course, but oil's strategic role in transportation as quickly and as thoroughly as possible. The national security reasons to destroy oil's strategic role are substantial. Over two-thirds of the world's proven reserves of conventional oil lie in the turbulent states of the Persian Gulf, as does much of the oil's international infrastructure.*
>
> *Increasing dependence on this part of the world for our transportation needs is subject to a wide range of perils. Just over a year ago, in response to bin Laden's many calls for attack on such infrastructure, al Qaeda attacked Abqaiq, the world's largest oil production facility, in northeastern Saudi Arabia. Had it succeeded in destroying, e.g., the sulfur-clearing towers there through which about two-thirds of Saudi crude passes—say with a simple mortar attack—it would have succeeded in driving the price of oil to over $100 per barrel for many months, perhaps close to bin Laden's goal of $200 per barrel. What we need is a transportation fuel that is as secure as possible, as clean as possible and as cheap as possible.*

Today, oil meets none of these needs (US Senate Committee on Finance 2007).

For another perspective on TSI, we suggest you visit Section 60 in Arlington Cemetery. You can pay your respects to thousands of heroes who paid the ultimate price by having their lives prematurely cut short fighting wars in the Middle East to protect the world's supplies of imported crude oil.

TSI HEALTHCARE COSTS

There are several studies that also exemplify the TSI of healthcare costs attributed to pollution.

Terry Tamminen, former secretary of the California Environmental Protection Agency and special advisor to California Governor Arnold Schwarzenegger, addressed the health effects and TSI costs in his book, *Lives Per Gallon: The True Cost of Our Addiction to Oil*. Tamminen cites data from The Institute for Transportation Studies at the University of California at Davis that places the minimum external cost of air pollution from motor vehicles in the US at $24.3 billion each year. "That alone is a healthcare tax of seventeen cents more per gallon" (Tamminen 2008). Please note US Congress has not been able to raise the gasoline tax in decades.

Loren Cobb authored an insightful article "Oil Addiction, the External Costs of Petroleum Use" published in the *Quaker Economist* in 2006. According to Cobb, "Health costs of air pollution from petroleum use is $300 billion per year. Government spending on roadway construction, maintenance, and research: $75 billion per year." Cobb noted these are taxpayer costs not including fuel taxes, tolls, and registration fees. Net economic impact of petroleum-related global warming, excluding discounted future effects, is $25 billion per year (Cobb 2006).

The costs associated with gasoline use are as pervasive as the emissions they produce.

People who escape becoming ill directly from the effects of gasoline-related emissions will still have to pay for the ones who were not so lucky. Healthcare costs are a burden across the populace, and with increasing science and medical data supporting their linkage to gasoline, it is only going to get worse if EPA does not act.

This point is reinforced in Alan Lockwood's *Atlantic Journal* article, "How the Clean Air Act Has Saved $22 Trillion in Health-Care Costs" when he reported, "According to data cited by the Council of Economic Advisors in 2009, 18 percent of Americans under the age of sixty-five are Medicare or Medicaid beneficiaries (i.e., poverty line) or received health care from the military. About 16 percent are not insured, and the rest are self-paying healthcare plans or their employers are paying for the plan as part of a benefit (Lockwood 2012).

These external costs have consensus internationally.

- According to the World Health Organization, the annual economic cost of premature deaths from air pollution across the countries of the WHO European Region was US $1.431 trillion (World Health Organization Report 2015).

- In 2015, the International Monetary Fund (IMF) estimates US federal subsidies for fossil fuels at $500 billion. Eliminating global energy subsidies could reduce deaths related to fossil-fuel emissions by over 50 percent and fossil-fuel related carbon emissions by over 20 percent and increase revenue by US $2.9 trillion (International Monetary Fund 2015).

- In 2016, Laura Tuck, the World Bank's vice president for Sustainable Development, stated, "Air pollution is a challenge that threatens basic human welfare, damages natural and physical capital, and constrains economic growth. We hope this study will translate the cost of premature deaths into an economic language that resonates with policy makers so that more resources will be devoted to improving air quality. By supporting healthier cities and investments in cleaner sources of energy, we can reduce dangerous emissions, slow climate change, and most importantly save lives" (The World Bank 2016).

Regardless of insurance plan or age, we all pay some percentage more for our healthcare premiums because of air pollution. We pay for the same reason several state attorney generals sued tobacco companies and received $260 billion in settlement of the lawsuit (see "Chapter 14: Moving Forward").

TSI COSTS VERSUS SAVINGS FROM CLEANER FUEL AND REDUCED POLLUTION

In 2007, the US Office of Management and Budget (OMB) reported the benefits and costs of all federal regulations to Congress. The largest benefit was because of a reduction in air pollution from a single air pollutant, also called fine particulate matter, or PM. The benefits were between $18.8 billion and $167.4 billion per year, compared to a previous cost of $7.3 billion per year (US Office of Management and Budget 2007). The Harvard team calculated estimated EPA savings into a return on investment at twenty-five to one. That return on investment should also translate into the government, and hopefully you too, investing into cleaner gasoline with less aromatics/BTEX.

According to EPA's 2011 report to Congress, "Benefits and Costs of the Clean Air Act 1990–2020 (CAA), the Second Prospective Study," the agency predicted by 2020, the legislation would avoid 230,000 premature deaths among adults thirty and older *annually*. The report states, "EPA's estimated cost of meeting the CAA air quality standards $65 billion for the period 1990 to 2020 and the benefits at $2 trillion" (US Environmental Protection Agency 2011). As we wrote this book in 2022, we are included in EPA's estimated avoided premature deaths. We hope in each year to come that you and your family are too.

In its 2013 "Cost Benefit Analysis" report to Congress, EPA states, "Efforts to reduce air pollution from transportation have proven to be cost effective. For every dollar spent on programs to reduce emissions from mobile sources results in the American people receiving nine dollars of benefits to public health, the environment, productivity, and consumer savings" (US Environmental Protection Agency 2011).

Jerry Useem's February 3, 2003, article in *Fortune Magazine* sums up the TSI cost of oil when he documented a prediction by OPEC co-founder Juan Pablo Perez Alfonzo in the 1970s. Mr. Alfonso stated, "Oil will bring us ruin... it's the devil's excrement" (Useem 2003).

MORE ETHANOL REDUCES THE PRICE OF GASOLINE

Here is the good news about the true cost of your gasoline: Adding ethanol makes the price go down. Several studies have been conducted to validate what we think should be a simple supply and demand equation driven by common sense.

According to a 2008 study conducted by McKinsey and Company for the DOE National Renewable Energy Laboratory, adding ethanol reduced gasoline prices by twenty to fifty cents per gallon. As you would expect, additional ethanol supplies also lower the demand and price of crude oil. McKinsey cited several other studies, some of which are listed below (National Renewable Energy Laboratory 2008).

- Merrill Lynch: US retail gasoline prices today would be fifty cents per gallon higher without ethanol.

- US Departments of Energy & Agriculture: Without ethanol, today's gasoline prices would be twenty cents to thirty-five cents per gallon higher.

- LECG Study: E10 gasoline in Missouri will be seven cents per gallon cheaper than conventional gasoline over the next ten years. Ethanol blending at E10 in South Dakota saved consumers eleven cents per gallon from March 2007 to March 2008.

- Iowa State University: Ethanol blending reduced gasoline prices on average by twenty-nine to forty cents per gallon, depending on the region in US, during the 1995–2007 time period.

- Renewable Fuels Association: Consumers should be realizing a thirteen cents per gallon saving by utilizing E10 if refiners are passing through savings.

Reducing gasoline demand reduces crude oil demand too. Therefore, reducing the price of crude oil can reduce the price of every commodity transported to the market or produced from petroleum products. The litmus test is in oil embargoes, the recent loss of Russia's oil supplies, and disruptions by hurricanes, all impacting the price of crude oil and gasoline.

So why would detractors keep making claims that ethanol drives up the price of gasoline?

TAKEAWAYS

- Air pollution has a cost to society, and a portion must be attributed to gasoline and its aromatic/BTEX components.

- The total society impact (TSI) gasoline costs are much higher than what you pay at the retail gasoline station.

- Adding ethanol to gasoline reduces the price of crude oil, and, therefore the price of gasoline and every other product produced from crude oil or transported to market.

- Federal subsidies artificially lower the price of crude oil and gasoline to thwart the development of alternative fuels.

WHAT'S NEXT

- The road to less sickness, disease, death, premature deaths, pollution, war, *and* lower-priced gasoline could be paved with more renewable biofuels—not less.

- The oil industry has fought to keep the de facto monopoly on transportation fuel market regardless of their product's true cost and impact on their customer.

CHAPTER 3
The Anti-Ethanol War

Duped, Hoodwinked, Bamboozled—Gaslit

In 1996, the book *The Cigarette Papers* shocked the world. After working for a tobacco company for thirty years, the anonymous "Mr. Butts" became a whistleblower. He provided documents to well-known anti-smoking activist Professor Stanton Glantz. *The Cigarette Papers* documented how and why tobacco companies hid the grave dangers of smoking. The tobacco industry used gaslighting to ignite the cigarettes of their misinformed customers. They used deception to manipulate politicians, the media, and even the medical community, until they got caught (Glantz 1996). We are still waiting for our message from Mr. or Mrs. BTEX.

HOW PEOPLE GOT AND CONTINUE TO GET DUPED ABOUT ETHANOL AND BIOFUELS
Disinformation and legislative influence are imbedded in the battle over how to reduce the nation's reliance on fossil fuels and develop cleaner, lower cost, better, and safer alternatives to crude oil, gasoline, and especially aromatics/BTEX.

The following example and definitions are important to keep in mind while reading the rest of *Gasolinegate*. They will help you assess what negative impressions you may have about fuel ethanol and the likely source of that information. They also help us explain the ethical and moral conflict between Congress, Corporate America, and Americans.

1. Corporations have neither bodies to be punished, nor souls to be condemned; they therefore do as they like. — Edward, Lord Thurlow, 1731–1806, English jurist (Oxford 2016).
2. Willful ignorance (uncountable) (idiomatic, law). Noun: A bad faith decision to avoid becoming informed about something to avoid having to make undesirable decisions that such information might prompt. It may also be shown as for a person to have no clue in a decision but still goes ahead in their decision. Synonyms: (bad faith decision to remain ignorant): vincible ignorance (Lawyerment 2022).
3. Merriam Webster defines gaslighting as psychological manipulation of a person usually over an extended period of time that causes the victim to question the validity of their own thoughts, perception of reality, or memories and typically leads to confusion, loss of confidence and self-esteem, uncertainty of one's emotional or mental stability, and a dependency on the perpetrator. Please note Merriam-Webster named "gaslighting" the Word of the Year for 2022 (Merriam-Webster 2022).

It is understandable to have faith in your doctor, parents, or best friend. But anyone can gaslight. Politicians have been known to gaslight by denying events even when recorded or witnessed by multiple people. Doctors may gaslight you by suggesting you have imaginary symptoms, or are exaggerating pain, or if they tend to recommend therapy instead of medical treatment. Gaslighting works because people want to trust and earn the approval of the gaslighters (Morris 2021).

Corporate, legislative, and bureaucratic bodies can actively use gaslighting to protect their markets, profit, or power. They can engage in intellectual bullying by using technical industry jargon to twist facts. There are many ways to create confusion, fear, and doubt. Most of us do not have the time and resources to fact-check, so we believe the ones we trust. Unconditional trust is the oxygen for the gaslight's flame.

When national security experts refer to Russia's disinformation campaign as weaponized, we believe the weapon is gaslighting, which will impress upon anyone the power this tactic holds (Gamberini 2020). People who refuse to accept science give oxygen to the gaslight and pass the torch to those they know.

The recent accusations about the fossil fuel industry's role in hiding, denying, or influencing policy makers about climate change data is an excellent example of gaslighting. In September 2022, the House Natural Resources and Oversight and Reform Committees requested representatives of the fossil fuel industry to testify about their industry's role in thwarting climate change action. Natural Resources Chair Raúl Grijalva (D-Ariz.) and subcommittee Chair Katie Porter (D-Calif.) sought documents from several companies detailing their work for fossil fuel companies and industry trade associations (Sobczyk 2022).

What the oil industry has done to influence EPA to ignore the public health and national security threat connected to oil, gasoline, and specifically BTEX is no different than what they have done with the climate change issue.

Why is it so hard for the US to stop repeating history?

> "A lie can travel halfway around the world while the truth is putting on its shoes" is attributed to a host of credible and notable people in history like Mark Twain, Jonathan Swift, Thomas Jefferson, and Winston Churchill (Quote Investigator 2015).

We will provide examples of the abundant and credible information in the public domain that could help policy makers and EPA make better decisions. You will notice many of the citations are from EPA and other government websites. We do not want to lose you in technical doublespeak and data overload. Because of the volumes of information and space restrictions, we will show you the tip of the information iceberg and provide you with an easy online path to deeper research.

What is our biggest challenge in telling our story and advancing alternative fuels? Mark Twain said it best.

It's easier to fool people than to convince them that they have been fooled.
—MARK TWAIN (QUOTE INVESTIGATOR 2015).

Illustration by Antony Razwadowski.

Timing is everything when it comes to influencing Congress.

Here is a fitting example of a coordinated anti-ethanol campaign attack during the battles over expanding the Renewable Fuel Standard (RFS). On May 15, 2008, Senator Charles Grassley (R-IA) placed his "Scapegoating of Ethanol" statement in *The Congressional Record,* Senate, Vol. 154, Pt. 10, page S4243.

"But, as was recently reported, this anti-ethanol campaign is not a coincidence. It has been well-thought-out, well-programmed, and that program is going on. It turns out that a $300,000, six-month retainer of a beltway public relations firm is behind the smear campaign against ethanol. And they have been hired by a trade association referred to as the Grocery Manufacturers Association. They have outlined their strategy of using environmental, hunger, and food aid groups to demonstrate their contrived crisis. And it is right here in a twenty-six-page document [request for proposal] put out by the Glover Park Group, called "The Food and Fuel Campaign." They enlist the support of these other nonprofit groups involved with the environment and hunger" (Grassley 2008).

Senator Grassley's press release referenced in the appendix also addresses the multitude of myths about ethanol that circulated the halls of Congress.

A more recent example was in February 2022. Tyler Lark, a scientist in the Great Lakes Bioenergy Research Center and the Nelson Institute for Environmental Studies at UW—Madison, released a study stating corn ethanol increases greenhouse gases by 24 percent. Based on Jill Sakai's article in the *University of Wisconsin at Madison-Wisconsin News*, it appears Lark agrees with us: When it comes to influencing Congress, timing is everything.

The results are especially timely because the Renewable Fuel Standard mandates specific annual biofuel volumes through 2022; once these requirements expire, the Environmental Protection Agency will take over the role of determining how much and which types of biofuels should be produced each year to meet the standard (Sakai 2022).

Note that Congress gave EPA the authority to oversee the Renewable Fuel Standard and reduce mobile source toxic emissions to the greatest extent possible.

We interviewed Ron Alverson to capture the current data readers need to combat this myth. Ron has a degree in Agronomy/Soil Science and was a founder of the South Dakota Corn Growers Association and Dakota Ethanol/ Lake Area Corn Processors ethanol plant. As a board member of the ethanol plant, Alverson studied and monitored the ongoing work in government and academia focusing on full lifecycle greenhouse gas (GHG) accounting for ethanol produced from corn.

Full lifecycle accounting is like accounting for TSI, total society impact costs. As described in further detail in "Chapter 2: The True Cost of Gasoline," TSI is the total cost of ownership, similar to adding up the cost of all the ingredients that go into a cake (e.g., egg, flower, milk, oven, etc.). Ron stated, "despite recent claims that ethanol production and use increases carbon, in 2022 ethanol produced from corn reduced GHG emissions by about half compared to gasoline." Ron provided us with an overview of the three most respected authorities and studies on the subject, which we review in more detail in "Chapter 5: Ethanol Myth Busters." Alverson also explained the increase in agriculture efficiency related to ethanol production saying,

"Farmers are planting on fewer acres, using fewer fertilizers, and growing more corn. Ethanol production increased from less than one billion gallons per year in 1990 to fifteen billion per year in 2022. During that same time period, total cropland planted decreased from 311 million acers to 194 million acers. Total bushels per acre increased from 118 to 171. The total bushels of feed corn produced increased from 8.8 billion to 15.5 billion. Fertilizer use decreased from 2.28 pounds per bushel to 1.78. In 2021 ethanol production also produced 35 million short tons of high-protein animal feed valued at nine billion dollars. Farmers are producing more food products and the fuel is a bonus. Ethanol production allows farmers to get the squeal out of the corn and put it back in the pig. We think that is full lifecycle accounting for farmers."

We believe the anti-ethanol misinformation campaign waged by the oil industry interests against ethanol is unprecedented in any other industry. Could you imagine misinformation campaigns with faulty product claims between Coke and Pepsi, McDonald's and Wendy's, or Apple and Android in full public view? (See "Chapter 4: Tales from the Battlefield.")

PEOPLE DON'T KNOW JACK ABOUT WHAT'S IN THEIR GASOLINE

Consider your sources and who is for you or against you. Years ago, most people believed the world was flat, smoking was cool, seat belts were unnecessary, and climate change was not real. In the same vein, in the 1920s, 1970s, and today, far too many people think fuel ethanol would ruin their engine, that it is bad public policy, unnecessary, and it will never replace a significant amount of gasoline.

In the past forty years, we have lobbied Congress and spoken with thousands of people from all walks of life. We continue to hear the same ethanol myths handed down like folklore for decades. We are amazed how many people think they know a lot about ethanol, yet do not know jack about what is in their gasoline. That is why we invented Jack the fuel test dummy videos. You can watch our ten-minute *You Don't Know Jack About What's in Your Gasoline* animated video that explains our issue using the QR code below or the URL in the chapter appendix (Clean Fuels Development Coalition 2019).

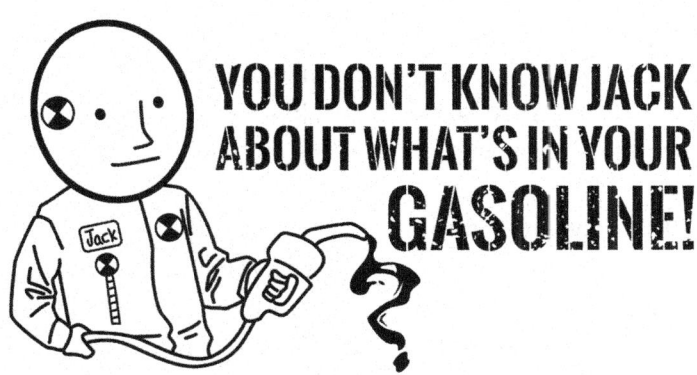

Jack the Fuel Test Dummy: You Don't Know Jack About What's in Your Gasoline. *Illustration by Antony Razwadowski.*

Jack the Fuel Test Dummy Goes to Washington Video. (Clean Fuels Development Coalition 2019).

When interviewing people, it is extraordinarily rare they can conversationally explain the negative impacts their gasoline use has on their health, energy, and economic security. The vast majority state they have not heard the word benzene. Therefore, they certainly were not going to know anything about benzene being associated with gasoline, aromatics, BTEX, octane, mobile source toxic emissions, the total societal cost of oil, or the detrimental health effects from the ultrafine particles from gasoline emissions going into their bloodstream.

Take a moment and think about some of the amazing education and awareness campaigns that changed consumer behavior based on advertising directly by or sponsored by the federal government. These include campaigns to stop people from smoking cigarettes and taking drugs, encouraging drivers to wear seatbelts, and for everyone to prevent forest fires and keep vaccinations current. It is not unreasonable to ask why a federal agency or a publicly funded nonprofit organization has not taken up this important message to get benzene out of gasoline.

Does the nine-tenth of a cent price on gasoline puzzle you? It angers us and provides a great opportunity. Like the tobacco company lawsuit settlement (see "Chapter 14: Moving Forward"), if that nine-tenths of a cent per gallon was captured and applied to a safer gasoline education and awareness campaign, it could raise $1.4 billion to help fight the nation's addition to crude oil and make gasoline safer.

Have you ever noticed how many of the gasoline stations in your area have the same price right down to nine-tenths of a penny? Oil companies don't have a monopoly, but gasoline does.
Photo by Burl Haigwood.

As noted earlier, most anti-ethanol media campaigns are relaunched while Congress is in session debating how to solve current economic, energy, agriculture, environmental, or public health crises.

Many policy makers are guilty of DUIs, or as we like to call it, "Debating Under the Influence of Political Contributions." Elected officials not under the influence have found ways to increase the use of renewable biofuels like ethanol and biodiesel to solve those problems. Why? Biofuels are available, scalable, practical, quick to market, and positively impact their constituents when compared to other alternatives.

When reading anti-ethanol articles, it is very important to always keep in mind the phrase "compared to what." Most articles are trying to compare ethanol to perfect, not progress, and surely not gasoline.

As noted in Senator Grassley's press release, the anti-ethanol fearmongers rely on their anti-ethanol myth playbook. The go-to anti-ethanol myths are food versus fuel, negative energy balance, vehicle performance, lack of refueling infrastructure, land use—code for carbon—and increased gasoline prices. We will refute the ethanol myths at length in "Chapter 5: Ethanol Myth Busters." The two most hypocritical, wackadoodle anti-ethanol rants are price increases and complaining about federal government subsidies for ethanol, which are both covered in "Chapter 2: The True Cost of Gasoline."

Policymakers and biofuel advocates trying to make change are forced into a defensive crab trap set by ethanol detractors. They must defend their alternative fuel, but their opponent is a perfect, mythical unicorn fuel instead of the imperfect gasoline we use in reality. Gasoline is much less perfect in comparison to ethanol, and yet, it does not face the same scrutiny.

Creating national policy is complex and multidimensional. While some refer to it as a sausage factory, we feel it is more like a Rubik's Cube. Legislators need to consider and align the holistic impacts of potential solutions, much in the way a Rubik's Cube is only solved by taking stock of each side. Promoters of anti-ethanol political agenda dissect potential policies for every flaw, forcing ethanol into a monolithic silo of "not good enough." Until we can forget the pipe dream of perfect, we will never address the real benefits of renewable energy and problems with crude oil. Renewable energy, including ethanol, solves many of the negative problems created by the reliance on fossil fuels and the myriad of other problems it causes.

Making more profits, protecting market shares, defeating the competition, and setting unrealistic comparisons makes business sense for ethanol's competitors. However, the fuel industry is betraying their customers and their country. In their words, they defend capitalism and the free market, but in their actions, they defy capitalism and the government in trying to control the market. They are fighting a cheaper—less expensive, not inferior—faster-to-market, and safer—less toxic and polluting—product. Consider the current focus on climate change and how the fossil fuel industry, of which petroleum is the key player, is dealing with it. A Texas group called the Advanced Power Alliance is fighting back against what they say is a massive disinformation campaign from a fossil fuel front group called the Texas Public Policy Foundation. The group makes what it calls "the moral case for fossil fuels," which holds that American prosperity is rooted in an economy based on oil, gas, and coal, and that poor communities and developing nations deserve the same opportunities to grow.

"When you look at their advocacy, it is consistently a false choice between being environmentally responsible and enjoying economic prosperity," said Jeff Clark, chief executive of Advanced Power Alliance, an Austin-based trade group for renewable energy companies. "They're against offshore wind, yet they spent decades advocating for offshore oil drilling. They are against subsidies, but only when it applies to renewables. They're for looser restrictions on fracking and drilling, but greater restrictions for solar and wind. This organization exists to defend fossil fuels from any threat to their market share" (Gelles 2022).

We are reminded of the cow in the fast-food commercial trying to get people to "eat mor chikin."

The legislative achievements listed below were courageous bipartisan efforts intended to help end the nation's dangerous addiction to imported crude oil and stop a one-hundred-year gasoline-BTEX de facto mandate. These achievements met public policy objectives like rural development, economic stimulation, enhancing national security, and protecting the environment. The table below documents the many battles policy makers had to fight to take the oxygen out of the ethanol detractor's gaslights. Many of those policy makers are recognized in our special thanks and acknowledgment sections.

LEGISLATIVE AND REGULATORY HISTORY OF FUEL ETHANOL-RELATED INITIATIVES AND THE BATTLES TO PROTECT THEM
1970: US Environmental Protection Agency Established

1973: OPEC Oil Embargo and Recession

1978: US Department of Energy Established

1978: Energy Tax Act (first fuel ethanol incentive)

1979: OPEC Oil Embargo and World Recession

1980: Crude Oil Windfall Profits Tax Act and Energy Security Act

1980: Gasohol Anti-Competition Act

1985–1990: Battle in the States over Ethanol Incentives and Oxy-Fuel Mandates

1988: Battle to Remove "No Alcohol in Our Gas" Pump Labels

1988: Battle to Create a National Oxygenated Fuel Standard for Gasoline

1988: Alternative Motor Fuels Act

1990: Omnibus Budget Reconciliation Act

1990: Clean Air Act Amendments of 1990 (Oxy-Fuel Program)

1992: Energy Policy Act

1994: Battle for Renewable Oxygen Requirement (ROR)

1995: Nationwide Reformulated Gasoline Program Begins

1998: Transportation Efficiency Act of the Twenty-First Century

2004: Volumetric Ethanol Excise Tax Credit Established (VEETC)

2004: Jobs Creation Act

2005: Energy Policy Act Creates First Renewable Fuel Standard (RFS 1)

2007: Energy Policy Act Creates Second RFS (RFS 2) and Increases Volumes

2007: Mobile Source Air Toxic (MSAT) Rule and PM2.5 Rule

2008: Battle over Indirect Land Use Carbon Penalty Attacks

2008: Battle over Food versus Fuel Attacks

2008–2010: Institute of Medicine "Anti-Backsliding" Study

2008–2012: Battle over Energy Policy Act and MOVES Model Findings

2010–2012: Renewable Fuels Standard Waiver rejection

2012: Greenhouse Gas Corporate Average Fuel Economy (I) Standard Rulemaking

2012: Second Renewable Fuel Standard Final Rulemaking

2012: Repeal of Ethanol Tax Credit (VEETC)

2013: EPA Tier 3 Rulemaking

2015–2018: Battle against Efforts to Repeal the RFS

2016–2018: GHICAFE Standard Reconsideration

2017: Congressionally Mandated EPA Update of MSAT Cost Benefit Analysis Is Ten Years Overdue

2018: US House of Representative Octane Hearing to Repeal RFS

2018: EPA REG Rule to Limit Ethanol Use to 15 percent

2018: Legislative Reforms to Repeal the RFS

2019: Battle over EPA Granting RFS Waivers to Refiners

2021: Battle Lost to Include Higher Octane Gasoline Standard in CAFE

2022: Congressionally Mandated EPA Update of MSAT Cost Benefit Analysis Is Twenty-Two Years Overdue

2022: EPA Takes Control of RFS

2023: EPA to Release Findings to Consider Continuation of RFS

2023: Next Battle to Modify CAFE to Include Higher-Octane Standard for Gasoline

Regardless of these legislation achievements and our on-going efforts, the anti-ethanol war continues.

The most recent and egregious examples of the anti-ethanol campaign were a series of TV commercials calling President Biden to "fix" the RFS—code word for getting rid of ethanol. We considered the commercials almost a *Gasolinegate* promotion gift from ethanol detractors. The commercials ran on late-night TV in the Washington, DC, area before the midterm elections in 2022. As we noted, timing is everything. The commercials made it to primetime and aired during the National News reporting the polls on the evening of November 9, 2022. The commercials claimed fixing the RFS would lower gasoline prices by thirty cents per gallon (Fueling American Jobs Coalition 2022).

The clues of this disinformation campaign were evident to us:

- the www.FuelingUSJobs.com website and organization names do not match,

- there is no address or phone number, and

- to get more information, we were required to fill out a form, forcing us to sign up to receive emails.

We signed up Jack, our fuel test dummy, to receive email updates. These emails now act as our "insider insight" into the other side's thought process. We also follow the group on Twitter @FuelingUSJobs and watch them blast ethanol and the RFS almost daily.

We signed up to receive other emails in response to a commercial that blames high gasoline prices on *The Real Cost of Washington*. We felt as if they beta-read our "Chapter 2: The True Cost of Gasoline." We began to receive emails from Americans for Prosperity. This experience helped us connect the dots between the objectives of Americans for Prosperity and its funding base.

These campaigns are not unique to the RFS or ethanol. These groups oppose alternatives using all kinds of front groups. As noted in the Gelles article referenced earlier, "Just as the tobacco industry had front groups and the opioid industry had front groups, this is part of the fossil fuel disinformation playbook," said David Michaels, an epidemiologist at the George Washington School of Public Health who has studied corporate influence campaigns. "The role of these so-called policy organizations is not to provide useful information to the public, but to promote the interests of their sponsors, which are often antithetical to public health" (Gelles 2022).

TAKEAWAYS
- For over one hundred years, oil interests and their cronies have claimed ethanol is an inferior product and will not work. Today, 10 percent ethanol is in nearly every gallon of gasoline sold in the United States. A few exceptions exist where gasoline retailers sell ethanol-free gasoline

for as much as a dollar per gallon more, which proves ethanol costs less.

- Ethanol is not perfect, but it is a better, less expensive, and safer fuel than aromatics/BTEX.

WHAT'S NEXT?
- The oil industry has tried hard to stop the growth of modern fuel ethanol since first introduced in Nebraska in the 1970s.

CHAPTER 4

Tales from the Battlefield

The Fight for States' Cleaner Gasoline Rights

Three things must work together to get ethanol into retail gasoline stations: government policies, fuel production, and marketing to the petroleum industry, which is also a rabid competitor in a cutthroat motor fuel market.

Governments can establish requirements and incentives, but getting your competitor to replace their product with yours redefines the word challenge. Replacing his product with yours goes against business principles and common sense unless he has good reasons to do so.

In our interview with Terry Ruse he makes the obvious but painful observation, "It is an extremely difficult proposition where your largest customer is also, by the way, your greatest adversary!" (Ruse 2022).

THE BATTLE FOR NEBRASKA

Nebraska is one of the birthplaces of the ethanol movement and also its earliest battlegrounds. In the 1930s, the state legislature established a tax incentive to use an ethanol-gasoline blend called *Agrol*. The program allowed Nebraska to use its corn to make the food and fuel needed to boost the state's agriculture industry. The program extended fuel supplies, and the economic benefits went far beyond just agriculture in Nebraska (Sneller 2019).

One of the true pioneers that propelled ethanol from a niche fuel to an established component of gasoline was Loran Schmit. Schmit was a state legislator who led the effort to bring fuel ethanol into the mainstream. In 1969, he authored legislation to establish a statewide ethanol agency and create financial incentives for the petroleum industry to blend ethanol. Interestingly, even back then, he was a vocal proponent of getting lead out of gasoline and recognized its terrible toll on human health.

As we noted in several sections throughout this book, the "subsidies" for ethanol primarily took the form of tax incentives to the petroleum industry to get them to use the product from our perspective that is entirely appropriate and defensible. As a nation, the States use the tax code to drive policies, be it tax write-offs for home mortgages or deductions for contributing to your 401(k). In this case, taxing the petroleum industry less to get them to use a product that has national benefits is a good government policy.

In our interview with Senator Schmit in August of 2022, he recounts the difficulty he had getting buy-in from fellow legislators. Those from urban areas like Omaha had less interest in promoting corn and were clearly influenced by oil industry lobbying that utilized the whole bag of false flag arguments against ethanol. He ultimately prevailed by pulling together a coalition made up of everyone from unions to wheat farmers who wanted corn farmers to keep growing corn and not wheat!

Despite that success, the state petroleum council and the major oil companies they served shrugged off the value of the tax incentives, preferring to maintain total market share. In addition to badmouthing ethanol at every opportunity, they took tangible action such as not allowing stations to sell ethanol out of their pumps, denying credit card purchases for gasoline containing ethanol, and creating labels and warnings implying—and sometimes claiming outright—that ethanol was a harmful product. Stations that did not offer ethanol often proudly displayed signs saying, "our gas contains no ethanol," a mantra that continues to this day.

As the Nebraska ethanol program began to gain traction because of massive oil supply disruptions in the 1970s, oil representatives frequently visited Lincoln to lobby state legislators. By then, Loran Schmit was recognized as one of the most committed ethanol advocates in the legislature. Oil lobbyists often invited him to evening dinners where they routinely lobbied legislators. Schmit made it a practice to decline these invitations because of the pressure and intensity of lobbying. Schmit often said, "I may be a poor farmer, but I can afford to buy my own damn steak."

When the direct approach to persuade Schmit was unsuccessful, oil lobbyists made a more subtle but devious approach via the affiliated state oil lobby associations. A prominent state association executive contacted Schmit requesting a private meeting. Schmit recounted that the executive laid out why the ethanol program was a flawed concept that had no chance of success, particularly given the opposition and resources of the oil industry. The lobbyist urged Schmit to "be smart" and back off the idea of pushing an ethanol program in Nebraska. The lobbyist, according to Schmit, made it clear that it would benefit Schmit if he "played it smart."

Schmit had at that time served two terms in the legislature but in retrospect, stated, "I must have been a real neophyte to not recognize what was being proposed. It never occurred to me that the stage was being set for a bribe." That became clear to Schmit as a check was laid on the desk and the lobbyist said he was leaving his office for a minute. He urged Schmit to "pick it up," referring to the check, as the lobbyist stepped out. Schmit said he looked at the check in disbelief and then promptly left the petroleum association office without it. As Schmit related this story many times in later years, he laughed about the experience. "I was astounded that those guys would take that approach, but I'm also a little insulted." The check was for $5,000. Schmit said, "If they thought I was that important, maybe they should have upped the ante a bit."

We had the pleasure of working with Todd Sneller in his capacity as chairman of the Clean Fuels Development Coalition and advisor to the Clean Fuels Foundation. Todd started working with the Nebraska ethanol development program in 1976 with the Nebraska Agricultural Products Industrial Utilization Committee, now the Nebraska Ethanol Board. Sneller kept Senator Schmit's torch blazing until his retirement in 2018.

Sneller assisted the Nebraska Department of Economic Development as an industrial development consultant before returning to the Nebraska Agricultural Products Industrial Utilization Committee as the agency's administrator. He also served as technical advisor of the Nebraska Ethanol Authority and Development Board, where he managed a $20 million equity investment fund. Sneller's forty-two-year career included ethanol plant recruitment, legislative and regulatory assistance to ethanol producers, marketing and policy program development, and public outreach activities. The ethanol program Senator Schmit started, which Todd Sneller and others fought to keep, became a significant return on investment for Nebraska taxpayers. Todd wrote an excellent paper on the history of the ethanol program from 1969–2019. You can read "Ethanol Development in Nebraska: 1969–2019" online with the QR code provided below (Sneller 2019):

THE BATTLE FOR NEW MEXICO

The oil industry has numerous levers they can pull to slow or even stop the blending of fuel ethanol. One of the first battles in New Mexico was over the oil industry demanding mandatory ethanol labels on each gasoline pump dispensing the product. Ruse, who we introduced you to in chapter 1, told us,

> "The refiners wanted bright orange labels with the words, "Warning: this product contains ethanol." Discussions also included labels that would have had the likeness of a skull and cross bones image. They intended to warn the driving public against the dangers of using ethanol. We eventually compromised on not having orange or other images and just have the words "This Product Contains Up to 10% Ethanol." Other states were not so lucky. In addition to pump labels, billboards, and street signs also started playing a role in oil industry anti-ethanol campaigns, some of which continue to this day.
>
> Today, I believe the more people understand what is in their gasoline and what ethanol replaces, the ethanol label on every gasoline dispenser in America will become a positive statement. It's branding by karma."

Ruse also explained how Diamond Shamrock, a major refiner and New Mexico supplier, literally put an ethanol plant Terry was managing out of business by choosing not to provide "clean gasoline" suitable for blending with ethanol. Ruse told us,

"For all the negative signs and bad publicity generated by the oil industry desperately trying to maintain their monopoly, the ultimate trump card was their ability to ship gasoline unsuitable for ethanol blending through the pipeline system to wholesale gasoline terminals before it was delivered in trucks to retail gasoline stations. The EPA deemed MTBE and ethanol incompatible, therefore, not approved to be commingled. Offenders faced $10,000 per day penalties. Refiners sending gasoline containing MTBE through the pipeline made adding ethanol at the wholesale gasoline terminal illegal."

For background, methyl tertiary butyl ether (MTBE) is made from methanol and excess butane from the refining process or purchased from chemical manufacturers as an octane-enhancing additive. Both of which are controlled by the refining complex itself.

Ruse and the owners of the ethanol plant in New Mexico engaged in an extensive marketing and education program centered on Albuquerque. They collected and provided proven data on the ability of ethanol to address the region's carbon monoxide program and conducted tutorials to station owners and auto dealers. They had to go as far as to guarantee their ethanol blends against any mechanical problems. When that did not work, they went further by offering retailers a fifty cent per gallon incentive to buy their product. The more ground they gained, the more the petroleum industry fought to take it back. Then the ability to blend hit a wall.

"Overnight the 'clean gasoline' supply went away and all the ethanol blending along the pipeline stopped! No gasoline retailers were going to risk a $10,000-a-day fine for co-mingling ethanol and MTBE. They stopped blending immediately," Ruse recalls. "Repeated pleas for a clean gasoline stream went unanswered. In a meeting with the New Mexico Governor's representative and the refiner responsible for injecting MTBE into its gasoline stream, the refiner reportedly replied his company was very concerned about market share. If he made clean gasoline available, his company might lose some of it!" (Ruse 2022).

This became the proven game plan replicated throughout the country: Badmouth the product by stoking fears of cars blowing up or stalling out, leaving women and children stranded on the side of the road. Outrageous claims of higher prices. Guilt tripping over using "food for fuel." They also warned their retail customers they would cut off their fuel supplies if they used branded credit cards. If all else fails, don't supply a suitable blendstock, and do not allow corporate branded retailers to sell ethanol blends at their stations.

These oil industry shenanigans continued for decades despite national legislation that created the Gasohol Competition Act of 1980 (Cornell Law School 2022). The Act protects independent gasoline marketers that want to sell ethanol blends from unfair trade practices of their suppliers. The Act was one of the first examples of Congress protecting its intent with legislation to combat the oil industry's obvious and relentless public bias against ethanol. However, enforcement was difficult, and the MTBE in gasoline was perfectly legal at the time.

Terry Ruse provided a more detailed overview of his experience in an essay titled *A Journey of a Thousand Steps* referenced in the chapter appendix. You can read his essay using the QR code below or the URL in the appendix (Ruse 2022):

THE BATTLE FOR COLORADO

In the late 1980s, before the Clean Air Act Amendments of 1990 (CAAA) that established national requirements, many states were trying to tackle their pollution problems. For many western high-elevation states, carbon monoxide was a nagging problem. Ethanol, with its chemical property as an oxygenate, was proven to reduce carbon monoxide emissions. Ethanol increased combustion and therefore reduced tailpipe emissions. Ruse and his company in New Mexico discovered the air pollution and health benefits early, and so did the environmentally conscious state of Colorado.

Carbon monoxide was primarily a wintertime pollutant. In places like Denver, the cold, thin air trapped emissions at a greater frequency than in warmer months. For the petroleum industry, as much as they disdained ethanol, it was a seasonal solution. As soon as the wintertime control requirements ended, they dropped ethanol immediately.

In 1990, forty-four cities in the US were deemed as being out of compliance with carbon monoxide (CO) standards. Cities that exceeded CO air quality standards were designated by EPA as carbon monoxide nonattainment areas. Almost every major city was affected, but especially western cities in higher elevations, some of them considerably smaller like Boise, Idaho.

Not many options were available to allow these polluted areas to come into compliance. Among big emitters were bakeries and dry cleaners, but shutting them down was bad for business.

That left cutting gasoline as an easy solution. Now oil companies found themselves using a product they were maligning in other parts of the country. The way around was not to market ethanol blend as a good thing, but rather not to mention it at all. These companies simply made it a ubiquitous part of gasoline, and no one noticed. They were silent when ethanol was in their product. When it was not, they fueled their gaslight lanterns with it.

That is not to say the oil industry did not try to shift the blame to the stationary sources of pollution. CFDC was called to testify at hearings in Denver, Phoenix, Santa Fe, Albuquerque, Boise, and other cities to make the case for protecting public health. Studies done on 10 percent ethanol blends had shown reductions of CO by more than 20 percent. At those hearings, we went up against outgunned and underprepared oil company representatives. These were usually local representatives who had never been challenged about their product. Like the public, they knew nothing about air pollution or what was in their gasoline. They repeatedly used the same talking points provided by corporate headquarters. These claims were easily debunked using the mounting evidence and public record from other hearings. During a conference CFDC sponsored in Denver, Colorado, Governor Roy Roemer, an unsung hero of the effort to clean up gasoline, called out the oil industry representatives in the audience for their doublespeak and hypocritical actions. He warned them, "If you want to wear a white hat and help us then great; if you don't, then wear your black hat so we know who you are."

ALL BATTLE ROADS LED TO WASHINGTON, DC

Our efforts to create a year-round Reformulated Gasoline Program (RFG) that required oxygenates turned the state ethanol battles into a full-fledged war. The RFG program was a tipping point. Ethanol went from a tolerable annoyance to a major threat. No longer was it a wintertime program that lasted only four to five months. Oil companies could hold their nose all the way to the bank. They made more profits by collecting and keeping the tax exemption for ethanol. Adding ethanol also increased the octane of their gasoline. This benefit allowed them to increase the price to their customers. All that was good—in small doses.

The Clean Air Act required nine cities with the highest level of ozone, or summertime smog, to use a new clean formula that required the addition of an "oxygenated fuel." Trench warfare began when cities on the borderline of violation were allowed to voluntarily adopt the new federal clean gasoline standard. While most of the oxygen demand would be met by MTBE, it still represented a great opportunity for ethanol. That is when we returned to the local level as state environmental agencies had to decide on what they were going to do to get back into compliance. Once again, cleaning up gasoline was an easier path than shutting down or restricting operations of many stationary sources of air pollution.

The level of competition changed drastically from our early jousting with some of the state petroleum representatives. Refiners were now sending scientists and actual fuel experts to argue why they did not need fuel oxygenates. They claimed they could devise new gasoline formulations that would have the same air pollution reduction benefits. Refiners commissioned "independent" studies and bombarded state air quality officials and legislators. They overwhelmed them with studies, statistics, and technical doublespeak. And while they had an arsenal of red herring arguments like the food versus fuel, or excessive water usage, they always had an ace in the hole with cost.

As illustrated on the national stage with the dramatic price spikes in gasoline in 2022, few issues put the fear of God into politicians like rising gasoline prices. Because ethanol would require a slightly modified blend stock, segregated storage, and other adjustments, the petroleum industry could pin any higher number on gasoline they wanted.

CFDC served on a governor-appointed commission in Arizona to deal with the growing smog problem in Phoenix. Of course, we were advocating the federal RFG program, even though there was no guarantee the oxygenate would be ethanol. Many of the California refiners that supplied gasoline to Phoenix sent a small army of lobbyists and technical experts arguing that simply lowering the Reid vapor pressure (RVP) of their gasoline would provide all of the air pollution reduction benefits. The intended outcome would be an all-hydrocarbon all-gasoline product so they would not lose market share, while still being able to charge more.

However, we could prove oxygenates, be it ethanol or MTBE, provided greater reduction benefits. We worked with the most knowledgeable person we have ever met in terms of fuel science named Bill Piel of Arco Chemical Co. Arco had been very interested in using ethanol instead of methanol to make their fuels. Arco was a CFDC member and having Bill on our team was almost unfair to the oil guys when we got into technical arguments. The oil industry's low RVP strategy was simply not effective. We showed case after case where it failed to provide the promised reductions.

Ultimately, truth prevailed. When Phoenix adopted federal RFG with the fuel oxygenate requirement, they eliminated ozone exceedances for the first time. However, two years later, the oil industry persuaded Arizona to opt out of that program and adopt the oil-only formula, and exceedances returned.

We went on to participate in a dozen more state commissions and committees established to decide what fuel strategy to employ. At every turn, it was the same oil industry game plan. They fearmongered about ethanol's performance, cost, and safety. Regulators authorized to make the decision feared the new and the unknown. Fear of failure and public ridicule, they usually resulted in defaulting to the status quo—a mandate for gasoline—despite having acknowledged the problem with air pollution was coming from gasoline. The outcome was letting those who caused the problem to decide how to solve it. This empowered the oil industry to make sure their competition did not get a toehold in their market regardless of the air pollution that had a stranglehold on their customers.

Fast-forward to 2018 and we are watching the US House of Representatives Congressional Hearing, "High Octane Fuels and High Efficiency Vehicles: Challenges and Opportunities." It was a public hearing about the future of cars and gasoline. It had little focus on what should have been the primary point of contention—public health. Beyond a reasonable doubt, it was another example of the oil industry boldly showing their cards and telegraphing their next move. They wanted to see the next thirty years just like the last hundred: all gasoline, more toxic/carcinogenic aromatic octane enhancers, and without a national renewable fuel standard (RFS). They asked Congress to repeal the RFS. The oil industry deftly put ethanol on trial. They dismissed any notion that gasoline needed to be cleaned up while eviscerating the available, cleaner, higher-octane, lower-carbon, and less expensive replacement for their benzene-laden BTEX additives.

TAKEAWAYS
- Science and data are readily available to help make decision-makers more educated and accountable.

- The battle for the world's largest gasoline market will likely never end.

- The choice to buy higher blends of renewable fuels would give consumers a weapon to use in the battle to get safer gasoline.

WHAT'S NEXT
- Science and data show that fuel ethanol can protect and improve environmental, energy, public health, economic, and national concerns.

CHAPTER 5

Ethanol Myth Busters

Combating Disinformation Campaigns

Ethanol is one of the most scrutinized products in our lifetime. It took over one hundred years to combat misinformation and disinformation campaigns and make renewable ethanol part of US gasoline quality standards. After reading about gasoline pump labeling requirements and the Battle for New Mexico, we hope you have an appreciation for the political courage and conviction it took to get the National Renewable Fuel Standard (RFS) though Congress and signed by the president—twice! We hope you also see the "Contains up to 10% Ethanol" label on every gasoline pump in the United States as an accomplishment, not the intended warning.

The information and photographs in this chapter will allow you to see beyond the price on gas station signs and help you consider what you know about gasoline and ethanol every time you pick up the nozzle.

It took almost one hundred years to get the lead out of gasoline and over three decades to add 10 percent ethanol.
Photo by Burl Haigwood.

Have you noticed other labels on your gasoline dispenser?

- Notice: This Gasoline Contains No Ethanol
- Caution: Contains up to 10% Ethanol
- Attention: E15—Up to 15% Ethanol
- Non-Ethanol Supreme Unleaded
- Ethanol Free Gasoline

The next time you buy gasoline look for the "Benzene Warning" label on the gasoline dispenser. Spoiler alert! Unless you live in California, you will not find one. Why?

If you are interested in viewing the evolution of the ethanol label on gasoline dispensers, you could conduct a Google search using these search strings, "Contains up to 10% Ethanol," "No Alcohol in Our Gasoline signs," and especially "1980s No Ethanol in My Gasoline Signs." You might spot our colleague Terry Ruse, who we introduced you to in the Battle for New Mexico, on his ladder trying to take down one of those signs.

Considering space restraints and our mission, we can only show you the tip of the disinformation iceberg that is trying to sink your *USS Ethanol*. We refuse to fall into the defend-ethanol disinformation trap set by ethanol detractors. That is a ploy to keep the focus away from crude oil, gasoline, and especially aromatics/BTEX. We focus on examples to help you recognize a biased or planted anti-ethanol article so you will not get duped or fooled again.

Because of the long anti-ethanol war, a tremendous amount of documented and validated research from trusted sources is in the public domain. We summarize the most popular ethanol myths in this chapter. Our citations in the appendix provide a clear research path to thousands of validated reports and statistics from industry, academia, and governments worldwide.

You can find the most important, peer reviewed, and trusted ethanol myth buster questions and answers in our Ethanol Fact Book series (Clean Fuels Development Coalition 2019), or the three additional sources cited below.

- US Department of Energy: Biofuels & Greenhouse Gas Emissions: Myths versus Facts (US Department of Energy 2008). The document was produced during the battles over the RFS I and RFS II. It was produced during the George H. Bush administration which supported ethanol and was instrumental in passing the RFS (White House 2007).

- People looking for more technical answers can find a collection of *Bobby Likis' Car Clinic Ethanol Myth Buster Series* on the Agwired website (Schroeder 2016).

- We interviewed Marc Rauch about his book, *The Ethanol Papers* (2019). Marc allowed us to provide the QR code on the next page to his eBook, or you can use the URL in the appendix for this chapter. *The Ethanol Papers* is over six hundred pages of in-depth, well-documented, no-holds-barred examination of ethanol versus gasoline and other associated myths.

Marc uses simple words and comparisons. We would consider him very funny if the topic were not so sad. His material is well suited for a skit on *Saturday Night Live* or Stephen Colbert's *Meanwhile*. According to Marc, "My book is Biofuels for Dummies. Even brain-washed scientists, academics, and politicians can understand." If you would like to support Marc's continued research, you can sign up to receive The Auto Channel Newsletter and buy his book on www.Amazon.com. You might enjoy two of his recent snippets on The Auto Channel website, *Battling Anti-Ethanol Snake Oil Myths* (Rauch 2022a) and *It's Time for Ethanol Honesty*

(Rauch 2022b). We refer to these articles as Marc's *Ethanol Chop Buster Series*.

The Ethanol Papers, By Mark Rauch

With your online ethanol myth buster reference library full, we will focus on our mission to help you not breathe oxygen into the anti-ethanol gaslighter myths. The following explanations of tactics used and descriptions of ethanol myths will help you recognize anti-ethanol disinformation campaign articles when you read them.

USING DOUBLESPEAK

We have researched and documented alcohol fuel related issues since the late 1970s. Two of the most difficult disinformation tactics to combat are trust and doublespeak. Doublespeak is used by oil interests to argue against ethanol and use the same argument to protect the market share for gasoline. We also understand it is difficult not to trust companies that produce the products you buy most frequently.

For example, arguably one of the most recognizable faces and trusted spokespersons in the US for decades was actor and comedian Bob Hope. Apparently, Texaco's research department data showed consumers would trust Bob Hope because in 1975, he became *Mr. Texaco*. Hope's endorsement of Texaco—now Chevron/Texaco—was part of the *Trust Your Car to the Man Who Wears the Star* advertising campaign from 1960 through 1980 (Texaco 2022). In 1979, Bob Hope endorsed *Gasohol* for Texaco on national television, touting corn as a renewable resource. Hope concludes the commercial by saying, "Gasohol. 10 percent ethanol and 90 percent gasoline is one of the ways Texaco is working to keep your trust" (The Auto Channel 2018).

Dave Hallberg, the founder and CEO of the Renewable Fuels Association (RFA) told us Texaco was one of his first members. He said, "Texaco owned 50 percent of Pekin Energy, one of the first commercial ethanol plants. However, when the price of oil went down, Texaco's interest went with it. They divested in ethanol and their membership in the RFA."

USING THE ART OF IMPERFECTION

If an anti-ethanol article tries to compare ethanol to a theoretically perfect fuel instead of gasoline or aromatics/BTEX, it is not fair, impartial, or based on modern science. If an anti-ethanol article does not reference benzene, aromatics, BTEX, foreign oil, OPEC, mobile source air toxics (MSATs), total societal impact, or gasoline's impact on air pollution, climate change, and public health, it is likely a hatchet job.

MYTH: ETHANOL USE IS MANDATED

Being labeled an "ethanol mandate" is one of the great misrepresentations of the RFS. The RFS requires certain refiners and importers to integrate *renewables* into their fuel mix. Renewables include biodiesel, biogas, methanol, butanol, and ethanol. Therefore, the RFS could be met without ethanol. Compared to the renewable alternatives, fuel ethanol is easily integrated into the existing refueling system and every car is compatible. Refiners and importers choose renewable ethanol because it costs less than the gasoline being replaced *and* because of its higher-octane rating, they can sell ethanol blends at a higher price. They make money hand over fist, with some in each fist.

Therefore, when an anti-ethanol article refers to the RFS as an ethanol mandate, it is technically incorrect, and they are not telling the other side of the story. Without the RFS, the market must exclusively use petroleum-based fuels and that is a de facto gasoline and aromatics/BTEX mandate.

MYTH: ETHANOL BLENDS INCREASE POLLUTION

If you review the Clean Fuels Development Coalition report, *What's in Our Gasoline Is Killing Us: Mobile Source Air Toxics (MSATs) and the Threat to Public Health*, you will understand the emissions from ethanol are much less toxic and polluting compared to gasoline (Durante and Haigwood 2019).

When you read "Chapter 8: The Smoking Gun and the Poison Squad," you will understand how and why some people still believe ethanol blends are considered more polluting. Emails received by the Urban Air Initiative from a Freedom of Information Act request show EPA collaborating with oil interests to develop designer test fuels to make ethanol-blended gasoline emissions appear worse than gasoline without ethanol. You will learn EPA does not use commercially available gasoline to certify vehicle emissions. EPA also does not conduct "real world" road tests that would determine comparable emission or efficiency ratings consumers would achieve driving those same vehicles. That is why your mileage is not what you see on the showroom sticker.

As a result of that information, in 2018, the Urban Air Initiative commissioned studies by North Carolina State University (NCSU) and the University of California Riverside (UCR). Both studies evaluated tailpipe emissions using fuels similar to what consumers could buy at their gas stations. Both tests showed ethanol blends reduce toxic tailpipe emissions by up to 50 percent, significantly improving air quality and protecting public health (Urban Air Initiative 2018).

You can find a multitude of studies from the past two decades in *The Ethanol Fact Book* and *The Ethanol Papers* cited earlier.

MYTH: ETHANOL HARMS CARS AND WILL NEVER WORK ON A LARGE SCALE

Our interview with Plinio Nastari, a world-renowned expert on ethanol and the Brazilian ethanol program, revealed the following:

"Brazil is now the world's second largest ethanol producer in the world. Since 2006, the US is first. Brazil began using fuel ethanol in 1924 in the Northeastern states of Alagoas, Pernambuco and Paraiba. For the following fifty years, ethanol was used in various percentages as a blend component in gasoline. During World War II ethanol blends reached levels above 40 percent, due to constraints in gasoline supplies.

In 1975, after the first oil shock, under President Ernesto Geisel, Brazil created Proálcool, its National Alcohol Program, aimed at raising ethanol blends to 20 percent, and above, in all the gasoline pool and the introduction of cars capable of using pure ethanol, or E100. Proálcool ended in 1983, but its consequences endured.

Since January 1978, ethanol blends in Brazil have been at 20 percent or higher. Since July 1984, 22 percent; since June 1998, 24 percent; since July 2002, 25 percent. In August 1979, Brazil launched neat ethanol (E100) cars, which were a popular success in the mid-1980s. In March 2003, automakers based in Brazil (all international brands, such as GM, Ford, Toyota, Honda, Nissan, Fiat, BMW, Peugeot, Citroen, KIA, Hyundai, and others) produced flexible-fuel vehicles (FFVs) capable of using any percentage of ethanol up to 100 percent.

Since March 2015, the blend level in common gasoline rose to 27 percent. Currently, over 83 percent of Brazil´s light vehicle fleet are FFVs. In 2020, from using E27 all over the country and E100 in the flex-fuel fleet, Brazil achieved 48 percent substitution of gasoline. In Brazil, some states have higher gasoline substitution rates: São Paulo 64 percent; Goias 64.8 percent, Minas Gerais 56 percent; Mato Grosso 70.5 percent. India, Thailand, Indonesia, Paraguay, Argentina, Colombia, Belgium, Bulgaria, and France are trying to achieve the same objectives."

We find it interesting the ethanol and FFV incentives were always on the legislative chopping block. Yet, federal subsidies for crude oil, gasoline, and by extension BTEX have been in place for decades. The thought US automakers cannot make cars to efficiently use higher blends of ethanol is as ridiculous as the notion that it would not be accepted by consumers.

In our interview with Dave VanderGriend of ICM in Kansas, he provided data showing "the sales of E30 are double that of E10 or E15." He also told us about the tests conducted in Nebraska, South Dakota, and Kansas, where consumers voluntarily purchase E30—30 percent ethanol—for their vehicles that are not FVVs. Retail gasoline station reports indicate no vehicle problems and sales data show widespread consumer acceptance.

Ethanol is a proven high-octane fuel for virtually any application—road transport, aviation, and even marine engines. Consider the following:

- The US Department of Energy Co-Optimization of Fuels & Engines (Co-Optima) initiative website. This program explores how higher blends of ethanol can boost fuel economy and vehicle performance while reducing emissions, advancing the underlying science needed to deliver better fuels and better engines sooner (US Department of Energy 2022).

- Plinio Nastari's presentation at the Federal Aviation Administration's International Conference on Alternative Aviation Fuels in 1998 (Nastari 1999).

- A video about Dr. Maxwell Shauck and his wife Grazia Zanin's transatlantic flight using 100 percent ethanol in 1993 (Stromeyer 2016). Please note the smoke from their plane during air shows is for effect. The smoke allows viewers to track the plane in the sky. The smoke is not produced because of ethanol use.

If Henry Ford could make his cars ethanol capable in 1925, pilots could transverse the Atlantic on 100 percent ethanol in the 1990s, Brazilians use a minimum of 27 percent ethanol in cars today, India is moving to 20 percent ethanol blends just a couple of years, and the Department of Energy is documenting the use and outcomes of higher blend use in the future, there is not much left to prove. Except, that is, why you don't have the choice to use higher blends of ethanol (see part 3).

Therefore, myth busted. Ethanol can and does work on a large scale.

MYTH: ADDING ETHANOL TO GASOLINE INCREASES GREENHOUSE GASES

We shared information from our interview with Ron Alverson in chapter 3. Here are the three GHG models Alverson believes are the most validated and credible sources of trusted information.

- According to the Department of Energy's Argonne National Laboratory's Greenhouse Gases, Regulated Emissions, and Energy Use in Technologies Model (GREET), typical corn ethanol provides a 44 percent greenhouse gas (GHG) savings compared to gasoline. And that includes the controversial land use change emissions, which are not often included in analyses of crude oil and gasoline.

- Researchers affiliated with Harvard University, Massachusetts Institute of Technology (MIT), and Tufts University concluded that current corn-based ethanol production has an average GHG reduction of 46 percent compared to gasoline.

- The California Air Resources Board's (CARB)—often not a fan of ethanol—research found that, on average, ethanol used in the state in 2020 reduced emissions by 41 percent compared to gasoline. From 2011 to 2020, CARB data show that the use of ethanol cut GHG emissions from the California transportation sector by 27 million tons. That is more than any other fuel used to meet the state's Low Carbon Fuel Standard requirements.

Alverson told us, "Ethanol detractors often hold ethanol to much higher standards when it comes to full lifecycle GHG analysis when compared to gasoline, crude oil, or electric vehicles (EVs). Detractor studies often compare apples to oranges and do not include all the fruits in their basket.

Reputable studies have a similar apples-to-apples baseline, which is why the reduction benefits are similar in the studies I referenced."

Alverson also helped us place a carbon value on ethanol at the pump. Carbon credits fluctuate, and for this example, we estimate the value of a carbon credit at $190 per ton. Using the GREET model as the baseline, replacing gasoline with 288.8 gallons of ethanol reduces carbon by one ton. Therefore, the carbon reduction value of ethanol is worth sixty-five cents per gallon. Would you pay sixty-five cents more per gallon to reduce a ton of carbon? You don't have to; it's already cheaper than gasoline or aromatics/BTEX and has been for a decade according to our interview with Terry Ruse. Therefore, ethanol's carbon reduction is free, and the reduction in toxic air pollution is a bonus. Like frequent flyer programs, consider cleaner air part of your biofuel frequent driver miles dividend.

Carbon reductions can come from processing a variety of feedstocks. Phil Madson, president of Katzen International, has designed ethanol plants worldwide and dealt with various feedstocks. Madson was an early skeptic that the RFS defined advanced biofuels as meeting a 56 percent GHG reduction and also that it must come from a cellulosic and non-corn starch feedstock.

In Madson's 2012 CFDC White Paper *Generation 1.5 Ethanol: The Bridge to Cellulosic Biofuels*, he makes a compelling argument that the insistence of cellulosic feedstocks denies the carbon reduction benefits from a range of other products that can meet the 50 percent GHG reduction. He termed it *Generation 1.5* rather than assuming a second generation of fuels produced solely from cellulose would be possible, stating,

> "Despite the emphasis on the development of Gen 2 the reality is that the volume of cellulosic biofuels required by the RFS2 schedule has not been and will not be available. Because of the lack of available cellulosic biofuels, US refiners can make a strong argument that they are being forced to buy something that does not exist; and, therefore, the requirement should be eliminated. It is simply wrong to mandate implementation of RFS2 via the use of unknown or unproven technology (Madson 2012)."

Madson was right on target with that prediction in 2012. Refiners have indeed argued that the cellulosic requirement is a small fraction of the original targets.

Technologists continue to make advances toward producing fuel ethanol from agricultural wastes and other cellulosic materials. Meanwhile, there are no valid reasons to penalize ethanol produced from feed corn.

MYTH: FOOD VERSUS FUEL

Perhaps no ethanol myth is more based in "moral" outrage than that of food versus fuel. Naysayers argue that a bushel of corn could feed a starving family, but the nation chooses to selfishly convert it to fuel so we can drive our SUVs. Anti-ethanol policies supported by this misconception are presented by so-called "anti-hunger" groups who, without fail, have never taken the time to learn how ethanol is produced. The truth is that *field* or *cow* corn, grown to feed cows or produce ethanol, is not *sweet corn* grown for human consumption. In fact, less than 10 percent of corn produced is for human consumption because there is only a small market.

This myth was further debunked during the battle for the RFS in 2008 and extensively referenced in Marc Rauch's *The Ethanol Papers*. Various government and private studies determined food price increases are because of the increases in crude oil prices—not ethanol. As DOE and other organizations proved in chapter 2, ethanol production decreases the demand for crude oil, thus lowering the price of not only crude oil but also every product that relies on it to arrive at the marketplace. Therefore, ethanol production lowers the price of your fuel *and* your food and, frankly, nearly everything else you buy, too.

We have been involved in more than twenty studies investors needed to determine the profitability of ethanol plants being considered for financing. Here is the simple economics. One-third of a bushel of corn contains the starch used to make the fuel, and the remaining two-thirds is high-protein animal feed, hopefully soon to be human-grade if approved by FDA. Therefore, US ethanol production from feed corn creates more food and fuel.

In our interview with Dave Vander Griend of ICM, whose company built about half of the fuel ethanol plants in the United States and many more in several countries, he explained their research turning high-protein animal feed into high-protein human-grade food. He notes, "the world is not lacking in starch: It is lacking in more protein." Vander Griend points out, if ethanol producers could not make or sell the high-protein feed needed to keep up with growing worldwide demand, the economics would not work.

Fuel ethanol production is the means by which farmers may be more efficient and profitable, thus keeping their farms in business. The more farmers lose work, the more farmland is taken out of production and developed for other uses. Less ethanol production would not only hurt food security for the world, but it would also turn farmland into shopping centers and housing developments, thus exacerbating climate change.

By virtue of their ignorance, ethanol detractors are asking their elected officials to vote for policies that would encourage farmers to grow less food and increase the prices of everyday goods.

MYTH: ETHANOL INCREASES LAND USE
If an anti-ethanol article talks about ethanol production's impact on land use, it is outdated or designed as disinformation. Another telltale sign of misleading information about ethanol is a source that will not make any comparison to the impact of crude oil on land use.

Two self-proclaimed land-use experts have weighed in on this issue. One is a longtime critic of ethanol, Dr. Timothy D. Searchinger. The media used Dr. Searchinger's study as a reference extensively during the RFS battles. The second expert is Dr. Lark, introduced in chapter 3. Unfortunately,

Lark's work has not had the longevity of Searchinger's in the mind of the public.

Although Searchinger's report is decades old and even highly criticized at the time, it has lasted past its time. The erroneous study was even cited in a recent Reuters special report: "How US Ethanol Plants Are Allowed to Pollute More than Oil Refineries" (Reuters 2022). "'The ethanol mandate was just a mistake,' said Timothy Searchinger, a senior researcher at Princeton University's Center for Policy Research on Energy and the Environment. 'We created a terrible model.'"

The Reuters special report was soon retracted and is no longer available on their website. However, that bad data already lapped the earth a couple of times at cyber speed. It is still referenced on the CleanTechnica website (Hanley 2022). Even Mark Twain would have been impressed.

The US Department of Energy's Argonne National Laboratory, Purdue University, and the University of Illinois system published an assessment of the "Environmental Outcomes of the US Renewable Fuel Standard," a report by Tyler Lark of the University of Wisconsin mentioned earlier. The authors of the Argonne study released the following:

After a detailed technical review of the modeling practices and data used by Lark et al., we conclude that the results and conclusions provided by the authors are based on several questionable assumptions and a simple modeling approach that has resulted in overestimating the GHG emissions of corn ethanol.

"The land-use changes identified by Lark et al. likely reflect the conversion of fallow or idle land to crops rather than permanent grasslands.

Lark et al. likely overestimated soil organic carbon (SOC) loss by a factor of two to eight because of the incorrect application of carbon response functions.

The validation of the SOC emissions model used by Lark et al. … showed a remarkably poor fit to measured SOC change. This is important since a foundational assertion in the recent study was that emissions related to land-use change are higher than commonly recognized.

Lark appeared to have double-counted the emissions of nitrous oxide—a greenhouse gas—from the use of fertilizer in corn production by adding them in, while overlooking the fact that they are already included in the corn-farming-related emissions in the main lifecycle assessment models (Taheripour 2022)."

MYTH: ETHANOL INCREASES THE PRICE OF YOUR GASOLINE

If an anti-ethanol article is about ethanol driving gasoline prices up, it is a relic. As we discussed in "Chapter 2: The True Cost of Gasoline," adding ethanol to gasoline drives down the price of gasoline and world crude oil.

Free market revelers would like you to believe that supply and demand work for everything except ethanol. How could adding 10 percent of the highest-octane fuel to the gasoline pool increase prices if the baseline price is lower? It is math at its most basic level. If you take out a gallon of three-dollar gasoline and replace it with a gallon of two-dollar ethanol, how can that possibly increase the price? Detractors would argue the ethanol has a lower energy content and gets less milage. The facts show it is offset by its octane value, and any mileage loss is negligible. It is hypocritical doublespeak.

In our interview with Terry Ruse, who is now the manager of operations for Benchmark Renewable Energy, an advanced biofuel campus facility in Raeford, North Carolina, he said,

"The average price of ethanol over the past ten years has been lower than unblended gasoline by twenty-six cents per gallon on average. Based on retail postings, octane's indicated value is nearly twenty cents per octane point, depending on the gasoline grade. This translates into an additional unrealized value of 18 cents per ethanol gallon in a 10 percent blend!"

The lower price and higher value of ethanol do not increase the cost of gasoline to retail stations.

If the oil industry claims ethanol costs more, why does it cost less? What could possibly be the price difference of fuel ethanol between Oklahoma and Maryland in the same week?
Photos by Burl Haigwood.

MYTH: FUEL ETHANOL RELIES ON FEDERAL GOVERNMENT SUBSIDIES

To spur research, production, and use of ethanol, Congress included a tax incentive in the Energy Policy Act of 1978. The Congressional intent was for the oil industry to offset additional costs. It was unfortunately called the ethanol tax exemption, though the oil industry took the money and left the ethanol industry to bear that cross. As ethanol matured, the cost consistently fell below that of gasoline, but the petroleum industry was happy to continue to pocket most, if not all, the subsidy.

As we discussed in "Chapter 2: The True Cost of Gasoline," studies show fossil fuels, oil, and thus gasoline and aromatics/BTEX have received trillions of dollars in federal government subsidies to artificially keep the price of gasoline lower than alternatives.

In 2019, the Environmental and Energy Study Institute (EESI) estimated federal subsidies for the fossil fuel industry at $20 billion per year (Coleman 2019). The EESI analysis did not include defense spending to protect oil supplies from the Middle East region.

Another example is provided in the International Center for Technology Assessment study "The Real Price of Gasoline" (Harrje 1998):

- Total annual government spending on subsidies: $38 billion to $114.6 billion

- Total annual protection costs (military): $88.5 billion to $140.8 billion

- The real price of gasoline per gallon
  - Low estimate: $5.60
  - High estimate: $15.14
  - Including price spike: $15.37

Those estimates were before Iraq's invasion of Kuwait on August 2, 1990, and the dozens of conflicts in the decades to follow. The argument about federal subsidies is another example of doublespeak.

MYTH: THE NATION DOES NOT NEED ETHANOL OR A RENEWABLE FUEL STANDARD

We have been at countless Congressional hearings and heard the same baseless claims that the US and oil industry do not need ethanol or an RFS because we have plenty of gasoline right here at home.

At the time the RFS was passed, the petroleum industry had shown no inclination to produce domestic renewable fuels so there was most certainly a need to reduce our level of dependence on foreign oil. The RFS, while not restricted to fuels produced in the US, was designed to and succeeded in propelling domestically produced alternatives to crude oil and gasoline. US percentage of imports fell from 60 percent to 45 percent from 2005 to 2011.

Getting Congress to pass RFS legislation was a five-year battle. For many years, organizations that should have been supporting our effort were missing in action (see "Chapter 15: Missing in Action"). Since its passage, it has once again become an annual battle to keep the RFS. When Congress is in session, it is an opportunity for oil companies to try to repeal the RFS, making it open season on ethanol. In the most recent case, it was also election season.

During the Congressional debates on the RFS in 2005, net US oil imports were roughly 60 percent, according to a 2012 Congressional Research Service (CRS). The CRS report states,

> "Oil is a critical resource for the US economy, but despite policy makers' long-standing concern, US oil imports had generally increased for decades until peaking in 2005. Despite the decline in net import volumes, the cost of net imports has increased due to rising oil prices. The aggregate national cost of oil imports is a function of the volume of oil imported and the price of that oil. The United States spent about $327 billion on net oil imports in 2011. Being a net importer of a particular good is not necessarily negative for an economy, but greater national oil import dependence can amplify the negative economic impacts of oil price increases (Congressional Research Service 2012)."

Simply stated, when the US lowers demand or reduces oil imports, OPEC can simply raise the price because there are still no significant alternatives and ethanol use is essentially capped at 10 percent.

The hypocrisy associated with this myth becomes obvious when oil industry executives complain about legislation designed to support ethanol during Congressional hearings. They often said ethanol was not necessary, and it was increasing the price of their customer's gasoline. Suppose the oil industry does not believe ethanol is essential to keep their costs low and their refiners of plentiful supply of lower priced octane. Why would they need to charge you upwards of one dollar per gallon more for premium gasoline? Furthermore, why would they charge consumers upwards of one dollar per gallon when they don't add ethanol? The following snapshots in time paint a somewhat hypocritical and unethical picture.

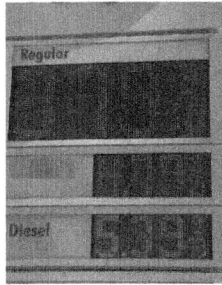

"Octane is the single most important property of gasoline when determining engine design" (Mercedes Benz 2013). If oil companies do not think having more supplies of high-octane fuel is important, why do they charge you $1 more for premium?
Photos by Burl Haigwood.

MYTH: ETHANOL IS A WASTE OF TAXPAYER MONEY

Taxpayers receive a healthy return on their ethanol investment. According to the 2021 *Contribution of the Ethanol Industry to the Economy of the United States* study by John Urbanchuk, managing partner at ABF Economics:

- In the past three decades, the return of the taxpayers' investment in ethanol has been fivefold. Americans see about $14 billion in savings at the fuel pump.

- The estimated cost of the two major federal incentives in 2008, the Volumetric Ethanol Excise Tax Credit (VEETC) and ethanol Small Producer Credit, totaled $4.7 billion. Consequently, the ethanol industry generated a surplus of $7.1 billion for the federal treasury.

- Fifteen billion gallons of ethanol displaced nearly 500 million barrels of crude oil at an estimated value of $33 billion.

- The impact of spending for annual operations of ethanol production, co-product output, exports, and R&D is estimated to have contributed nearly $52 billion to the nation's GDP.

- The ethanol industry spent $37.6 billion on raw materials, other inputs, and goods and services.

- The largest share of spending was on corn and other feedstocks. The ethanol industry used 5.1 billion bushels of corn valued at $30.8 billion.

- USDA Trade Multipliers suggests that the $4.4 billion of export value-added $10.7 billion to the GDP and supported twenty-seven thousand jobs in all sectors of the economy (Urbanchuk 2022).

Ethanol production creates geopolitical power. US farmers and ethanol producers feed our strongest allies, including Canada, Mexico, Japan, South Korea, Turkey, and Vietnam. Relying on crude oil and gasoline creates a geopolitical vulnerability that leads to our presidents begging for oil while being *held over a barrel*.

The Department of Energy's Alternative Fuel Data center website (https://afdc.energy.gov/stations/#/find/nearest) will help you locate the 4,125 gasoline stations in the United States that sell E85. How much more would you pay for gasoline that reduces your carbon emission by almost half? You don't have to because it costs *less*.
Photo by Marc Rauch.

TAKEAWAYS
- Considering the unified outrage against oil companies gaslighting about climate change to protect their oil market, we hope there will soon be a similar outrage about the gaslighting over ethanol and other alternative fuels.

- During the past four decades, competition and the free market brought consumers technological advancements in telephones, TVs, and the internet, and private companies are even launching rockets into space. Meanwhile, gasoline remains in the stone age.

WHAT'S NEXT?
- Can EPA protect public health and the environment and save the day?

PART 2

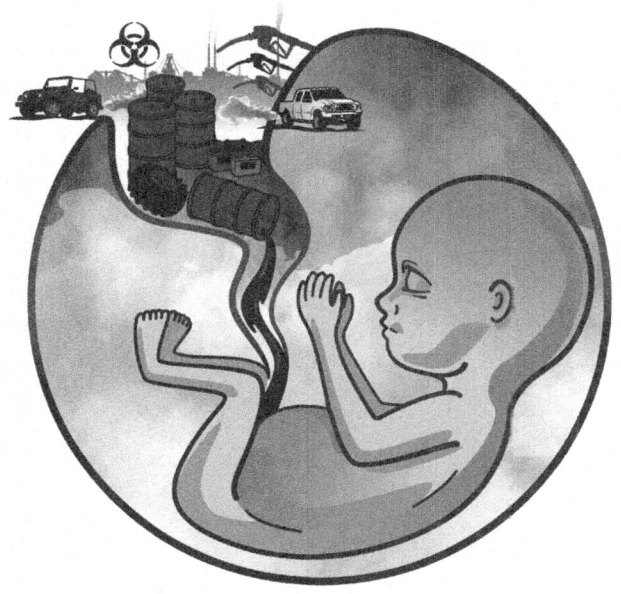

From conception to cradle to grave.
Illustration by Antony Razwadowki.

CHAPTER 6
A Sacred Oath

EPA Circumvents Energy and Environment Laws, Regulations, and Its Mission

On the surface, the legislative process is simple. Public pressure forces Congress to create solutions to the nation's problems. Congressional committees responsible for those problems hold hearings to receive testimony from the public and industries affected. Committee reports and the final legislation provide the roadmap with specific directions for federal agencies to implement the legislation. We believe EPA continues to defy or ignore explicit Congressional intent and documented history of not complying with the Clean Air Act (CAA) and Section 202 (l) in the Clean Air Act Amendments of 1990 (CAAA).

EPA OWNS THE CLEAN FUELS MISSION
EPA's jurisdiction, responsibility, and stated mission are to protect public health and the environment. As a result,

other agencies can't always step in and help fill the void (see "Chapter 12: The People versus Big Oil, Congress, and EPA").

"EPA's mission is to protect human health and the environment. When Congress writes an environmental law, we implement it by writing regulations. Often, we set national standards that states and tribes enforce through their own regulations. If they fail to meet the national standards, we can help them.

[We] teach people about the environment. Protecting the environment is everyone's responsibility and starts with understanding the issues. The basics include reducing how much energy and materials you use, reusing what you can, and recycling the rest (US Environmental Protection Agency 2022c)."

Despite its mission of protecting public health and the environment, EPA has not proactively supported ethanol use, leaving its environmental stewardship mission incomplete.

THE OFFICE OF AIR AND RADIATION'S OFFICE OF TRANSPORTATION AND AIR QUALITY (OTAQ) OWNS EPA'S PROGRAM RESPONSIBLE FOR CLEANING UP GASOLINE

The Office of Transportation and Air Quality (OTAQ) is within EPA's Office of Air and Radiation. According to OTAQ's "Toward a Cleaner Future" report published in 2005, OTAQ's mission is to:

Protect public health and the environment by reducing air pollution from motor vehicles, engines, and the fuels used to operate them and by encouraging business practices and travel choices that minimize emissions. The Clean Air Act requires EPA to regulate fuels and fuel additives for use in motor vehicle, motor vehicle engine, or nonroad engine or nonroad vehicle if such fuel, fuel additive or any emission products causes or contributes to air or water pollution that may endanger the public health or welfare (National Service Center for Environmental Publications 2005).

Based on our experience and research, EPA's vehicle emissions testing fails to protect public health to the greatest extent possible as required by the Clean Air Act Amendments of 1990 (CAAA). Therefore, EPA's failure defies explicit Congressional directives in legislation. Because of this failure, millions of people are at risk for sickness, disease, and premature death from mobile source air toxics (MSAT) attributed to aromatics/BTEX.

We will uncover the tip of the information iceberg and provide resources for further in-depth and validated research.

THE MISSION STARTS WITH AN OATH

Every individual who works for the federal government in any capacity must take an oath "to support and defend the Constitution of the United States against all enemies, foreign and domestic." While this might not seem to apply to a government agency like EPA, the second part of that oath is "that I will well and faithfully discharge the duties of the office on which I am about to enter." It is not a stretch to expect EPA to do everything within its power and ability to protect public health in response to this oath.

Thousands of dedicated civil servants working for the EPA have executed their duties to the best of their ability. We believe most of the opportunity for correction and responsibility for not complying with the Clean Air Act Amendments (CAAA) is in the hands of the EPA/OTAQ team in Ann Arbor, Michigan.

THE US CONGRESS GAVE EPA/OTAQ THE AUTHORITY TO REDUCE AROMATICS/BTEX

Section 202(l) in Title II of the CAAA contains Congressional language stating EPA *shall* use maximum achievable control technology (MACT) and "Technology-Forcing" regulatory adjustments to reduce toxics in gasoline as they present themselves. The EPA administrator can decide on the greatest degree of emission reduction achievable through the application of technology, considering many variables that include commercial availability and cost. However, using *shall* as opposed to *may* is significant because it obligates EPA to take action. According to many legal experts, the "shall" is an endangerment finding and is not an option.

THE MAKING OF THE CLEAN AIR ACT AMENDMENTS OF 1990 (CAAA)

The Clean Air Act (CAA) was passed in 1963. Congress designed the CAA to curb four major environmental and health threats to millions of Americans: acid rain, urban air pollution, toxic air emissions, and stratospheric ozone depletion. The amendments also established a national operating permits program to make the law more workable and strengthened enforcement to help ensure better compliance with the CAA.

Like any significant legislative effort, amending the CAA was not a rapid process and took years. Congress amended the CAA with overwhelming bipartisan support. President George H. W. Bush signed the law on November 15, 1990. The amendments featured new, progressive, and innovative approaches for effectively achieving the air quality goals and regulatory reform expected from these far-reaching amendments.

President Bush claimed responsibility and deep roots to the legislation, given that as vice president to Ronald Reagan, he headed up the Regulatory Reform Task Force in 1981. Staff at the US EPA's Office of Transportation and Air Quality had equally deep roots to the bill, but for a different reason. EPA/OTAQ's regulatory failure instigated the public, the president, and Congress to act.

Our organization, the Clean Fuels Development Coalition, was part of a diverse group of industry stakeholders that worked closely with the White House, Congress, and other federal agencies interested in reaching the national policy goals of the CAAA. We identified common-ground strategies to strengthen enforcement, prevent loopholes, keep the oil industry from "backsliding" on regulations, and meet the intent of Congress.

Congressional action resulted from public outcry stemming from the oil embargoes of 1973 and 1979 and economic recessions that followed the price spikes. In addition to public health and environmental protection goals in the CAAA, Congress also recognized the nation had reached a dangerous dependence on imported crude oil and, by default, forced a de facto mandate for crude oil, gasoline, and especially aromatics/BTEX. As a result, Congress passed major energy and environmental legislation as illustrated in the table in chapter 3, "Legislative and Regulatory History of Fuel Ethanol-Related Initiatives and the Battles to Protect Them."

An essential part of history is that before the CAAA passing, we were actively engaged in a near miss in 1987 to reduce aromatics/BTEX. Legislation passed by the House of Representatives established an oxygenated fuel standard that would have resulted in ethanol replacing toxic aromatics. Still, the Senate did not take it up when Congress adjourned in 1988. However, that effort laid the foundation for the clean octane provision in the CAAA.

The effort to clean up gasoline and couple it with domestic energy policy had begun in earnest when in 1987, Freshman Senator Tom Daschle implored then Vice President George H. W. Bush to focus on the looming public health threat of high levels of toxic and carcinogenic aromatics/BTEX in gasoline. The key to replacing those toxics was ethanol and methanol, another less-popular biofuel.

The support of President Bush for the CAAA and the inclusion of clean fuel provisions was all thanks to his White House Counsel, C. Boyden Gray. A colorful, knowledgeable, and dedicated lawyer, Boyden Gray drove a ten-year-old Chevrolet converted to run on methanol. He became a huge supporter as he learned more about ethanol and its high octane and oxygenate properties. Because of his direct efforts, the president embraced alternative fuels, and ethanol specifically. Gray's hands-on work with Congress as a liaison to the administration fashioned the most critical parts of the legislation. He is without question the nation's authority on the Clean Air Act, having drafted many of the provisions himself. He went on to advise George W. Bush and served as US Ambassador to the European Union. He remains a staunch supporter of ethanol and a harsh critic of EPA's Office of Transportation and Air Quality.

"Of course, ethanol has faced opposition from oil companies," he told us in an interview in July of 2022, "but the biggest problem has been EPA and the environmental community. EPA never truly supported ethanol and between rigged models and skewed full lifecycle analyses, ethanol never got a fair and accurate accounting."

Senator Daschle's frustration in the late 1980s, a frustration shared by Boyden Gray and many members of the Senate Environment Committee, was what Gray has termed trading a poison for a carcinogen. EPA/OTAQ failed to acknowledge that the removal of lead from gasoline resulted in significantly higher aromatics levels because refiners needed to find new sources of octane. Their anger and frustration were based on a 1971 Senate Environment Committee report stating when lead was in gasoline, the aromatic content averaged 22 percent but increased to 37 percent by 1987. Despite recognizing the increase, EPA proposed increasing test fuel's allowable aromatic content to 45 percent (Clean Fuels Development Coalition 2015).

EPA estimated it would cost refiners $450 million to $600 million annually from 1986 to 1992 to meet the lead phasedown standards (Daniels 1985). Although the number seemed high, a 1984 EPA cost-benefit report stated that eliminating lead would increase the manufacturing cost of gasoline by just 1 percent, and the health benefits would exceed the costs (US Environmental Protection Agency 1984).

Despite of all the studies refuting the benefits of lead, in 1984, the oil industry was still trying to defend adding lead to gasoline (Berry 1984). The need for phasing down aromatics/BTEX should be based on the same public health rationale and cost benefits as lead phasedown.

Did you know EPA still allows lead in aviation fuels? That makes airports even more dangerous.

LEGISLATIVELY MOVING FROM LEAD ADDITIVES TO ALTERNATIVES

Negotiations among the senators and staff had been underway for some time, and the basic framework of an agreement to remove lead from gasoline had been drawn up as the CAA amendments were nearing floor action. Though removing lead was a given, few concentrated on what would replace it. However, key members of the Senate had been studying and seized the opportunity the amendments presented to not just address a problem but to provide a solution.

Senator Tom Daschle, already immersed in energy and transportation fuel issues, crafted an amendment that would change the composition of motor fuels in the United States. Senator Daschle, Health Committee Chairman Tom Harkin of Iowa, Tim Wirth of Colorado, and many others understood that refiners would continue to use the worst part of the oil barrel—aromatics—to replace octane lost to lead removal. Therefore, it was crucial for public health to ensure that the already high aromatic content did not get even higher. As Health Committee Chairman Harkin stated in a floor statement during the CAAA deliberations:

> "Aromatic hydrocarbons in gasoline include benzene, toluene, and xylene. Benzene is a known carcinogen, one of the worst air toxics. Eighty-five percent of all benzene in the air we breathe comes from motor vehicle exhaust. Xylene from automobile exhaust in the morning rush hour will form ozone [smog] in sunlight to choke our lungs by the afternoon trip home. Toluene, another aromatic, usually forms benzene during the combustion process and thus becomes carcinogenic along with benzene in the gasoline" (Congressional Record, 101st Congress, Clean Air Act Amendment March 29, 1990).

The Daschle amendment is commonly called "the clean octane amendment" because it defined what would replace the lead and limited toxic aromatic compounds. Senator Daschle propelled the amendment forward by getting then-Senate Majority Leader Bob Dole to cosponsor it. Senator Harkin decided to cosponsor as well. The Daschle-Dole-Harkin amendment was a bipartisan health and energy initiative that specified a gasoline recipe and established a scheduled phase. Additionally, mandatory studies aimed at mobile source air toxics (MSATs) directed EPA/OTAQ to determine which MSATs to regulate and at what levels. As previously noted, EPA received specific Congressional direction in Section 202(l) in Title II of the CAAA.

Senator Daschle and his colleagues made no apologies for telling the petroleum industry how to clean up gasoline and the EPA how to enforce it. Senator Daschle's floor statement is recorded in the *Congressional Record* on March 29, 1990.

"Unfortunately, EPA has known about this problem for more than a decade and has repeatedly failed to address it. Despite the fact that mobile source toxics account for more than half the air pollution-related cancer deaths annually, EPA does not regulate mobile source toxics. I simply do not trust EPA to implement a program that has been stonewalled for more than a decade... The oil industry is one of the most powerful industries in the world. The EPA is not immune to pressure, both from well financed lobbying and from divergent interests within the Administration itself" (*Congressional Record* 1990).

A BIPARTISAN LANDSLIDE VOTE

Despite strong opposition from oil state senators, the amendment to establish reformulated gasoline (RFG) with a year-round oxygen content passed by a huge margin: sixty-nine to thirty. It was a historic "clean octane" requirement. It was not an ethanol mandate as the methanol-based additive MTBE was the preferred oxygenate by the petroleum industry. However, both ethanol and MTBE provided octane and displaced petroleum products.

It is critical to recognize Congress had made its endangerment finding by clearly defining the health dangers of toxic aromatic compounds in gasoline. In addition to the specified recipe to include oxygenates, EPA still had the task of reducing these harmful compounds. It was an order, not an option. But before the RFG requirements even took effect in 1992, the agency was dragging its feet. EPA/OTAQ was to have completed a rulemaking on toxics by May of 1995. EPA/OTAQ conducted a partial study in 1993 and 1995 but did not issue a preliminary rule until August 2000. The EPA rule was finalized five years late and included an inexplicable and complicated "toxics averaging scheme." That scheme skirted clear Congressional intent: to remove toxic aromatic/BTEX compounds from gasoline "to the greatest extent possible."

Instead, EPA gave the refining industry a pass. Rather than requiring the maximum toxics reductions possible, EPA let refiners get away with raising some levels of various toxics and then averaging them as the means to not increase overall toxic emissions. Yet the averaging did precisely that, with benzene topping 3 to 4 percent in some areas (Hallberg 2014).

We ran into the oil industry everywhere during this era. Lobbying expenses, as reported to Congress, were increasing (see "Revolving Door" in chapter 7). Beginning with the floor debate over the cost of RFG and adding oxygenates, refiners commissioned studies claiming outrageous costs to comply with all the new requirements. Then US Senator Don Nickles cited American Petroleum Industry estimates that this new gasoline formulation would cost $100 billion and at least $1 billion per refinery (Congressional Record Mar 29, 1990). Because many areas were not required to adopt RFG but were considering it, this threat of soaring prices passed on to consumers was an effective scare tactic.

EPA consistently supported the oil companies throughout the process by not supporting ethanol, and that lack of support was clear to us. We believe EPA protected the oil industry from a future cost they had not quantified.

Nowhere was this more obvious than in the areas selling reformulated gasoline (RFG). The law required the most polluted "non-attainment areas," i.e., cities in America as measured by ozone exceedances, to use RFG. Other areas, while not classified as *severe,* were *serious* and could opt-in to the RFG program. We believe the oil industry badgered EPA/OTAQ to agree that simply lowering evaporative emissions, or Reid vapor pressure (RVP), was enough of a control strategy. This cemented a fixation on the part of EPA/OTAQ that evaporative emissions/RVP rather than tailpipe emissions were the most critical fuel property to control. As noted in chapter 5, that notion was disproved in many non-attainment area battles. One such example we were directly involved with was in Phoenix, Arizona. When the state adopted RFG, it achieved air quality standards. When the petroleum industry convinced the next governor to opt out of the program two years later, they fell back into noncompliance (Clean Fuels Development Coalition 1995).

The idea of simply lowering gasoline's vapor pressure while ignoring toxics and failing to increase combustion through oxygenates defied science, public policy objectives, and common sense. Real-world data proved the oxygenated fuel content, as required with RFG fuels, was eating up carbon monoxide (CO). While carbon monoxide had its own wintertime compliance standard, it was clearly a precursor for ozone, or summertime smog, as well. The RFG formula not only included an oxygenated fuel but also capped benzene volumes and, by EPA/OTAQ's own models, reduced several other ozone precursors (Clean Fuels Development Coalition 1995).

Simply lowering vapor pressure through a low RVP program only addressed evaporative emissions, and only during the summer months. It was the oxygen in the fuel and the cap on benzene that protected the public from unburned hydrocarbons in the form of toxic-bearing particulates year-round. RFG included both vapor pressure and added oxygenates. Current EPA/OTAQ standards deem a low RVP program equal to the RFG formula, but the evidence shows RFG is notably superior.

Where were the environmental organizations during all this? Usually buried in their own, often singular, mission. While they might profess to protect the environment as a whole, many are special-interest groups, with some focusing on just water, land use, or even wildlife. These motor fuel-related provisions were technical, complex issues that many of these groups failed to understand.

We interviewed Scott Sklar, president of The Stella Group, Ltd and adjunct professor at George Washington University. Sklar was the former executive director and founder of the

Solar Lobby, several biomass nonprofits, and coauthor of *The Forbidden Fuel: A History of Power Alcohol*. Before becoming one of the nation's leading authorities on solar energy, during the 1970s, Sklar worked for US Senator Jacob Javits from New York. Sklar recognized then that ethanol provided a trifecta of energy, economic, and environmental benefits. He remains a respected lynchpin to the environmental community but noted their shortcomings when he told us, "So many of these groups cannot talk to each other, so there is little if any understanding of the other guy's issue. Environmental groups can become so siloed and buried in singular issues that they cannot see the big picture."

Ernie Shea, director of the 25x25 Campaign and former assistant secretary of Agriculture for Maryland, agrees. Shea also served as CEO of the National Association of Conservation Districts, whose mission is to "promote responsible management and conservation of natural resources of all lands." Consequently, he dealt directly with environmental groups and told us many of them have bought into misinformation campaigns funded by the fossil fuel industry. Shea told us,

> "Agriculture is a solutions platform. Biomass and biofuels could redefine the sector and positively contribute to climate change, energy, and food supply. But that message is not getting through. They are not monolithic, to some degree they are resistant to transformational change, including our fuels."

Like Sklar, Shea believes there are too many competing interests within the environmental community.

Boyden Gray takes it a step further, raising the specter of "agency capture," meaning EPA has identified itself with environmental groups to such an extent that they feel like that is their constituency and are hesitant to take an opposing position. Or, given that they are subject to so much influence from the petroleum industry, could that be their captor?

Because oxygenated fuels like ethanol displace petroleum, representing a loss in market share to an already heavily subsidized oil industry, there was plenty of incentive for the oil industry to fund disinformation efforts. Again, EPA rarely stepped in to set the record straight or offer additional information and perspective. We believe the only plausible explanation for how EPA/OTAQ could argue that low RVP sufficiently protected the public is either they have been personally persuaded by misinformation or they are chock-full of former oil industry employees. They certainly could not say they did not have enough information. After all, Congress told them how to get toxics out of gasoline, and they refused.

As evidence piled up in city after city that low RVP was failing to reduce smog while RFG was succeeding, they continued to support the petroleum industry's arguments that the two were equal. As we discussed in "Chapter 4: Tales from the Battlefield," the battles for cities to implement cleaner fuel standards ranged from Phoenix to Birmingham to Pittsburgh to Providence as we tried to help these, and many other cities, fight for clean air while EPA stood by.

In 1994, EPA/OTAQ made clear how it felt about petroleum alternatives. As the deadline to meet Congress's demands approached, EPA made a concerted effort to ensure that the multiple public policy objectives of the CAAA were met, namely the energy security benefits of reducing petroleum use and creating markets for renewable and domestic ethanol.

Under pressure from Congress, which had nearly passed legislation to require a certain percentage of oxygenates in the clean fuel programs to be renewable, EPA/OTAQ proposed a rule to require 30 percent of the oxygen demand be renewable based. However, the courts considered EPA overreaching and struck down the rule. Many in our coalition noted EPA's rule was riddled with weak links, and their obsession with evaporative emissions and ozone control rather than reducing the more dangerous mobile source air toxics caused by aromatics/BTEX in gasoline being the weakest. One of ethanol's few demerits is when added to gasoline, it raises the Reid vapor pressure (RVP), but the benefits of increased combustion from an oxygenated fuel far outweigh the impacts of evaporative emissions.

In a 1987 EPA report to Congress, the agency stated, "In analyzing the effect of gasoline volatility controls on cancer incidences caused by benzene, the Agency found that controlling volatility will have little or no impact on the number of incidents" (Congressional Record, March 29, 1990, S3513). EPA/OTAQ's fixation on emissions that do nothing to reduce tailpipe carcinogens is difficult to reconcile, especially when their 2009 report references benzene 243 times (US Environmental Protection Agency 2009).

We believe by 2000, EPA/OTAQ had established a pattern of obstructing ethanol's market growth. Based on our interactions and their actions, and notable inactions discussed in the next chapter, it seemed clear to us and others in our coalition that the EPA could be sheltering the oil industry from investing in modern technology, the exact opposite of "technology-forcing" provisions in the CAAA.

We are not alone in noticing EPA's reluctance to see the ethanol glass as half full; several people we interviewed agreed. Eric Washburn worked for Senator Tom Daschle during the height of the implementation phase of the RFG program. Washburn was the point person for Daschle when they introduced the RFS. Washburn was well respected by Congressional staff and EPA personnel and a steadying influence at a time when debates and negotiations often got heated. He later worked for other Congressional members and gained enormous insights into the process and conflicts between industry, government, and nonprofits. In our interview with Washburn, he concedes EPA has held back the growth of ethanol.

California had enormous influence over fuel regulations, and Washburn agrees that EPA was "culturally close to California." California regulators and Congressional representatives seemed to regard Midwest ethanol as coming from a foreign country and resisted ethanol at every turn. Washburn told us he felt EPA's attitude toward ethanol was "not to give it the benefit of the doubt unless you can prove it is not a problem. [Until] then we are going to assume there is."

Fast-forward to 2015. Carol Werner was the executive director of the Environmental and Energy Study Institute in Washington, DC, a non-profit education and policy organization. In Davis Burroughs's *Morning Consult*, Werner states,

"Benzene is today's lead." Even though EPA had capped the amount of benzene in gasoline, according to the *Morning Consult* review of components that make up gasoline sold by five major oil and gas companies, a gallon of unleaded averaged about 25 percent aromatics (Burroughs 2015). Recall Senator Harkin's floor statement, among other sources, which notes benzene is not just a volumetric measurement because benzene is formed in the air by the combustion of other aromatics/BTEX.

In 2016, EPA/OTAQ indicated they intended to propose a REGS rule (Renewables Enhancement and Growth Support Rule, 81 Fed. Reg. 80828). The rule would cap ethanol blends in conventional vehicles at 15 percent. That would equate to an ethanol roadblock and mandate for an 85 percent market share for gasoline and still no aromatics/BTEX reductions. This rule also would have classified any ethanol blend above 15 percent as an alternative fuel. This classification would subject ethanol use to many extraneous and burdensome regulatory requirements. This is a classic case of EPA answering a question no one asked and considering themselves helpful. There is no room for "enhancement and growth" for an industry with a rule that stunts it.

Meanwhile, researchers from nine national laboratories discovered ways to boost efficiency and lower emissions using conventional and advanced engines for vehicles that burn petroleum-based fuel blended with up to 30 percent of components produced from sustainable sources. The US Department of Energy's engine and fuel testing team has been hard at work on EPA's mission since 2016. DOE is bringing clean, efficient, affordable fuels and engines to market sooner.

The first-of-its-kind Co-Optimization of Fuels & Engines (Co-Optima) Program provides the American industry with the scientific underpinnings needed to maximize vehicle performance and efficiency, leverage domestic fuel resources, and reduce lifecycle emissions. Co-Optima partners include the National Renewable Energy Laboratory; DOE labs at Argonne, Idaho, Lawrence Berkeley, Lawrence Livermore, Los Alamos, Oak Ridge, Pacific Northwest, and Sandia National Laboratories; as well as more than twenty university and industry partners. EPA is once again MIA.

According to DOE, Co-Optima can:

- help improve fuel economy by 10 percent or more for light-duty (LD) vehicles,

- trim engine-out criteria pollutant emissions by as much as 99 percent for medium-duty (MD) and heavy-duty (HD) engines, and

- supply new fuel components with GHG emissions 60 percent lower than petroleum fuels for all cars and trucks (US Department of Energy 2022).

DOE's immediate objective was to give American industry and policy makers the scientific knowledge, data, and tools needed to identify the most beneficial alternatives. Commercial adoption of Co-Optima innovations makes it possible to reduce pollution and the use of imported oil, helping the nation mitigate climate change and strengthen energy security. Congress stated those same objectives in the CAAA and asked EPA to include them in developing the rules. When we met with DOE for their input on requiring a high-octane standard in the upcoming CAFE, or US Corporate Average Fuel Economy, rule in 2021, they told us, "we were not asked for our input by EPA or DOT."

Rather than seek to develop ways to use more ethanol for its benefits, why would EPA develop the REGS rule to effectively kill any chance of growth for renewable biofuels?

EPA did not support our coalition with developing the oxygenated fuel program, the reformulated gasoline program, or the renewable fuel standard. Yet it takes credit for the sickness, disease, and healthcare cost savings resulting from those programs. EPA's doublespeak is demonstrated in their Regulation of Fuels and Additives Report. In summary,

- EPA takes credit for the health benefits projected from the RFS.

- EPA requires the labeling of fuel dispensing systems for oxygenated gasoline—mandatory ethanol pump labeling—but not for the toxic emissions or carcinogenic exposure to aromatics/BTEX.

- EPA provides a loophole in the US Code of Regulations. "Nothing in this part is intended to preempt the ability of state or local governments to control or prohibit any fuel or fuel additive for use in motor vehicles and motor vehicle engines which is not explicitly regulated by this part." And hopefully, by now, you too would not be surprised to learn that in that over-one-hundred-page document regulating gasoline, the words benzene, BTEX, or aromatics did not appear even once. But the keyword "renewable" appears in their report 1,201 times (US Code of Regulations 2022).

OCTANE WARS

United by our shared mission to recognize the contribution of clean fuels on vehicle technology and reducing air toxics, Ford, General Motors, and Chrysler were members of CFDC for over a decade. We worked closely with the auto industry in asking EPA/OTAQ to increase octane. Automakers know more than anyone that higher octane would allow them to increase compression in conventional engines and get significantly better mileage. Ethanol would be the only legally permissible and cheapest source of octane if EPA enforced toxic limits. The only way oil interests would agree to requests by automakers to increase the baseline octane of gasoline was by coupling it with killing the RFS and then limiting ethanol blends to 15 percent. This would then pave the way for the oil industry to add more aromatics/BTEX to gasoline, especially knowing EPA/OTAQ had not indicated any willingness to enforce CAAA Section 202 (l) requirements as established in the Daschle amendment to the CAAA.

TAKEAWAYS

- EPA/OTAQ has had the information, responsibility, funding, and opportunity to address mobile source air toxics (MSAT) and make gasoline cleaner and safer.

- As a result of EPA's actions and inactions, individuals and federal and state governments pay more for health care, gasoline, and other total social impacts like national defense and climate change.

WHAT'S NEXT?

- Hindsight has its advantages. It helps us identify opportunities and anticipate delay tactics and strategies.

- We have documented the many opportunities EPA missed to make gasoline safer by supporting the increased use of renewable fuels.

- How has EPA failed to "protect human health and the environment" despite obvious options that would have made their mission possible?

CHAPTER 7

EPA's Actions Obstruct Environmental and Alternative Energy Progress

A History of Missed Opportunities, Noncompliance, and Creating Regulatory Hurdles

Mr. Butts changed the tobacco industry with *The Cigarette Papers*, but we have not yet received a message from our Mr. or Mrs. BTEX. However, we have the analysis of ten thousand emails from EPA through a Freedom of Information Act request. Emails and correspondence show at times, EPA/OTAQ has worked *with* the oil industry they took a sworn oath to regulate, resulting in negative impacts on public health, the environment, and the economy. Meanwhile, history shows that EPA had opportunities to utilize research and industry experts, including our coalition, but still do not proactively seek ways to leverage ethanol to meet their mission and comply with the Clean Air Act Amendments of 1990 (CAAA).

In this chapter, we will look at six key events that provided EPA/OTAQ the opportunity to enforce the Clean Octane Amendment in the CAAA as directed by Congress. These missed opportunities could have created "technology-forcing" actions, making gasoline cheaper (less expensive), better (higher octane and more efficient), cleaner (lower emissions), and safer (lower toxic emissions) to the greatest extent possible. Instead, they relied on forcing technology on automakers to make them responsible for incinerating the oil industry's dirty fuel.

Reducing mobile source air toxics (MSAT) is not a new issue. It should have been EPA's high priority for years. We hope new directives to reduce greenhouse gases (GHG) does not take the focus off reducing aromatics/BTEX/MSATs. EPA needs to broaden its view of ethanol and adopt an approach that embraces three key benefits. The first objective would be to stand firmly on climate benefits, the second on health benefits, and the third on reducing gasoline consumption. Lowering the price of gasoline with higher ethanol blends would be an environmental incentive instead of the traditionally perceived penalty. Higher blend volumes of ethanol could increase if EPA raises the minimum octane requirement *and* enforces Section 202(l) in Title II of the CAAA.

EPA's analysis of the CAA health and cost savings covered in chapter 2 proves the Renewable Fuel Standard (RFS) is effective. Enacting existing clean octane provisions in the CAAA would help meet the goal of that program by using thirty-six billion gallons or equivalent in the transportation fuel pool.

We still hope EPA will embrace ethanol because it is the only viable commercial replacement for aromatics/BTEX, especially when the science and data consensus shows the solution at hand is a lower-cost, lower-toxic, lower-carbon, and higher-octane product made in the United States.

Regardless of whether you feel EPA's inactions are because of ignorance, arrogance, or collusion, their actions thwart ethanol with the same results as the oil company actions illustrated in chapters 3, 4, and 5.

LEGISLATIVE AND REGULATORY OPPORTUNITIES TO PROTECT THE PUBLIC

Laws and subsequent regulations are often not applauded by industries or readily accepted by the public. As we discussed in chapter 6, when Congress passes legislation, they include directives to federal agencies to enforce it. While this process is transparent, it can also be open for interpretation and have ambiguous language leading to loopholes for a given industry to take advantage of. This is particularly evident in the rulemaking process, where an agency must develop a program to meet Congressional intent.

While we believe gasoline standards with respect to aromatics/BTEX have been ignored, in the meantime, the public is enjoying the shared benefits from other safety-related laws and regulation improvements. Improvements in seat belts, airbags, safety caps on medicine, food safety, child toy safety, occupational safety, health regulations, DUI laws, child restraint systems, and airline safety have been positive developments since the CAAA passed in 1990. Yet, thirty-three years later, we have failed to make meaningful improvements in gasoline even after Congress directed EPA to do so.

The following events are just a few of the significant opportunities EPA had to improve gasoline standards to protect the environment from climate change and the public from sickness, disease, and premature death of possibly millions of people in the United States. These opportunities were turned into obstacles, roadblocks, or unnecessary hurdles in each case. The result has hindered efforts to expand the market for ethanol despite Congressional intent, as evidenced since the CAAA and various energy initiatives passed by Congress, including the RFS.

1990 CAAA TOXICS RULE

As described in the previous chapter, Section 202 (l) of the Clean Air Act directs EPA to reduce mobile source air toxics. This section of the Act reaches the heart of our concern, but we believe measures to meet that directive are woefully inadequate. The legislation directed EPA to develop a rule fifty-four months after enactment, which would have been in May of 1995. They missed that deadline *by five years*.

We are not alone in our assessment. The Sierra Club, the Natural Resource Defense Council, the Public Interest Research

Group, and the states of New York and Connecticut sued EPA on the grounds that the control measures they eventually did adopt were insufficient in the final rule they produced in March of 2001. Sky Stanfield provides an extensive and comprehensive review and analysis of the unsuccessful lawsuit in the *Ecology Law Quarterly* in 2004. These groups were far from ethanol advocates; they simply recognized the health hazards of MSATs and challenged the rule on several fundamental arguments. One key argument stated the studies EPA were directed to perform were the basis for the flawed rule. The group argued the rule failed to meet the intent of the law in several areas. Those areas include that it be technology-forcing, while the costs assumed to the petroleum industry were excessive, and importantly, the rule failed to "achieve the greatest degree of emission reductions achievable" (Stanfield 2004).

We agreed with the analysis of the *Ecology Law Quarterly* review when they stated that maintaining levels, rather than reducing them, helped refiners avoid new capital investment and therefore incur no new cost. We ran into this poor logic repeatedly throughout our decades of working on these issues. Often when we discussed an environmental regulation that would protect public health, opponents would seem horrified that it would cost something to do so. The idea of protecting the party causing harm by not imposing costs on them contradicts the mission at hand.

The rule developed a Toxic Performance Requirement for gasoline that results in no greater emissions when burned than were present in the fuel content for 1998–2000. The rule created an averaging system that allowed refiners to increase certain pollutants and lower others as long as the combined total emissions met the cap.

Inexplicably, the lawsuit was unsuccessful, and the court rejected the plaintiffs' arguments. In true bureaucratic doublespeak, EPA argued that an anti-backsliding program—meaning not achieving future reductions but instead not going backward—was sufficient. As reported in Stanfield's review, EPA said, "The economic burden (to refineries) would be inconsistent with our finding that an anti-backsliding program at negligible cost is the most stringent program that we can justify in the near term." Stanfield summed up the conundrum and shed a bright light on why we continue to fight this battle.

> "How does the Greatest Reduction Become No Reduction? The Court found EPA acted within its mandate... despite the fact that the rule did not actually require any reduction in emission levels. By allowing an excessive consideration of costs, a continued deferral of rulemaking, and a perpetual search for more information, the court failed to ensure that emissions be reduced through technological innovation as the statute directs (Stanfield 2004)."

One of the many interesting people we got to interview and work with in the early years was Ed Rothschild, one of the first consumer energy advocates. Through his organization, Citizen Action, Rothschild gave significant credibility to our issue because he was not affiliated with the ethanol industry. By the 1990s, Citizens Action had affiliates in more than thirty states and had about two million members. Thirty-three years ago, Rothschild was ringing the alarm bell about the public health threat from benzene and aromatics in gasoline. As the director of energy policy, Rothschild published a report titled "Cancer at the Pump" in 1989, and he was not shy in carrying this message. Citizen Action's advocacy was not limited to consumer prices: The group recognized that consumer protection included their health (Rothschild 1989).

It had been about twenty years since we worked with Ed. Like us, he has no explanation for why gasoline depends on carcinogenic additives. Ed told us, "The EPA did not treat ethanol [as] seriously as they could have. They did not think it was the answer and should have looked at it as at least part of the answer." Rothschild followed his initial *Cancer at the Pump* report up with the second edition and continued to be a voice for change. He agrees there were small victories with RFG and other clean fuel programs, but much greater progress could have been achieved.

2007 MOBILE SOURCE AIR TOXICS (MSAT) RULE

In the 2001 rule, EPA committed to following up with additional rulemakings as directed in the 202 (l) provisions. By 2007, the first RFS had passed with a five-billion-gallon renewable fuel target. Interest in increasing octane was growing and considered in the update of the MSAT rule. However, when EPA released its 2007 MSAT Final Rule, they concluded there was an insufficient supply of ethanol to replace the aromatics/BTEX refiners were using for octane, again in the face of the requirements to reduce MSATs.

In conducting cost-benefit analyses, EPA failed to assume an increase in ethanol supplies, assumed crude oil was nineteen dollars per barrel, and that replacing aromatics required two gallons of ethanol instead of one (US Environmental Protection Agency 2007).

We considered these assumptions inaccurate then. They have become absurd with time.

However, and this is key, in the rulemaking process, EPA acknowledged ethanol was a superior octane enhancer, and they would revisit the MSAT provision if new science confirmed the linkage of aromatics to secondary organic aerosols (SOAs) and ultrafine particulate matter (UFP). The ethanol industry doubled in size in a few short years, making the supply argument a nonissue. Furthermore, a growing body of science indeed linked aromatics/BTEX to SOAs and PM. As recently as 2022, General Motors released a study concluding that 96 percent of particulate matter from gasoline was because of aromatics (Leach 2022).

Our view stated throughout this book has been consistent. As the regulatory authority over the RFS, EPA was aware of the significant increases in ethanol supply, and crude oil prices increased dramatically, making the previous cost-benefit analysis obsolete. Suppose EPA wanted to help move the ethanol industry along and truly clean up gasoline. In that case, it is within their authority to conduct a new cost-benefit analysis and even promulgate an octane rule. They did neither.

2007 PARTICULATE MATTER 2.5 (PM2.5) RULE

Particulate matter (PM) has become one of the most important air pollutants Congress is trying to control. Diesel fuel is a primary culprit, but gasoline also produces particulates. When it comes to PM, size matters. The smaller the particulate matter, the more it can get into your lungs. Particulate matter smaller than 2.5 micrometers is considered ultrafine particles (UFP) and can get directly into your bloodstream and wreak havoc (see "Chapter 11: Environmental Injustice").

As part of its periodic updating of National Ambient Air Quality Standards (NAAQS), EPA looked at their control technologies and determined more stringent reductions are necessary. They intended to limit their assessment of PM2.5 to diesel fuel with little focus on gasoline. This is relevant to our story because after EPA finalized its PM2.5 rule, it acknowledged that its computer model substantially under-predicted emissions of secondary organic aerosols (SOAs) and fine particulate matter from organic sources (Regulations.gov 2008).

However, EPA refused to correct its computer model—Community Multi-Scale Air Quality (CMAQ)—used to predict those emissions. EPA's top computer modeler for PM was an individual named Prakash Bhave. Bhave insisted most of urban PM2.5 came from either biogenic—trees—or diesel sources. Bhave also believed gasoline's only contribution to PM was primary organic aerosols (POAs). The EPA/OTAQ director at that time, Christopher Grundler, conceded EPA's mistake in not calculating secondary aerosols rather just primary aerosols in a March 15, 2018, letter responding to an inquiry from South Dakota Farmers Union President

Doug Sombke (Clean Fuels Development Coalition 2018). But nothing of significance has changed.

2008: INDIRECT LAND USE AND CARBON PENALTIES

We briefly reviewed the importance of land use and carbon reduction in chapters 3 and 5 so you would understand their impact relative to EPA's role. In the RFS, Congress instructed EPA to develop a lifecycle assessment (LCA) computer model to evaluate the carbon intensity factors for all liquid fuels, including corn ethanol.

EPA, the California Air Resources Board (CARB), environmentalists, and the oil industry relied on a report by Princeton University Professor Tim Searchinger, who had little practical background in the subject. His studies and theory essentially said biofuels were causing massive land-use changes, such as the deforestation of the Brazilian rainforest and new land or set aside lands being used to grow corn. This led to increased greenhouse gas emissions and potential food versus fuel issues. EPA ignored strong objections from several land use and climate experts warning Searchinger's assessments were invalid. They presented findings of their flawed Lifecycle Assessment model to the National Academies of Science (NAS) Institute of Medicine. It asserted the US would see 245 premature mortalities annually from increased ethanol use driven by the second Renewable Fuel (RFS).

Six years later, the comments submitted in response to an EPA Request for Correction of Information submitted by the Energy Futures Coalition, Urban Air Initiative, and the Governors' Biofuel Coalition summed up the problems with EPA's approach:

"A review of the scientific literature confirms that EPA fundamentally erred in the conclusions it reached about the lifecycle emissions of GHGs and other pollutants from ethanol. Despite significant improvements in the relevant technology and a growing body of updated scientific studies, EPA continues to regulate on the basis of its 2010 Lifecycle Analysis, relying on it as recently as last month in a new fuel pathway determination and last year in the 2014–2016 RFS Standards. And EPA continues to publish its outdated 2011 Report to Congress online, having failed to correct its inaccurate information in a follow-up triennial report, as the law requires. Petitioners therefore urge EPA to correct its analysis of the comparative lifecycle pollution effects of ethanol and gasoline in light of the best available science. Continued dissemination of and reliance on erroneous estimates undermines the scientific basis for important policy decisions in the critical area of fuel regulation (Energy Futures Coalition 2016)."

Energy Futures Coalition Executive Director Reid Detchon has spent decades trying to get EPA to focus on aromatics. He has held positions in the US Senate, as deputy assistant secretary for renewable energy at the Department of Energy and senior advisor for climate solutions at the United Nations Foundation.

During the National Clean Fuels Technology & Health Effects Leadership Forum cosponsored by the United Nations Foundation held in Washington, DC, on February 6, 2020, Detchon revealed what he termed the "smoking gun" (Detchon 2020). An EPA staff researcher, in a 2015 EPA workshop on ultra-fine particles, presented findings that had been published in a peer reviewed journal. According to Detchon, those findings were an admission that for many years, available atmospheric models could not predict SOA formation. Recent studies demonstrate that these assumptions were wrong (Environmental and Energy Study Institute 2020).

Those are two clear examples of how the EPA could have either pushed back in the case of flawed land-use claims or admitted their models were deficient. In both cases, EPA thwarted the development of ethanol, exposing the public to unnecessarily high levels of toxic gasoline.

Yet another missed opportunity to focus on aromatics/BTEX and therefore force technologies that would replace them, as required by law, is to address the universal cry from stakeholders to adopt the Department of Energy's Argonne National Laboratory's Greenhouse Gases, Regulated Emissions, and Energy Use in Transportation Model (GREET) (Urgun-Demirtas 2019). Per its mission statement, EPA/OTAQ could have relied on the GREET model. The computer model was considered a credible and validated computer then and is regarded as the gold standard today. Instead, it took decades to try to remove the tar and feathers EPA/OTAQ's analysis applied to ethanol.

2013: EPA TIER 3 RULEMAKING

After establishing national emission standards for non-road or off-road vehicles in 1994, referred to as Tier 1 of a nationwide effort to regulate gasoline emissions, EPA continued regulating emissions with a Tier 2 Vehicle and Gasoline Sulfur Program.

As described in the EPA website, "Tier 2 is a landmark program that began in January 2004 and affects every new passenger vehicle and every gallon of gasoline sold in the US. By designing cleaner cars that run on cleaner fuels, the result is much cleaner air" (US Environmental Protection Agency 2022). It was followed by a Tier 3 update and a forthcoming Tier 4.

Without question, EPA's Tier 3 standards offered significant national public health benefits. According to the Union of Concerned Scientists, "EPA's estimates show Tier 3 standards will prevent up to 2,000 premature deaths, avoid up to 2,200 hospital admissions, and eliminate 19,000 asthma attacks by 2030."

However, each year, oil companies and their allies in Congress actively worked against the EPA's Tier 3 standards, including making misleading and discredited claims about the impact these standards will have on consumers. Counter to these claims, a study commissioned by the Emission Control Technology Association and conducted by Navigant Economics finds that the cost of complying with Tier 3 standards for US oil companies is "in the vicinity of one cent per gallon" and may not even pass through to consumers.

EPA agreed in its analysis that it would cost about two-thirds of one cent per gallon (Union of Concerned Scientists 2013).

As positive as the Tier 3 rulemaking was, in 2013, EPA/OTAG asked for comments on the role of octane in its Tier 3 rulemaking. We were excited when, in the course of soliciting comments on the forthcoming rule, they discussed the potential role of octane and specifically asked for comments on 30 percent ethanol blends, or E30. This is extremely significant because an E30 blend would provide a huge octane boost to gasoline without a vapor pressure increase while lowering the carbon content and reducing various pollutants, most notably aromatics/BTEX.

We thought perhaps this was the breakthrough we had been looking for since 1990. During an industry briefing we attended at the White House in September of 2013, then-EPA Administrator Gina McCarthy said, "It looks like a 30 percent blend of ethanol in gasoline (E30) might be the sweet spot for fuel ethanol." In the end, the administrator was obviously overruled by what appears to be prejudices from the EPA's OTAQ team in Ann Arbor, Michigan. Despite soliciting comments in the notice of proposed rule, absolutely no mention of it appeared in the final rule.

This flip-flop on E30 was particularly frustrating given that as far back as 2008, several high-ranking EPA officials from the OTAQ office in Michigan applied for a patent on a high-efficiency alcohol fuel engine using 20 percent ethanol or more.

Charles Gray, director of EPA's National Vehicle and Fuel Emissions Laboratory, was one of the applicants for the patent. A truly interesting individual who we worked with during those crucial years leading up to and then implementing the fuel programs established in the Clean Air Act, he suggested that at least some folks in Ann Arbor thought higher than 10 percent blends could be practical in the future. According to the Patent Application's abstract:

> "In an internal combustion engine adapted to combust alcohol blend fuels (i.e., fuels containing greater than 20 percent alcohol by volume) ... to enable the use of a high compression ratio (greater than 15:1), for improved efficiency ... Thermal braking efficiency significantly exceeds that for conventional gasoline engines, thereby improving the potential cost-effectiveness of alcohol fuels (Google Patents 2022)."

2009–2021: CHANGES TO THE US CORPORATE AVERAGE FUEL ECONOMY STANDARDS (CAFE) STANDARDS

US Corporate Average Fuel Economy (CAFE) standards were first enacted by the US Congress in 1975 in response to the 1973–74 Arab Oil Embargo. The goal was to improve the average fuel economy of cars and light duty vehicles for the obvious purpose of reducing oil consumption. CAFE standards are a "technology-forcing" law that effectively moved automakers into a new era of efficiency to the benefit of the driving public. It was in their interest to produce automobiles that got better mileage and provided their customers with a lower cost of operation. But it took an act of Congress that included penalties for noncompliance to get it done.

While the original CAFE standards aimed at reducing crude oil and transportation fuel consumption, other public policy benefits created domestic jobs and reduced pollution.

The events mentioned prior have significance because they all impacted the three most tangible opportunities EPA/OTAQ had to protect human health and the environment during the administrations of Presidents Barack Obama, Donald Trump, and Joseph Biden. The original legislation required periodic updates, and either by requirement or seen as a positive initiative, each administration addressed CAFE standards.

Regardless, these events provided EPA/OTAQ with the chance to use their "technology-forcing" authority in the CAAA. EPA/OTAQ could help automakers improve vehicle efficiency by providing them with clean higher-octane gasoline automakers were asking for in the rulemaking process. In addition to reducing crude oil imports, the new standard would also create jobs, reduce GHGs, and reduce mobile source air toxics by forcing the aromatic/BTEX content of gasoline down.

In 2012, the Clean Fuels Development Coalition (CFDC) led a broad industry effort to make these points in the 2012 GHG Corporate Average Fuel Economy (CAFE) Rulemaking. In our comments to EPA/OTAQ, we focused on the critically important carbon reduction issue affecting transportation fuels. The CFDC et al. comments made the unique argument that as EPA was setting fuel economy and greenhouse gas standards, it would be an opportune time to finally enact the Congressional directive to reduce toxics, since high-octane fuels would otherwise be met with aromatics produced by the petroleum industry. Despite admitting in 2007 ethanol was a good octane enhancer if there were enough supplies, EPA/OTAQ rejected our comments, stating octane was "outside the scope" of the rulemaking (Clean Fuels Development Coalition 2012).

We then enlisted help in making our health argument, including working with the National Conference of Mayors and joining their business council. We presented at their annual meeting in Orlando, Florida, in 2012 and conducted over thirty briefings during that time.

The 2012 rulemaking was an unusually long period of regulation in that it established requirements thirteen years into the future. Recognizing that this was an unusual forward-looking endeavor, industry and government agreed to conduct a midterm evaluation (MTE) to determine if the assumptions and calculations they made in 2012 were still valid halfway through the regulated period.

Once again, we had an opportunity to present EPA with current, validated information on how the aggressive fuel economy standards the regulations called for could be met with higher-octane fuels. Many of the assumptions EPA had made in 2012 with respect to electric vehicle penetration had not materialized, and the standards were going to be difficult to meet. Our call for EPA to raise the minimum octane standard while enforcing the 202 (l) toxic controls went nowhere. We were trying to help the Obama Administration succeed in their fuel economy efforts by providing more tools, yet EPA ignored us.

In 2018, under the Trump Administration, EPA proposed to not only *not* increase efficiency standards but to roll them back. Ultimately, they proposed extremely modest increases under what they termed as the Safe Affordable Fuel Efficiency Rule (SAFE). Note the use of the word *Affordable*, an example of its concerns that environmental protection comes with a cost.

The Trump Administration's disdain for electric vehicles is a matter of record then and now (Lambert 2022). In the Notice of Proposed Rulemaking (NPRM) for this rule, EPA asked for comments on how higher-octane fuels could help meet the objectives of the program, and, of course, we provided comments (Clean Fuels Development Coalition 2017) (Clean Fuels Development Coalition 2018). Given the Trump Administration's leanings toward fossil fuels, we thought this would be a great fit for their ideology of how to achieve fuel economy since it kept us tied to the internal combustion engine. Once again, EPA ignored us.

Fast-forward to the Biden Administration. Determined to make fuel economy a centerpiece of their climate change efforts, the Biden Administration EPA in 2020 began work on blowing up the Trump CAFE program and developed a greenhouse gas (GHG) based system. It still equated to a mileage increase and working with the National Highway Traffic Safety Administration, which has joint jurisdiction on fuel economy. They established a standard requiring an 8 percent increase in 2024 and a 10 percent increase in 2026. We believe these are substantial increases.

CFDC, working with numerous other industry groups, put on a full-court press to get EPA to understand the efficiency gains possible with high octane. Ford Motor Company, for example, estimates a 7 percent increase in conventional vehicles with a ninety-three-octane fuel. Such a fuel can be economically produced with a 30 percent ethanol blend that contains much lower toxics. We had multiple meetings with EPA officials, looked them right in the eye, and asked that they request comments on the benefits that might be gained from clean, high-octane fuel. We made it even easier by saying, "We know you are not going to raise octane in this rule, but if you at least ask for information, it will allow us to build a record for next time." It was like asking for a ride and saying, "you do not have to pick me up, but at least wave at me while driving by."

The proposed rule did not even do that, and the final rule, with its fixation on electric vehicles (EVs), did not mention the word octane once in a 1,300-page rule (Govinfo.gov 2020).

TAKEAWAYS

- Despite their mission statement, EPA/OTAQ has never taken a leadership role in promoting fuel ethanol to environmental or public health organizations, Congress, media, or the American public via a national education campaign about health effects from the emissions of gasoline and especially aromatics/BTEX.

- The original CAFE standards focused on reducing crude oil in transportation fuels. Later, they also focused on reducing greenhouse gases and creating jobs. Even though EPA has unique authority to assess and regulate gasoline, they were missing in action when it came time to fulfill their purpose. Over time, the United Nations, USDA, and other credible organizations have categorically rejected the linkage of food prices to ethanol production.

- EPA has not made an effort to recognize or promote corn ethanol for its value in reducing carbon through sequestration, saving energy at the refining level, and ushering in a new era of efficient farming.

WHAT'S NEXT
- What would EPA do next to thwart the development of ethanol?

CHAPTER 8

The Smoking Gun and the Poison Squad

We Are What We Eat

When it comes to influencing Congress and changing history, timing is everything.

In 1901, chemist Dr. Harvey Wiley started a two-decade education and awareness campaign. His goal was to get the federal government to force food manufacturers to take toxic chemicals out of processed food and stop killing their customers. Dr. Wiley knew people had no idea what they were eating. To prove his point, Dr. Wiley conducted human trials on twelve people. The media dubbed the food testers the "Poison Squad" (Blum 2018). As the food safety issue was heating up, Upton Sinclair published *The Jungle*. Sinclair's book exposed the meat packing and canning industry's disregard for food safety and their customers (Sinclair 1984). In a hearing before Congress, Dr. Wiley stated, "There are hundreds and thousands of consumers who do not wish to use these chemicals in their food. It is the consumers and not the producers that should be venting their wrath."

Public outrage forced President Theodore Roosevelt to threaten Congress by releasing a government report (Public Broadcasting System 2020). On June 29, 1906, the US House of Representatives passed the Pure Food and Drug Act of 1906 (PL 59-384) 240 to 17, and the president signed it the next day (US House of Representatives 2022).

Is this analogous to our efforts to clean up gasoline? You bet it is. The good news is we do not need to create another federal agency. We do not even need new legislation. We just need to enforce the protective measures already established, such as the toxic control provisions in the Clean Air Act, and stop poisoning people with death-by-breath.

WE ARE WHAT WE EAT

The bad news is that we ingest more air than food or water. Romain Lacombe, the founder of Plume Labs, explains this alarming statistic in his TED talk, "Global Pandemic—Air Pollution." Lacombe graduated from École Polytechnique and received his master's degree at the Massachusetts Institute of Technology. Lacombe states, "People consume about 2.2 pounds of food, 4.4 pounds of water, and 20.44 pounds of air daily. We consume ten times more air compared to food and water." Citing a 2014 World Health Organization report, Lacombe shared another alarming statistic stating, "For the first time, air pollution is the world's number one preventable health risk. Breathing is more dangerous than poor diet, lack of exercise, high blood pressure, and tobacco. More people die every year from breathing air pollution than cigarettes" (Lacombe 2015).

We hope you can now understand the similarities between our fight to reduce the amount of aromatic/BTEX in gasoline, the Poison Squad, our Fuel Test Dummy Jack (chapter 3), and you. We also hope you are beginning to share our concern about EPA's role in preventing the development of technologies that would take harmful chemicals out of our gasoline and bodies.

As illustrated in the previous chapter, we believe EPA missed many opportunities to be proactive in replacing the harmful elements in gasoline. We acknowledge the composition of gasoline is a highly complex issue. However, we also believe EPA and the oil industry have taken advantage of that complexity to back their positions over the years.

A reasonable question for anyone reading *Gasolinegate* to ask, particularly after the last chapter and the inexplicable failure to take advantage of the fuel economy rules, is why? How can this inaction be justified? The answer is that their "science" supports it, which would be fine if it was accurate. We can point to no more relevant example than the computer model EPA uses to certify emissions from fuels and vehicles.

IMPACT OF EPA/OTAQS MOVES MODEL

"EPA's **Mo**tor **V**ehicle **E**mission **S**imulator (MOVES) is a state-of-the-science emission modeling system that estimates emissions for mobile sources at the national, county, and project level for criteria air pollutants, greenhouse gases, and air toxics." (US Environmental Protection Agency 2022).

EPA uses its MOVES model for the RFG program, Energy Policy Act (EPAct) studies, and Tier 3 certification fuel. In discussions with other clean fuel stakeholders, we discovered the MOVES model unnecessarily limited their assessment of potential fuel efficiency gains to regular-grade gasoline. EPA clearly ignored the recommendations of the National Highway Traffic Safety Administration (NHTSA) and defied the National Research Council's recommendations that higher-octane gasoline would positively impact efficiency and emissions.

This issue came to light at a Health Effects Institute (HEI) workshop in December 2016. The HEI workshop brought together some of the leading fuel emissions experts in the nation. The consensus was EPA must use real-world fuels under real-world driving conditions to get accurate measurements to certify fuels and vehicles for emissions. EPA/OTAQ's models were broken and therefore did not accurately reflect what consumers put in their gas tanks.

In addition to health groups, the auto industry has also weighed in. A 2015 study by the EPA assessing the emissions of higher blends of ethanol in which they added aromatics produced a completely skewed emissions profile. Automakers in a Society of Automotive Engineers (SAE) paper, *Issues with T50 and T90 as Match Criteria for Ethanol-Gasoline Blends*, went on record to complain that no one would ever make a fuel in that manner (Anderson 2014).

Steve Vander Griend, director of technical services at the Urban Air Initiative, rang the alarm early regarding the flawed EPA practice of match blending. He was also involved in writing the SAE paper. "Splash blending more ethanol on an already certified fuel only makes that fuel better by diluting aromatics, sulfur, and increasing octane," he told us. "Adding ethanol in a lab while adding aromatics, then blaming ethanol for various emission increases is going to produce their desired result."

Eventually, it came to light the EPA/OTAQ MOVEs computer model was underreporting toxic and particulate emissions by half. These flawed emission profiles were exposed in 2016 when Boyden Gray & Associates provided an analysis of EPA/OTAQ emails received by the Urban Air Initiative in its Freedom of Information Act (FOIA) request. As previously noted, C. Boyden Gray was the former counsel to President George H.W. Bush and played a crucial role in developing the Oxygenated Fuel, Reformulation Gasoline, and Renewable Fuel Standard programs. Ambassador Gray remains a staunch advocate for ethanol being the most suitable replacement for aromatics/BTEX. "The MOVES Model is a rigged system in the way it was developed," Boyden told us in our interview.

In essence, the FOIA emails caught EPA/OTAQ working with the oil industry to create "unicorn" fuels, meaning gasoline blends that do not exist in the commercial marketplace. Another player in this modeling exercise was the Coordinating Research Council (CRC). The CRC is a joint auto and oil industry research effort that is very involved in fuel formulation. In our interview with former Chrysler Executive Reg Modlin, he explained how the oil industry provided most of the funding for any work the CRC did and directed the bulk of their work on vehicle emissions. Most of the key personnel involved in the development of the model and the testing of the fuels either previously worked for Chevron and BP or did at the time. The subcontractors for EPA were former Chevron employees, and the project manager for EPA was a former BP employee.

By certifying vehicles on gasoline formulations that do not exist, these vehicles then go out into the real world and fall short of intended emissions standards. Sound familiar? This is the definition of the Dieselgate scandal and software scam Volkswagen got caught running on the public. The software was dubbed a "defeat device." The specifically engineered software allowed Volkswagen's vehicles to be certified under false pretenses. They were later proven to be polluting. In Volkswagen's case, the defeat device was on the vehicle. In *Gasolinegate*, the defeat device is a specifically engineered fuel without real-world results. The media and public were scammed on emissions, the related health threat, and the higher cost of gasoline by not using an alternative—ethanol.

How can we make that claim? The internal emails from EPA tell the story. The Boyden Gray law firm's analysis of the emails offers the following observations:

BOYDEN GRAY & ASSOCIATES ANALYSIS
Excerpts from the Executive Summary

1. EPA's emails reveal that the Agency directly solicited financial contributions and technical input, "especially on the fuel matrix," from the CRC. The oil industry had an incentive to participate because, as the EPA emphasized,

the "results generated will be critical to future policy decisions," including policies related to "future biofuel use."

2. The CRC executives in turn visited EPA personnel, expressing their "interest in this project and...in participating with some additions to the fuel matrix." Two CRC test fuels were ultimately selected by a Chevron employee and added to EPA's matrix. The CRC's investment in the design of the EPAct study explains why the CRC purchased all of the test vehicles so EPA could complete testing.

3. EPA hosted conference calls with oil industry employees "to resolve several outstanding issues related to this fuel matrix." EPA then redesigned the matrix based on their "feedback" and asked several oil industry employees what test fuels they would "prefer to see tested." The oil industry employees responded with detailed input on the test fuel parameters, outlining possible "compromises." EPA and its oil industry collaborators expected their test fuels to produce bad results for ethanol. When preliminary testing showed that higher ethanol fuels lowered emissions of nitrogen oxide and other pollutants, EPA considered "changing the program midstream" to obtain different results "if we continue seeing no NOX effect."

4. In the end, EPA decided to exclude the relevant test fuels from the program and otherwise altered its slate of test fuels to "emphasize ethanol effects."

5. EPA had provided thousands of emails and other internal records to UAI through litigation that Boyden Gray &

Associates initiated when EPA failed to timely respond to UAI's FOIA request. But EPA has withheld hundreds of other responsive documents and partially redacted hundreds more. UAI and EPA each recently filed motions for summary judgment asking the US District Court to decide their dispute about the scope of EPA's document production obligation under FOIA. The resolution of this case should uncover even more information about the oil industry's influence over EPA's emissions modeling.

6. EPA's exclusive and secretive reliance on the oil industry to design the Energy Policy Act (EPAct) study's test fuels violates the Federal Advisory Committee Act and EPA's own Scientific Integrity Policy and Information Quality Guidelines (Boyden Gray & Associates 2016).

BOYDEN GRAY & ASSOCIATES ANALYSIS
Discussion Highlights

- EPA's Design of the EPAct Study
  - The oil industry influenced the EPAct study's design from the beginning.
  - Higher ethanol content prompted more oil industry intervention.
  - EPA redesigned the matrix to address the oil industry's concerns.
  - EPA redesigned its fuel matrix when it proved impossible to blend.
  - EPA delegated the design of the EPAct study to an oil industry employee.

- EPA abandoned test results and test fuels that challenged its prior assumptions about ethanol's emissions effects.
- EPA made arbitrary, eleventh-hour, experimental design changes to control costs.

BOYDEN GRAY & ASSOCIATES ANALYSIS
Summary of Legal Implications

- We believe that EPA's secret consultation with a group of oil company employees about the test fuel parameters violated the requirement of the Federal Advisory Committee Act and EPA's Scientific Integrity Policy that such committees be balanced, that they be publicly announced, and that their meetings be open to the public.

- EPA's exclusive reliance on oil industry employees with an incentive to generate results favorable to petroleum and unfavorable to ethanol violated the objectivity requirement of the Agency's Information Quality Guidelines. It also violated EPA's Scientific Integrity Policy, which requires all employees, including scientists and managers, to "[a]void conflicts of interest and ensure impartiality."

- EPA's reliance on oil industry consultants was kept secret, in violation of the Scientific Integrity Policy's requirement that scientific findings, be "generated and disseminated in a timely and transparent manner."

- The EPAct study contributed directly to the emissions factors in the EPA's new vehicular emissions model,

MOVES2014, which states must use in constructing implementation plans for compliance with the EPA's air quality standards. The EPA's unlawful reliance on the oil industry to design the EPAct study compounds the agency's failure to give the public notice and an opportunity to comment on the MOVES2014 model, as required by law.

Our battle to fix the MOVES model continued. On January 19, 2017, the states of Kansas and Nebraska, joined by the Energy Future Coalition and Urban Air Initiative, filed a formal Request for Correction of Information, petitioning EPA to withdraw false estimates of ethanol's emissions effects.

For years, the EPA has required states to rely on these inaccurate emissions factors predicting that ethanol increases pollution, even though ethanol's pollution-reducing qualities have been repeatedly demonstrated. These erroneous emissions factors originated with the EPA's fuel effects study known as the "EPAct study" and the Agency's vehicular emissions computer model called MOVES2014. Prompt correction of these erroneous emissions factors is critically important because it encourages federal and state fuel policies that impair the nation's air quality.

The Request for Correction explains in detail the fundamental flaws in the design of the EPAct study that produced EPA's inaccurate emissions estimates. The filing also sheds light on the origin of these design flaws: EPA's collusion with oil industry employees in the study's design, as revealed by emails and other documents BG&A obtained through the aforementioned Freedom of Information Act request and related litigation (Boyden Gray & Associates 2017).

We initially provided access to the analysis of the emails in our *Gasolinegate Report* published in 2019. Although our outreach campaign generated over twelve million impressions on the internet, it did not go viral as we had hoped. We were surprised and very disappointed it generated little fanfare from Congress, the media, or the fuel ethanol industry. This was another reason we decided to write *Gasolinegate*. People needed to know.

People also need to know why there is a label for ethanol and oxygenated fuel on every gasoline pump—as if it is a warning—yet California is the only state requiring a warning label about gasoline, which explicitly includes benzene. We think there should be a "benzene warning" label on every gasoline pump, like the warning the Surgeon General made tobacco companies put on every package of cigarettes.

> "WARNING: Breathing the air in this area or skin contact with petroleum products can expose you to chemicals including benzene, motor vehicle exhaust, and carbon monoxide, which are known to the State of California to cause cancer and birth defects or other reproductive harm. Do not stay in this area longer than necessary. For more information go to www.P65Warnings.ca.gov/service-station (California Proposition 65 2016)."

An article in the *American Medical Association Journal of Ethics* by authors James F. Thrasher, PhD, Amira Osman, MPH, and Dien Anshari, MS provided the following information. As your research continues in *Gasolinegate*, we are sure you will see the correlation between the need for a warning label on cigarettes and gasoline pumps.

"The US Food and Drug Administration (FDA) was given regulatory authority over tobacco products in the Family Smoking Prevention and Tobacco Control Act of 2009. The act's mandate to the FDA included selection of "color graphics depicting the negative health consequences of smoking" to accompany nine different text messages for health warning labels (HWLs) that will cover 50 percent of the front and back of cigarette packages. The messages consist of the word "WARNING" paired with one of the following: "Cigarettes are addictive," "Tobacco smoke can harm your children," "Cigarettes cause fatal lung disease," "Cigarettes cause cancer," "Cigarettes cause strokes and heart disease," "Smoking during pregnancy can harm your baby," "Smoking can kill you," and "Tobacco smoke causes fatal lung disease in nonsmokers." This policy is consistent with recommendations by the World Health Organization Framework Convention on Tobacco Control (WHO-FCTC), the world's first global health treaty. As of 2012, 56 countries had implemented prominent pictorial HWLs on cigarette packs, and seven more countries are scheduled to do so in 2013. The US was to join these countries in 2012, but tobacco industry litigation has delayed implementation of this key tobacco control policy (Thrasher 2013)."

TAKEAWAYS

- Based on our research, it is our opinion EPA has a history of what appears to be unethical and unfair actions connected to the development and use of fuel ethanol in gasoline.

- Based on faulty inputs, the EPA model resulted in ethanol being deemed responsible for raising automobile emissions. EPA created a computer model that indicates federal reformulated gasoline is not beneficial.

- The EPA model, as designed, overestimates the impact of evaporative emissions to punish ethanol for its higher vapor pressure which, in comparison to benzene, we believe is negligible.

- EPA collaborated with oil interests which manipulated the computer model and the science and data produced to make a national policy decision that affects every citizen.

WHAT'S NEXT?

- Will EPA be moved by insight, analysis, and the Freedom of Information Act email analysis?

- Will EPA fix the MOVES Model?

CHAPTER 9

2018-2021: It's Déjà Vu All over Again

Should'a, Could'a, Would'a, Ought'a, and Didn't

New York Yankee's baseball Hall of Famer Yogi Berra popularly said, "It's déjà vu all over again" (Major League Baseball 2021). With that in mind, are you wondering how EPA/OTAQ responded to the MOVES model Request for Correction of Information? Once again, we hoped EPA/OTAQ should'a, could'a, would'a, and ought'a give a valid response to our request, but of course, they didn't.

In 2018, we worked extremely hard on comments to EPA regarding its upcoming Corporate Average Fuel Economy (CAFE) rulemaking. The Environmental and Energy Study Institute, Farmers Union Enterprises, Governors' Biofuels Coalition, Minnesota Farmers Union, Montana Farmers Union, National Farmers Union, Nebraska Ethanol Board, North Dakota Farmers Union, South Dakota Farmers Union, and the Urban Air Initiative signed on to the comments submitted by the Clean Fuels Development Coalition to request to include a modification to the national gasoline standard in CAFE standards (Clean Fuels Development Coalition 2018). As you can imagine, getting so many organizations and governors to agree on anything, much less an entire document, is challenging.

However, like Charlie Brown winding up to again try to kick a football held by Lucy hoping she would not pull it ways, we were hoping EPA/OTAQ would do the right thing with its next opportunity to improve the national gasoline standard by using their unique Congressional authority provided by Section 202 (l) of the CAAA of 1990.

Another way to lower mobile source air toxics is by restricting the volume of aromatics/BTEX in gasoline. Over the past thirty years, we accumulated an awe-inspiring arsenal of information. The consensus shows raising the minimum octane standard for gasoline would achieve EPA's stated mission (Clean Fuels Development Coalition 2018).

In formal comments requested by EPA/OTAQ from industry and the public for its CAFE rulemaking, CFDC et al., outlined several regulatory actions the agency should and could do that would reduce the amount of aromatics/BTEX in gasoline. This would improve the efficiency of vehicles, reduce gasoline consumption, greenhouse gases, mobile source toxics, and create jobs. The CAFE objective list was getting longer with the addition of greenhouse gas reductions and job creation, but our suggestions resulted in all the objective boxes being checked. Here is a summary of our recommendations. You can review the comments in their entirety with the URL link provided in the citation in the chapter appendix.

We believe EPA/OTAQ has the full statutory authority and moral obligation to act promptly on the attached ten-point Regulatory Reform Roadmap. By taking these actions, EPA/OTAQ could stimulate and protect the free market and fair trade and remove anticompetitive regulatory barriers restricting market access. In doing so, EPA would restore confidence and integrity to the oversight of programs designed to protect public health and the environment.

TEN-POINT REGULATORY REFORM ROADMAP

1. Like lead phasedown, establish a plan to transition to a minimum higher-octane standard of 98-100 RON.

2. Correct its misinterpretation of 211(f) substantially similar rule.

3. Extend the one psi RVP waiver for E10 and E15 to higher ethanol blends.

4. Approve a mid-level [higher than ten percent] Ethanol Blend Certification Fuel.

5. Update and reform its MOVES2014 Model.

6. Update its 2007 Mobile Source Air Toxics (MSAT) Cost-Benefit Analysis (CBA).

7. Update and reform its Corn Ethanol Life Cycle Analysis (LCA).

8. Comply with the Toxic Reduction Provisions in Section 202(l) of the CAAA.

9. Reinstate the incentives for automakers to produce FFVs.

10. Provide new incentives for automakers to produce engines optimized for higher-octane fuels.

We worked with Farmers Union Enterprises to publish the Gasolinegate Report in July of 2019. A table in the report "Actions EPA Can Take to Lower Toxic/Carcinogenic Aromatics and Save Lives, Save Consumers Money, and Create Jobs" updates our list above by calling on EPA to review the checks and balances.

> "EPA needs to review the checks and balance systems in the Clean Air Act Amendments of 1990 (CAAA) and determine who specifically monitors for backsliding and anti-dumping regulations for the increased use of aromatics in gasoline. New reports and data clearly indicate there is an increase in the volume of aromatics as well as the need to increase aromatic use in the gasoline pool to boost octane to make up for the growing low octane sources of crude oil refiners are buying from shale oil producers and from Canada (Farmers Union Enterprises 2019)."

To date, none of these suggestions have been adopted. As a result, the aromatic/BTEX levels remain the same and pollution is getting worse because their faulty atmospheric air pollution model is now included in the faulty MOVES model that certifies gasoline and vehicles. More context and perspective on the impact of repeated history are provided in the next chapter.

Meanwhile, the nation is now facing an "ethanol blend wall" because of EPA/OTAQs inaction on the items above. Ethanol blend wall is the term used to describe the marketplace when more ethanol has been produced than can fit into the gasoline market. More precisely, what they will allow in the gasoline market. EPA/OTAQ has in essence capped ethanol's share of the gasoline market at 10 percent. Because of the history of oil industry interference and EPA/OTAQs negligence, we thought this would never have been achieved. But it is clear that higher-blend volumes are achievable.

When Congress passed the RFS, EPA developed a system of credits and trading to provide maximum flexibility for obligated parties—refiners, importers of gasoline, others—to comply with the law. Every gallon of renewable fuel, be it ethanol, butanol, or biodiesel, is issued a Renewable Identification Number (RIN). A RIN is a tradeable credit, often called the currency of compliance, meaning the RIN is turned in to EPA showing the obligated party met their obligation. The volumes of the RFS are effectively translated to percentages; in other words, every refiner must augment its total of fuels with approximately 10 percent renewables. A refiner that blends more than required would generate extra RINS that can be sold to a refiner who either would not or could not blend ethanol.

In theory, the RIN system is good. However, certain fuels get more than one RIN credit, it skews the market. In the case of ethanol, these extra credits could eat into the actual gallons available for ethanol blending. For example, biodiesel gets 1.5 RINS—credits—per gallon. Once that obligation is met, those "extra" RINS are sold to someone who turns them in but no actual gallon of renewable fuel is used. In that case, those RINS are turned in to EPA, but no renewable fuel is used, and gasoline continues to contain high levels of toxic carcinogens. How does that protect the public from harmful emissions from the vehicles that remain on the road? This could be exacerbated if proposals to create RINS for electric vehicles come to pass. We address this challenge in more detail in "Chapter 13: Reality EV."

TAKEAWAYS

- Despite EPA/OTAQ having the science and data to make technology-forcing changes to automakers and fuel providers to take advantage of a higher-octane gasoline standard, they did not.

- The EPA's faulty models and inaction have resulted in its failure to protect public health and the environment.

WHAT'S NEXT?

- After years of fruitless work, the NHTSA repeals SAFE I Rule in 2021.

- Fast-forward from 2018 to 2021 because nothing resulted from our next attempts to improve national CAFE standards either.

- December 21, 2021: NHTSA Repeals SAFE I Rule

- "After reviewing all the public comments submitted on NHTSA's April 2021 Notice of Proposed Rulemaking, NHTSA finalizes the CAFE Preemption rulemaking to withdraw its portions of the so-called SAFE I Rule. The final rule concludes that the SAFE I Rule overstepped the agency's legal authority and established overly broad prohibitions that did not account for a variety of important state and local interests. The final rule ensures that the SAFE I Rule will no longer form an improper barrier to states exploring creative solutions to address their local communities' environmental and public health challenges" (National Highway and Transportation Safety Administration 2021).

CHAPTER 10
Environmental Justice

Death by Breath

The one thing we all share, regardless of race, creed, or color, is air. That air is polluted. The same air you are breathing now is the leading cause of significant health problems and premature deaths.

A 2013 assessment by WHO's International Agency for Research on Cancer (IARC) concluded that outdoor air pollution is carcinogenic to humans, with the particulate matter component of air pollution most closely associated with increased cancer incidence, especially lung cancer.

"Addressing all risk factors for noncommunicable diseases—including air pollution—is key to protecting public health" (World Health Organization 2022).

The health problems in your rearview mirror are much closer than they appear. This chapter reviews the major warning signs that brought us to this dangerous intersection of environmental, energy, economic, and public health policies.

On May 17, 2022, The Lancet Commission published "Pollution and Health: A Progress Update." Thirty contributing authors, their research team, and ninety-six peer-reviewed studies later reported,

> "Pollution cuts more lives short worldwide than war, terrorism, malaria, HIV, tuberculosis, drugs or alcohol... and is on par with smoking. Global efforts can synergize with other global environmental policy programs, especially as a large-scale, rapid transition away from all fossil fuels to clean, renewable energy is an effective strategy for preventing pollution while also slowing down climate change, and thus achieves a double benefit for planetary health. We cannot continue to ignore pollution. We are going backwards" (Fuller 2017).

Unfortunately, while everyone is affected by pollution, there is a disturbing history of urban, minority, and poor populations being disproportionately impacted. EPA established an Office of Environmental Justice (OEJ) in 1993, but "environmental justice" only became a mainstream buzzword in recent years. Its mission is "to address the disproportionately adverse human health and environmental impacts in overburdened communities by integrating environmental justice considerations throughout the Agency" (US Environmental Protection Agency 2017).

Hannah Perls's 2020 article, "EPA Undermines Its Own Environmental Justice Programs," outlines several obstacles that need to be cleared to achieve significant positive outcomes. Hannah stated, "There is no federal law governing environmental justice (EJ). This means that agencies, including EPA, have no authority to mandate actions or remedies addressing EJ concerns independent of their authorities under other statutes" (Perls 2020).

Others shared our concern over EPA's ability to execute the program alone. "In August 2011, seventeen federal agencies committed to updating their strategies for incorporating environmental justice into programs, policies, and activities. The agencies committed to providing meaningful opportunities for the public to comment on their environmental justice plans and efforts and to publish 'Annual Implementation Progress Reports' to inform the public on the status of their environmental justice strategies" (Jacobs 2015).

The OEJ programs often centered on real, identifiable problems like drinking water, soil and mill tailings, lead paint, and other obvious things. Many of these problems are found in urban areas with low-income and minority residents. The water quality problems residents experienced in Jackson, Mississippi, and Flint, Michigan, in 2022 were examples. To the extent air pollution could be traced to a power plant or a stationary source, they could be addressed. But the most dangerous source of urban air pollution is the primary culprit: gasoline emissions. Urban areas with tall buildings that trap air are incubators for such emissions (Sullivan 2022).

WHAT IS JUSTICE?

Then-presidential-candidate Joe Biden promised during his presidential campaign to address the pollution and drinking water concerns affecting poor communities. The assumption is that if lead were found in the drinking water of Beverly Hills or another rich, white suburb, EPA would be on it in a flash. Would rural areas in Mississippi get the same attention?

In 2021, the Biden Administration signed an Executive Order creating the Justice40 Initiative. Justice40 directs federal agencies to ensure that 40 percent of federal programs issuing grants or other federal investments in eight key areas benefit communities overburdened by pollution, climate change, and other environmental hazards. The Council on Environmental Quality then developed the Climate and Economic Justice Screening Tool. The tool's parameters include climate change, clean energy, energy efficiency, clean transit, affordable and sustainable housing, training and workforce development, the remediation and reduction of legacy pollution, [health burdens], and the development of critical clean water infrastructure (US Council on Environmental Quality 2022).

This new buzzword quickly received a lot of attention. The Biden Administration established the White House Environmental Justice Advisory Council to devote time and resources to this subject. The Inflation Reduction Act included $60 billion to fund Environmental Justice programs (White House 2021).

One objective for writing *Gasolinegate* is to help the media, public, health and environmental/health advocacy organizations (NGOs), and Congress understand the differences between generic "air pollution" and mobile source air toxic pollution. Everyone needs to understand and agree that all air pollution is not equal; some pollutants are much more toxic than others. Despite the Office of Environmental Justice mission, EPA's emphasis does not appear to be on gasoline or mobile source air toxics.

Following through on his commitment to action during his Journey to Justice Tour, on January 26, 2022, EPA Administrator Michael Regan announced a series of actions responding directly to concerns of communities historically and disproportionately impacted by pollution. According to EPA's press release, "The actions, which range from policy changes to community-driven efforts, reflect Administrator Regan's commitment to deliver environmental justice and work toward building a better America, and are part of the Biden-Harris Administration's whole-of-government approach to addressing these issues in communities that are marginalized, underserved, and overburdened by pollution." Administrator Regan stated,

> "In every community I visited during the Journey to Justice tour, the message was clear—residents have suffered far too long and local, state, and federal agencies have to do better. The pollution concerns have been impacting these communities for decades. Our actions will begin to help not only the communities I visited on this tour, but also others across the country who have suffered from environmental injustices (US Environmental Protection Agency 2022)."

Every time we hear the words "environment injustice," we hope the impact of gasoline will not be forgotten given it is one, if not the primary, source of such injustice. To date, that has not been the case. The EPA press release did not mention gasoline, aromatics/BTEX, or mobile source air toxics as if they did not exist.

How is gasoline not more of a priority considering the broad criteria of the Justice40 initiative? Some might push back and point to many cities that have adopted natural gas buses that replace diesel, which is a start. But the US consumes about 130 billion gallons of gasoline and forty-seven billion gallons of diesel (US Energy Information Administration 2022). How can the EPA not pay attention to passenger cars and light-duty vehicles? Our coalition believes the air pollution narrative got hijacked by change. Our research revealed the conversation is focused on climate change concerns nearly every time. We may drown in rising seas and floods, but people are now dying from mobile toxic air pollution. We are not alone in seeing a skewed set of priorities.

Writing for *The New York Times*, Binyamin Appelbaum, the lead writer on business and economic issues for the *Times* Editorial Board, posted this outstanding article on April 19, 2022, titled "Enough about Climate Change. Air Pollution Is Killing Us Now." Applebaum states,

> "The low quality of the air that we breathe should be regarded as a crisis. It also presents an opportunity. The existential threat of climate change has come to dominate debates about environmental regulation. Proposals to curb emissions, once presented as public health measures,

are now billed as efforts to limit global warming. The solution to both threats is the same: We need to stop burning fossil fuels, preferably yesterday. But there is cause to wonder whether a greater focus on the immediate dangers posed by air pollution, rather than the more distant specter of global warming, might help to muster the necessary support for changes that are going to be expensive and disruptive (Appelbaum 2022)."

We could not have said it better ourselves. We could start cleaning up gasoline this afternoon if EPA removed the regulatory barriers identified in the previous chapters and our elected officials put climate change, as sexy as it is for them to talk about, in proper perspective.

"We the people" pay the ultimate price for EPA's failure to protect the public from mobile source air toxics coming from aromatics/BTEX in gasoline. A gradual acceptance that carbon dioxide and fossil fuels are affecting climate change has evolved over the past decade. Similarly, we find little dispute over the fact that air pollution is killing people. Could any reasonable person then argue that mobile source emissions, of which gasoline is the primary source, should be the first place to focus if we are to provide environmental justice? Where is the justice for every man, woman, and child being subject to toxic emissions as they stand on a corner waiting to cross a street?

During the height of the COVID-19 pandemic, data proved that less driving had resulted in cleaner air in New Delhi, Kansas City, New York, or Beijing. Using computer models to generate a COVID-19-free 2020 for comparison, National

Aeronautics and Space Administration researchers found that from February to November 2020, pandemic restrictions reduced global nitrogen dioxide concentrations by about 20 percent (National Aeronautics and Space Administration 2020). Vistas that previously were only foggy images burst through as crystal-clear pictures of what clean air looks like. If we thought we were cleaning the air before, we now see we can do better.

While not officially defined as a pollutant, the COVID-19 pandemic made obvious the health issues that come with urban living. A second alarm sounded when New York City reported that inner-city minorities were experiencing the highest fatalities from COVID-19. The same was true for Midwestern cities like Chicago and Milwaukee. Were these people predisposed to getting sick by simply living in urban areas? Our research and history of observing the energy and environmental impacts suggested that could be the reason.

In November 2020, the Harvard University School of Public Health came to the same conclusion in its study, "Fine particulate matter and COVID-19 mortality in the United States: A national study on long-term exposure to air pollution and COVID-19 mortality in the United States." The School of Public Health published an article, "Air Pollution Linked with Higher COVID-19 Death Rates" summarizing the study.

> "The study looked at more than 3,000 counties across the country, comparing levels of fine particulate air pollution with coronavirus death counts for each area. Adjusting for population size, hospital beds, number of people tested

for COVID-19, weather, and socioeconomic and behavioral variables such as obesity and smoking, the researchers found that a small increase in long-term exposure to PM2.5 leads to a large increase in the COVID-19 death rate (Wu 2020)."

The study found, for example, that someone who lives for decades in a county with high levels of fine particulate pollution is 8 percent more likely to die from COVID-19 than someone who lives in a region with just one microgram per cubic meter less of such pollution. The reality is that minority communities were disproportionately contracting COVID-19 because of health conditions caused by poor air quality.

A study by the Max Planck Institute for Chemistry, Harvard University, and the Cyprus Institute's Climate and Atmosphere Research Center was another example. Ethen Lieser provided an analysis of the study in her article "Air Pollution Linked to 15 percent of All Coronavirus Deaths" in the *National Interest* on October 28, 2020. Lieser reported bad and good news stating,

> "Even after the virus is gone, people will still suffer from poor air quality... In East Asia, the percentage of coronavirus deaths related to pollution was about 27 percent, while Europe was 19 percent, North America 17 percent, and Australia 3 percent... The researchers stressed that millions of people will continue to die worldwide even after the pandemic if countries don't make a concerted effort to transition to clean and renewable energy sources (Lieser 2020)."

We believe pollution is much, much worse than what EPA measures. We believe the most important common ground finding in the studies is people living in counties in the US that have experienced a higher level of air pollution as measured by EPA have a higher COVID-19 mortality rate. Particulates associated with coal-fired power plants or diesel fuel are part of the story. Much smaller ultra-fine particulates are microscopic, equal to or lesser than one micron. Because ultrafine particles are underregulated and underreported, we focus heavily on them in our efforts to increase octane but limit toxic aromatic/BTEX compounds.

The COVID-19 pandemic is only one example of the connection between urban areas and higher—unjust—levels of pollution. As the Harvard studies make clear, most of the preexisting conditions that increase the risk of death from COVID-19 are the same diseases that are affected by long-term exposure to air pollution. They underscore the importance of enforcing existing air pollution regulations to protect human health and the environment during and after the COVID-19 crisis.

TAKEAWAYS

- Environmental justice is a nationwide responsibility, and its power is desperately needed in cities to focus on this issue.

- All Americans—minority or not—need to understand they are already at risk and will continue to be until we reduce tailpipe emissions by cleaning up gasoline *and* reducing consumption.

- Everyone directly or indirectly pays more for health care and social programs because of the root cause of environmental justice.

- The current condition is an injustice for sure.

WHAT'S NEXT?
- Is environmental justice a legal or constitutional right?

- What would constitute environmental injustice?

CHAPTER 11

Environmental Injustice

Can We Get an Amen?

What do experts really know about the link between air pollution, mobile source air pollution, and the emissions from aromatics/BTEX and what they do to the body?

First, let's agree that air pollution is a problem. We hope the previous chapter's World Health Organization (WHO) reports do not fool you into thinking these are problems in faraway places. In this chapter, the *WHO* is you. The problem is closer to home than you might be wishfully thinking. The American Lung Association's 2022 "State of the Air" report says:

> "Despite decades of progress on cleaning up sources of air pollution, more than 40 percent of Americans—over 137 million people—are living in places with failing grades for unhealthy levels of particle pollution or ozone. This is 2.1 million more people breathing unhealthy air compared to last year's report. Nearly 9 million more people

were impacted by daily spikes in deadly particle pollution than reported last year. In the three years covered by this report, Americans experienced more days of "very unhealthy" and "hazardous" air quality than ever before in the two-decade history of "State of the Air" (American Lung Association 2022)."

DEATH BY NUMBERS
We do not need a math expert or a computer model to understand what unhealthy air means to you. In its 2015 study, the Massachusetts Institute of Technology (MIT) estimates "premature deaths from air pollution in the US at 200,000 per year. According to MIT, emissions from road transportation were the most problematic, causing approximately 53,000 premature deaths in 2005, followed closely by power generation accounting for 52,000 of the totals" (Caiazzo 2013).

MIT's heat map graphics show the East and West Coasts of the US having more transportation-related emissions. The largest impact from power generation is in the east-central United States and the Midwest. MIT's data does not bode well for policy makers and environmental organizations relying on electric vehicles to be the silver bullet zero-emission vehicle of the near future.

Even closer to our home, MIT researchers mapped local emissions in 5,695 US cities, finding the highest emissions-related mortality rate in Baltimore, where 130 out of every 100,000 residents were likely to die in a given year because of long-term exposure to air pollution. While we do not live in Baltimore, we often visit the city for great sporting and social events and enjoy the hospitality of its residents. However, when not visiting, the wind often blows north to south and comes right down the beltway.

Jennifer Chu, a writer for the MIT News Office summarized the MIT's findings in her article "Study: Air Pollution Causes 200,000 Early Deaths Each Year in the US: New MIT Study Finds Vehicle Emissions Are the Biggest Contributor to These Premature Deaths." Chu quotes researcher Steven Barrett, an assistant professor of aeronautics and astronautics at MIT,

> "In the past five to ten years, the evidence linking air-pollution exposure to risk of early death has really solidified and gained scientific and political traction. There is a realization that air pollution is a major problem in any city, and there is a desire to do something about it. A person who dies from an air pollution-related cause typically dies about a decade earlier than he or she otherwise might have (Chu 2013)."

To determine the number of early deaths from air pollution, the MIT team obtained emissions data from the EPA's *National Emissions Inventory*, a catalog of emissions sources nationwide. The researchers collected data from 2005, the most recent data available at the time of the study.

MIT is not alone in its findings. EPA's "Benefits and Costs of the Clean Air Act (CAA) 1990–2020, the Second Prospective Study" proudly states the CAA will have prevented 230,000 deaths during that period (US Environmental Protection Agency 2011). However, we could not find a reference to the number of premature deaths caused. Our concern is that the conversation in the media appears to be in general about air pollution and not more focused on mobile source air toxic pollution.

As we mentioned earlier, writing *What's in Our Gasoline Is Killing Us: Mobile Source Air Toxics and The Threat to Public Health* inspired us to write *Gasolinegate* (Clean Fuels Development Coalition 2019). We reviewed hundreds of medical and technical reports that reference over a thousand peer-reviewed studies. We realized a clear connection to the rise in air pollution, mobile source air toxics, and the link to the health issues cited in the WHO reports. The data continued to point to mobile sources as the culprit. For example, the Pennsylvania Department of Environmental Protection's Toxic Pollutant Source website references EPA's data stating, "The EPA estimates that 50 percent of all man-made air toxic emissions come from mobile sources. Mobile sources produce air toxics through tailpipe emissions as well as evaporation from the engine, the fuel system, and when refueling" (Pennsylvania Department of Environmental Protection 2022).

Other stakeholders we interviewed shared our concerns after reviewing our publication and research. Doug Sombke of Farmers Union Enterprises said,

> "This research makes it clear that mobile source emissions are out of control—literally. Current EPA programs and models are faulty and fail to recognize the impacts of real-world fuels. If we did not learn anything from Dieselgate (the Volkswagen emissions scandal), when computers told us all is well when in reality, they were polluting the air,

then shame on us because the same thing is happening with gasoline."

The research path continues to track our thesis. According to EPA's How Mobile Source Pollution Affects Your Health website, "People who live, work, or attend school near major roads appear to have an increased incidence and severity of health problems associated with air pollution exposures related to roadway traffic. Children, older adults, people with pre-existing cardiopulmonary disease, and people of low socioeconomic status are among those at higher risk for health impacts from air pollution near roadways. These risks include:

- Higher rates of asthma onset and aggravation,
- Cardiovascular disease,
- Impaired lung development in children,
- Pre-term and low-birthweight infants,
- Childhood leukemia, and
- Premature death" (US Environmental Protection Agency 2022b).

The data continued to track in 2022. According to the US Energy Information Administration, "Transportation accounts for about half of mobile source toxics. Gasoline accounted for 58 percent of transportation energy use in 2021. Distillate fuels, mostly diesel, accounted for only 24 percent, and jet fuel accounted for only 11 percent. Ethanol's share is about 4 percent" (US Energy Information Administration 2021).

SIZE MATTERS

Department of Chemical Engineering, Carnegie Mellon University researchers Laura Posnera and Spyros Pandis' report, *Sources of ultrafine particles in the Eastern United States*, states, "Gasoline cars are the most important source of primary particle number." Their data show "Source contributions to ultrafine particle number concentrations for a summertime period in the Eastern US are gasoline automobiles (40 percent), industrial sources (33 percent), non-road diesel (16 percent), on-road diesel (10 percent), and (1 percent) from biomass burning and dust" (Posnera 2015).

As illustrated in chapter 9, EPA's unrealistic certification fuels and testing parameters did not accurately measure the emission data from the 287 million registered vehicles on the road in 2020. As a result, those vehicles are emitting more emissions than currently estimated.

In our interview with former Chrysler Director of Regulatory Affairs Reg Modlin, he acknowledged "EPA tends to pick and choose the issues they prioritize. We were aware that gasoline had health impacts but know a lot more now than we did then. We relied on groups like the Health Effects Institute (HEI), and they should have done more."

Even if EPA measurements were 100 percent effective at predicting real-world emissions, we believe EPA failed to recognize mobile source air toxics are responsible for the micro or ultrafine particles (UFPs) that fall below any regulated category. We think they're disproportionately dangerous. They defy particle size definitions but make up for their danger in total number and by their characteristic of being carriers of toxic carcinogens. Their microscopic size does not allow the human lung to filter them out, and they can directly enter the bloodstream. It is for this reason that gasoline-related emissions producing ultrafine particulates are not only associated with respiratory ailments but also neurological issues such as autism.

Carol Werner, executive director of the Environmental and Energy Study Institute, pointed out these same issues in EESI's 2015 comments to EPA when the agency proposed to update the air quality standards for ground-level ozone. The comments addressed to EPA Administrator Gina McCarthy stated,

> "The proposal leaves out the largest contributor to ground-level ozone in urban areas, gasoline exhaust... and according to EPA, in the United States alone, 45 million people are living, working or attending school within 300 feet of a major road, airport, or railroad."

Werner also pointed out that tightening the standards would provide increased protection from the negative health impacts of ground-level ozone, and she noted research showing fine particulate matter linked to autism and developmental disorders, low birth weight in newborns, and a range of other ailments.

> "Just as PM2.5 was a growing area of concern 20 years ago, ultrafine particle (UFP) exposure is a growing area of concern for public health researchers. Unlike larger particles, these ultrafine particles may stay airborne for weeks at a time, allowing them to travel long distances

and penetrate vehicles and buildings. Indeed, they are so small that they pass the blood barrier in the lungs and carry with them a toxic payload of PAHs, metals, and other products of incomplete gasoline combustion (Environmental and Energy Study Institute 2015)."

If you are concerned about your children's exposure to mobile source air toxics while at school, please refer to EPA's education and awareness information in their report, "Best Practices for Reducing Near-Road Pollution Exposure at Schools: Additional Resources" (US Environmental Protection Agency 2021).

Ultrafine particulate matter (UFP) and secondary organic aerosols (SOA) are linked to polycyclic aromatic hydrocarbons (PAHs). PAHs are in secondhand smoke. We believe a significant source of these lethal emissions is our gasoline's aromatic/BTEX components.

This carcinogenic aromatic-based alphabet soup exposes us to "endocrine disruptors" from when we are an embryo and follows us to our graves.

TIMING MATTERS

The focus of EPA's prioritization also needs to be on the importance of morbidity versus mortality. For example, just before reaching one's final destination of premature death, many must pay a pollution toll before paying the ultimate price. The pollution toll is the cost associated with the disease caused by air pollution. The toll comes with a hefty price tag that includes a doctor, specialists, specialty medicines, emergency room visits, and a costly extended hospital stay toward the end of life.

Most people have limited financial resources when the health effects of end-of-life begin. Thus, escalating healthcare costs burden the family and federal and state governments. The problem compounds when premature death comes earlier in life. This situation creates long-lasting financial and emotional stress and impacts younger family members.

What insurance do we have to cover us from "death by breath," and who should pay for it? We find it alarming that the health and property insurance companies are not pushing us down the halls of Congress, encouraging us to tell our story. Ernie Shea, whom we interviewed and introduced in chapter 6, made this point when he said, "The public Health Community needs to get engaged in these issues, and they have not." These potentially powerful allies of our cause are silent and missing in action (see "Chapter 15: Missing in Action").

Again, the problem starts early in life. In 2018, researchers in Belgium conducted tests on children's urine in a school near a roadway and found particulate matter. We can only guess what we would find in the US with similar tests. "Death by breath" is the outcome of the sickness and eventual diseases caused by air pollution. Premature death is not sudden like an opioid overdose, but they are equal in numbers. The air we breathe is not a choice of lifestyle, unhealthy habits, or product choice.

CAUSE OF DEATH MATTERS
The "Top 10 Causes of Death" in the US include heart disease, cancer, and various respiratory ailments; in fact, they are the top three of the ten (Nichols 2019). There is a clear association with research that links these causes to air pollution and mobile source air toxics (Clean Fuels Development Coalition 2019).

PREVENTABLE DEATHS MATTER
We found it alarming that preventable motor vehicle deaths in 2021—42,114—are less than those attributed to mobile source air pollution—53,000. Even more disturbing was that deaths from mobile sources were more than twice that of total gun deaths at 19,384. Deaths from natural disasters, for which some should be attributed to climate change, are estimated at 2,118 (Gramlich 2022).

We believe some portion of the "deaths by breath" from mobile source air toxics *should'a, could'a, and would'a* been preventable, but that *didn't* happen.

PROFILES IN ENVIRONMENTAL JUSTICE LEADERSHIP
The World Health Organization (WHO) report is not just about you; it's about your kids.

Dr. Linda S. Birnbaum was director of the National Institute of Environmental Health Sciences (NIEHS) of the National Institutes of Health, and the National Toxicology Program (NTP) from 2009 to 2019. Before she was appointed NIEHS and NTP director in 2009, Dr. Birnbaum spent nineteen years at EPA, where she directed the largest division focusing on environmental health research. In 2010, Dr. Linda Birnbaum testified before the Senate Environment and Public Works Committee stating, "In a 2009 study of the effects of PAHs on children's IQ in NYC... the mothers' exposure as measured during their pregnancies by wearing backpack monitors was associated with a decrease in IQ among the more exposed children. The extent of this effect was similar to that of low-level lead exposure" (National Institute of Health Sciences 2022).

Note Dr. Birnbaum's testimony to Congress was thirty-five years after unleaded gasoline was universally banned in 1975, indicating there has to be a linkage to the aromatics that replaced it.

Dr. Frederica Perera, PhD, was the founder of Columbia Center for Children's Environmental Health and served as director from 1998 to 2019. For decades, Dr. Perera has been one of the most outspoken advocates for children's health. We believe her leadership and research created new champions for public health and laid the foundation for groundbreaking new legislation.

Dr. Perera's 2017 study, "Multiple Threats to Child Health from Fossil Fuel Combustion: Impacts of Air Pollution and Climate Change," sums up our feelings and validates our research connecting the total societal cost and impacts of our dependence on crude oil and gasoline. It also explains what fuels our coalition to continue fighting for cheaper, faster, and safer alternatives to unnecessarily elevated levels of aromatics/BTEX in our gasoline.

Like the many-headed Hydra in Greek mythology, fossil fuel combustion inflicts a multitude of serious health and developmental harms in children through its emissions of toxic particles and gases and carbon dioxide (CO_2), a co-pollutant that is a major driver of climate change. Each of the myriad pollutants released from the burning of fossil fuels is capable of exerting multiple and cumulative adverse effects, either directly or indirectly. The developing fetus and young child, and especially the poor, are most vulnerable to the impacts of both toxic air pollutants and climate change. Were we, like Heracles, to succeed in slaying the Hydra, we would reap significant benefits for children (Perera 2017).

To that, we say AMEN!

For those who pray, let's pray for environmental justice because not much has changed since 2010. The research is clear, and the future can be bright.

It was challenging to paraphrase Dr. Perera's 2016 *Fossil Fuels Threaten Children's Health* video. Please take seven minutes and fifty-eight seconds to watch Dr. Perera's plea to the world to save our children so you can feel the passion and conviction in her voice, and your heart.

"The single most important action we can take for our children and their future is to cure our addiction to fossil fuels. Combustion of coal, oil, gasoline, diesel, and natural gas is the root cause of much of the ill health and developmental impairment of today's children and their highly uncertain future... Globally up to $230 billion of avoided health costs annually by 2030 could be accomplished with an increase to 36 percent in renewables in total energy consumption (American Association for the Advancement of Science 2016)."

Dr. Fredericka Perera's 2016
Fossil Fuels Threaten Children's Health video (Perera 2016).

Dr. Perera has not given up or changed her mind, and the collective we have not either.

"One billion children worldwide are exposed to very high levels of air pollution. Fortunately, *solutions are now available* to substantially reduce, and in some cases, eliminate these emissions" (Perera 2022).

As Dr. Perera notes, there can be no doubt about the connection between fossil fuels like gasoline and the myriad of adverse health effects. Biofuels can be the Hercules to slay the fossil fuel Hydra she so eloquently presents.

TAKEAWAYS

- The good news: EPA recognizes cleaning up gasoline from implementing the oxygenated fuel program, reformulated gasoline program, and the renewable fuels standard reduces pollution and saves lives. *But* they need to focus on the source of fine particulates, which is gasoline, and to enforce the requirement to reduce toxics to the greatest extent achievable!

- The bad news: air pollution is getting worse and has the similar negative health effects that the nation experienced when lead was added to gasoline to increase octane and smoking was cool.

WHAT'S NEXT?

- Will electric vehicles be the silver bullet policy makers and environmentalists hope to use to kill the mythical many-headed fossil-fueled hydra, or will they require more renewable fuels, or will they inadvertently protect status quo?

CHAPTER 12

The People versus Big Oil, Congress, and EPA

Preserving Power and Wealth at Any Cost

On March 29, 1990, while proposing the regulation of mobile source air toxics, US Senator Thomas A. Daschle (D-SD) stated, "I simply do not trust EPA to implement a program that has been stonewalled for more than a decade... the oil industry is one of the most powerful industries in the world. The EPA is not immune to pressure, both from well-financed lobbying and from divergent interests with the Administration itself" (Congressional Record. 1990).

Tom Daschle saw it then, and it has only worsened in the ensuing decades. The petroleum industry spends whatever is necessary to protect its market, and they have plenty of yours to spend.

History shows environment, energy, and public health policies are riddled with decades of political and financial influence designed to protect power, wealth, and market share at any price, including *the ultimate price* of sickness, disease, and premature death. Although tied to some dirty businesses, lobbying is not a dirty word.

Trade associations, private companies, labor unions, and other organizations spend billions of dollars each year influencing the presidential administration, Congress, and federal agencies. Anyone can approach their legislators and lobby for increased cancer research funding, education programs, or any wonderful causes. When that lobbying ignores the public good or perpetuates harmful practices, it needs to be called out. Laws require reporting lobbying activities. Data can be obtained from the United States Senate Office of Public Records.

Money spent on lobbying the federal government broke a record in the third quarter of 2022, surpassing $3 billion. The oil and gas industry was ranked fourth in a crowded pack behind pharmaceuticals, electronics, and insurance (Giorno 2022). What was the return on their investment? More Congressional friends to influence federal agencies to thwart the development of alternatives to crude oil, gasoline, and aromatics/BTEX.

FOX IN THE HEN HOUSE

OpenSecrets is a nonpartisan, independent, and nonprofit organization that tracks money in US politics (OpenSecrets, n.d.). Their data allow us to take a brief but deep dive into the lobbying and campaign contributions of the oil and gas industry.

According to OpenSecrets, the top twenty companies or entities registered as "oil and gas" spent $78 million on campaigns from 2019 to 2020. The American Petroleum Institute ranked fourth on their list.

From 1998 to 2022, the oil and gas industry spent nearly $3 billion on lobbying. In 2021, the oil and gas sector spent $120 million on more than two hundred firms with 756 registered lobbyists. Considering there are 535 members of Congress, that equates to one lobbyist for every member, with a few hundred more to work the agencies!

Over 60 percent of these lobbyists were former government employees (OpenSecrets 2021).

OpenSecrets refers to this practice as the "Revolving Door." The agencies they have collected data on have employed the most significant number of former lobbyists or sent the greatest number of former employees to lobby firms and interest groups. OpenSecrets profiles over two hundred people in their database just for the US Environmental Protection Agency (OpenSecrets 2022).

In our interview with former US Senator Ben Nelson of Nebraska, who also served two terms as governor, we asked him if, when in the Senate, they found this influence of oil in EPA troubling. "Of course, we knew the fox was guarding the henhouse," he said. "In terms of advancing ethanol, we never had the support of EPA. There was no common understanding of the value of an alternative like ethanol, and the oil industry simply yelled louder. We couldn't match that." Senator Daschle concurs, "It has been a consistent revolving door that arguably is one of the single biggest factors, and that is why, on a regulatory basis, we have not been able to make more progress".

During one of the many battles between refining and ethanol interests—in this case, a proposal by refiners to allow exports of renewable fuels to count toward their obligation to use it in the US—EPA was reportedly considering it. Senator Chuck Grassley (R-IA) was incensed upon learning of EPA's attempt to negotiate a compromise between refiner and ethanol interests. Dino Grandoni captured the political tension in his June 6, 2018, *Washington Post* article quoting the Senator saying,

> "You know how Big Oil has had Washington wired for a long time, and I think EPA is part of this Washington swamp delivering this blow to ethanol if it occurs. This is a case where the president is being ill-served by political appointees that aren't carrying out his agenda (Grandoni 2018)."

The drumbeat of petroleum industry opposition to "renewable-fuel mandates" is ironic, considering oil interests toss their one-sided mandate coin on the negotiating table yet protect the current de facto aromatic/BTEX mandate we all live under.

We heard reports US refiners worked out a deal with EPA Administrator Scott Pruitt—formerly the attorney general of Oklahoma, who sued EPA on numerous occasions over environmental regulations. One of Pruitt's most ardent supporters was Senator James Inhofe of Oklahoma, perhaps one of the most vocal opponents of the RFS in the Senate. Couple that with significant oil interests in Oklahoma, which seemed to stack the deck at EPA in oil's favor.

After Mr. Pruitt resigned over various ethical allegations, his deputy, a former Inhofe staffer, and fossil fuel lobbyist, took the job as EPA administrator. You can't make this up! In one of our interviews, a former environmental lobbyist called going from Mr. Pruitt to Mr. Wheeler "worse and worser." It is impossible to believe individuals coming out of a highly regulated industry can leave their beliefs and loyalties at the door. We believe the actions of many of these industry-executives-turned-bureaucrats illustrate that.

"For me, there is no greater responsibility than protecting human health and the environment, and I look forward to carrying out this essential task on behalf of the American public," Wheeler said in a statement upon his nomination to be EPA administrator (National Geographic 2019). Yet it was under Mr. Wheeler's watch that the SAFE Rule was introduced and initially attempted to roll back fuel economy standards and ultimately ignored our calls to protect public health from aromatics/BTEX.

Shortly after Wheeler's confirmation on April 14, 2018, EPA released a statement on Twitter.

> "The Senate does its duty: Andrew Wheeler confirmed by Senate as deputy administrator of @EPA. The Democrats couldn't block the confirmation of an environmental policy expert and former EPA staffer under both a

Republican and a Democrat president (US Environmental Protection Agency 2018)."

The string of replies that followed @EPA's official Twitter announcement of Administrator Wheeler's confirmation provides a fascinating snapshot and barometer of public opinion. Twitter users were disgruntled and disappointed but not surprised. The URL in the appendix will take you directly to the exchanges.

The article in *National Geographic* referenced earlier cites about one hundred actions taken by "Trump's EPA" that hurt EPA's mission to protect public health and the environment. Was President Trump or civil servants at EPA creating and carrying out these actions? Was it really Trump's EPA? One article in the collection caught our attention on January 15, 2019. The nonprofit Public Employees for Environmental Responsibility (PEER) reported that EPA's criminal prosecutions for various environmental infractions under the Trump administration had been the lowest in thirty years. That clearly indicates the ability to preserve wealth and power at any cost and influence the agency's inability to enforce laws.

As a note of interest, in March 2022, Mr. Wheeler was nominated to serve as the administrator for the Virginia Department of Natural Resources, the state equivalent of EPA, but failed to be approved by the Virginia Senate. According to Sarah Vogelsong's article in the *Virginia Mercury,* Wheeler "Was a polarizing figure, both in Washington and Richmond," and efforts to block him were based on "his record of rolling back environmental rules aimed at protecting air and water quality" (Vogelsong 2022).

RED, BLUE, OR YOU

Per our analysis of the actions of oil interest and EPA in chapters 7, 8, 9, and 10, we consider creating and protecting the national Renewable Fuel Standard (RFS) a modern-day bipartisan miracle. With that in mind, please place your political biases aside. Try not to use our examples as a scorecard to assign blame to one political party over another.

We are not picking on the GOP. We have been disappointed by both parties serving at several administrations' behest. Senator Daschle, the former Democratic leader in the Senate, told us he felt the Democratic administrations were less helpful than the Republicans in some cases. The examples we used are the most recent, relevant, and publicly documented examples of the impact of influence, regardless of who, how, and when; both political parties failed to make progress in cleaning up the nation's gasoline to the greatest extent possible.

Here is the simple math and history lesson to reinforce our thesis. The Organization of the Petroleum Exporting Countries (OPEC) banded together to weaponize their control over the United States' growing dependence on crude oil and gasoline to meet energy needs. Despite the devastating economic and geopolitical impact that lingers today, the US has done little to wean itself from that dependence. The most recent example is the outcome of President Biden's fist-bumping trip to Saudi Arabia in October 2022, fifty years after OPEC's first oil embargo on the United States. We think the media and political aftermath was best described in an analysis by Javier Blas, writing for Bloomberg and published in *The Washington Post*. Blas states,

> "The OPEC+ cartel has just delivered a massive snub to Western governments facing the worst energy crisis in half a century. Look past the buzzwords accompanying Wednesday's cut in oil production—preemptive move, uncertain outlook—and it's difficult to see the move as anything but an attack on a global economy that desperately needs the price of crude to remain subdued. Riyadh and its allies also extended for a year, until the end of 2023, their alliance with Russia, the "plus" in the OPEC+ acronym. The Riyadh-Moscow alliance, which started six years ago, is becoming a permanent axis, redrawing energy geopolitics. Make no mistake, these are dangerous developments for the future of energy security (Blas 2022). "

President Biden and the rest of us have remained in a de facto gasoline and aromatic/BTEX mandate for transportation fuels for over fifty years. During that period, we experienced many combinations of Republican and Democratic control of the US House of Representatives, US Senate, and the White House. According to our calculations, since the first OPEC oil embargo:

- Congress had twenty-four sessions to make progress.
- Republicans controlled ten sessions, Democrats fourteen.
- Democrats held the House and Senate eleven times, and Republicans eight.

- From 1995–2007 Republicans held the House and Senate for about half the time.
- Democrats controlled the White House, Senate, and House four times.
- Republicans controlled the White House, House, and Senate four times.
- Republicans controlled two of three (White House, House, and Senate) twelve times.
- Democrats controlled two of three (White House, House, and the Senate) thirteen times.
- A Republican was elected to the White House thirty-two of the fifty years referenced.

While we can vote for our elected officials, most voters can only choose gasoline as the fuel for their cars, and we sure can't choose the air we breathe. Who's to blame, and who will fix it? Only "we the people" can push for change.

WHO'S GOING TO LET THE HENS OUT?

The executive branch and the federal agencies should, to some extent, adopt policies and practices that reflect the ideology of the president, whoever that might be at the time. EPA's current laser focus on climate change reflects the Biden agenda, while the previous administration under Trump did not share that view.

Boyden Gray does an excellent job describing this conundrum in his interview with John Henry of the Committee for the Republic in 2021 (Henry 2021). Ambassador Gray often refers to this problem as "agency capture," when the industry an agency is supposed to be regulating has influenced the agency to the point it *loses its way*. An underlying problem allowing potential overreach by an agency was the result of a Supreme Court decision called "The Chevron Doctrine" in 1984 (Boyden Gray & Associates 2022). In effect, the doctrine said Congress delegated authority to the federal agencies by not giving explicit directives and instructions in the laws they passed. The doctrine empowers federal agencies to become the ultimate authority and decider when there is ambiguity in legislation passed by Congress. Ambiguity in legislation is commonly called loopholes, often created by industry's influence on the legislative process.

A recent Supreme Court decision essentially repealing an EPA rule to curtail power plant emissions effectively took authority away from EPA and gave it back to Congress. The court's decision was based on their finding that EPA needed specific and explicit directives if the rule involved "major questions" that impacted numerous sectors. For example, a ruling that might impact jobs, the economy, agriculture, or anything else could be considered outside the scope of the intent of the rule and the "major questions" such action raised had not been considered.

The good news, in the case of regulating mobile source air toxics, is Congress already gave EPA explicit directives to reduce aromatics/BTEX in gasoline in Section 202(l) of the Clean Air Act Amendments. New legislation is not necessary. With the Chevron Doctrine becoming less of a factor, courts may ultimately decide the outcome of federal legislation based on the bill and legality, not influence.

Senator Daschle has not waivered on his position that Congress gave EPA all the authority to take action because they included it in the legislation and directives. This has been frustrating for clean energy advocates like us for more than thirty years.

EPA'S WEB OF INFLUENCE

According to our analysis of OpenSecrets' data, after the passage of the second national Renewable Fuel Standard (RFS) in 2008, the amount of money spent on lobbying—as reported—by the entire oil and gas industry increased by about $100 million per year for several consecutive years.

Anyone who thinks lobbying reports are comprehensive does not work in Washington—or any state capitol. These reports only account for "covered officials" at the agency level. This means many career employees with long and protected positions can be lobbied directly or indirectly with no limit. This amount also does not include lobbying efforts at the state level, which often do not require reporting.

We discovered this challenge during our state battles for oxy-fuel, reformulated gasoline, and pump labeling. Many of these activities, while not tracked, certainly take place in and impact the intended outcome of market protection. We documented past and current efforts to thwart gasoline quality improvements to reduce mobile source air toxics in chapters 3, 4, and 5. We believe the increase in spending on lobbying after the passage of the second Renewable Fuel Standard (RFS) showed when the battle over Washington escalated.

As documented throughout *Gasolinegate*, laws made in the public interest to create positive outcomes for energy, environmental, economic, and public health are influenced by conflicted special interests (see "Chapter 15: Missing in Action").

It's not illegal to petition, question, or lobby our government. However, rules exist to protect the integrity of our political system. Most important is the transparency of money spent on specific bills, by specific industries, by specific people, with specific stated interests.

According to OpenSecret's data cited earlier, here are a few highlights from the American Petroleum Institute's (API) list of bills the organization lobbied for in 2017.

- Consumer and Fuel Retailer Choice Act
- Renewable Fuel Standard (RFS) Elimination Act
- Renewable Fuel Standard (RFS) Reform Act of 2017
- Ozone Standards Implementation Act of 2017

EPA'S REVOLVING DOOR

EPA experienced the same upswing in lobbying activity after 2007. According to OpenSecrets data, 655 entities lobbied EPA. Madeleine Sheehan Perkin, a reporter for the *San Francisco Chronicle*, drilled into some specifics in her June 27, 2017, article, "7 of 45 New EPA Top Staff Come from the Coal, Oil, and Chemical Industries." Perkin documents a parade of key executives from Hess Corp, National Rural Electric Cooperative Association, Ohio Coal Association, American Chemistry Council, and a former senior counsel for the American Petroleum Institute going into EPA to create or enforce environmental regulations.

It is common for key industry executives to take a tour of duty in essential government roles and then return to their industry. They can return to their industry better equipped to advise on how to get around the very rules they may have established. EPA is no exception. For example, Richard Wilson, a key official within the Office of Air and Radiation, which oversaw OTAQ and was directly involved in the deliberations of the CAAA, later went to work for API. OTAQ was the critical arm of the EPA that controlled everything from emissions testing and protocol to fuel modeling.

In addition to the American Petroleum Institute, a refiner's group also represents the oil industry. In 2012, Charles Drevna, president of the US-based National Petrochemical & Refiners Association (NPRA) trade group, announced NPRA changed its name to the American Fuel & Petrochemical Manufacturers (AFPM) stating, "Our new name will emphasize more than ever what we stand for. AFPM will be just as vigorous as NPRA in educating Congress, regulatory officials, and the American people about the vital role our members play in American life" (Hydrocarbon Processing 2012).

NPRA and AFPM were and remain formidable forces in fighting ethanol and any alternative fuel that threatens their market share. Another example of the Revolving Door challenge is Chet Thompson, the president and chief executive officer of the American Fuel & Petrochemical Manufacturers (AFPM). Mr. Thompson went from a prosperous

Washington, DC, law firm to become a political appointee at EPA for about two years and served as EPA's deputy general counsel. After his tour of duty at EPA, he returned to another law firm, Crowell & Moring LLP, with significant petroleum clients. There is nothing wrong or unethical about the process, but it would be naive or ignorant to think it does not substantially impact outcomes.

According to OpenSecrets data just for 2011, the firm's clients included the American Chemistry Council, BP, Dow Chemical, DuPont, FMC, Methanol Institute, National Petroleum Refiners Association (oil & gas), Penn. General Energy (oil & gas), Philip Morris International, Royal Dutch Shell (oil & gas), SC Johnson & Son (chemicals).

The other side of the double-edged sword of influence is not having the money or power to be included in the decision-making process. For example, Dr. Herbert L. Needleman, Department of Psychiatry, University of Pittsburgh School of Medicine, captured the essence of EPA's web of influence in his June 28, 1999, article, "The Removal of Lead from Gasoline: Historical and Personal Reflections," published in the *Environmental Research Journal*. Dr. Herbert states, "In 1980, OMB increased the pressure on EPA to do something about the complaints of the small refiners. Richard Wilson, EPA's acting director of enforcement for air, held 32 meetings with refiner representatives to discuss their problems, but none with public health or public interest officials" (Needleman 2000).

As discussed in "Chapter 3: The Anti-Ethanol War," Congress passed fourteen laws to support the development of alternative fuels and protect people from toxic air pollution from 1978 to 2007. To the extent ethanol was a substitute fuel, it was a big hill for ethanol to climb that included a huge twenty-year battle to get over the hurdles of burden-of-proof. As we have referenced so many times in this book, EPA could have seen the glass as half full and taken initiatives to get over the drivability, durability, emission testing, consumer acceptance, price stability, infrastructure compatibility, and performance issues—but didn't.

FOLLOW THE MONEY

We started research for *Gasolinegate* in 2017 because we were frustrated with the lack of progress on the Corporate Average Fuel Economy (CAFE) rules as well as in response to the relentless attacks on the RFS. We realized over half of the 535 Congressional offices have jurisdiction and oversight responsibilities regarding EPA.

- Twenty-one Congressional committees/subcommittees have jurisdiction over EPA.
- Ninety senators and House members sit on those committees.
- Sixteen House of Representative committees and subcommittees have jurisdiction over EPA.

This overlap creates an intricate and confusing spiderweb of closely-knit legislators and highly skilled lobbyists linked to a network of lawyers and representatives of private companies and representative organizations.

Based on our experience and conversations, this onslaught of technical doublespeak and campaign contributions makes it extremely hard for what is, on average, a young Congressional staff that experiences high turnover. They deal with a pile-on trying to keep up with multiple issues and the special interests of their bosses and constituents.

As we deal with all three branches of government in the age of emails, Zoom meetings, and other impersonal methods, we can't help but feel like we are not getting sufficient support from Congress. We asked almost everyone we interviewed who'd had any experience with Congress if they agreed that between the technical nature of fuel and health issues and the sheer overload staff face, those in Congress don't know enough to help. The answer was always yes.

The days of professional staff members on Congressional committees, in particular, seem gone. Professional staff often withstand the changing of the guard in terms of who is running the committees and stay on because they have expertise and skills. We would work with such folks who were close to being wholly objective and could influence—in a positive way—EPA. Not that they are not intelligent, but it is so different now for a staffer when you walk into the office in the morning and have a hundred emails on a hundred other subjects.

Senators Daschle and Nelson agreed, as did veterans like Scott Sklar and others, that the deep understanding of these issues by members and staff seems to be missing, leaving EPA somewhat insulated from sufficient oversight. Add to that the fractured nature of modern politics, and we do not find members reaching across the aisle to work together.

In his book, *The Death of the Senate,* Ben Nelson chronicles his twelve years in the US Senate as a downward spiral of cooperation among members. Beginning in 2000, right through his final year in 2012, he was frustrated that the parties grew further and further apart. This extends to staff that should be clearly bipartisan, such as protecting human health. However, they become caught up in other issues and fail to provide the attention required (Nelson 2021).

OTHER FEDERAL AGENCIES COULD NOT HELP FILL EPA'S VOID

Our coalition of environmental, public health, and clean fuel advocates frustrated with the lack of support from the EPA have tried enlisting the help of other agencies. Here are three examples:

HEALTH AND HUMAN SERVICES

The mission of the US Department of Health and Human Services (HHS) is to enhance the health and well-being of all Americans, by providing for effective health and human services and by fostering sound, sustained advances in the sciences underlying medicine, public health, and social services.

Based on its mission, HHS appeared to be the place to get help advancing the cleaner, safer gasoline cause. From 2009 to 2011, our small pack of cleaner gasoline brethren were emphasizing new research connecting the impact of increasing emissions of ultrafine particulate matter (UFP) and polycyclic aromatic hydrocarbons (PAHs) on public health. These dangerous pollutants were going unnoticed and unregulated by EPA, and the source was dirty gasoline.

In our interview with David Hallberg, introduced in chapter 5, Dave summarized his 2011 meeting with Dr. Howard Koh, assistant secretary for health, US Department of Health & Human Services and presentation, *Improving Public Health by Improving Fuel Quality: Secondhand Smoke & Mobile Source Ultrafine Particle Emissions: Common Links to a Multi-Billion Dollar Health Threat*. Hallberg states,

"I was excited about the possibility of getting support from HHS and optimistic about outcomes. We talked about the synergies between the HHS mission, President Obama's public health, oil use reduction, and economic goals and my mission. I shared research from the Society of Automotive Engineers, Honda, Ford, and other automotive experts who cited the need for changes to fuel composition to complement advanced engine designs, specifically noting the direct linkage between aromatic/BTEX gasoline compounds and increased UFP/PAH emissions. I thought I would get a better reaction when presenting the recent California Air Resource Board data showing ethanol blends of 35–85 percent reduced ultrafine particulates by 70–90 percent.

The warning about increased UFPs and PAHs was not just coming from automakers. I shared the Health Effects Institute's Fall 2011 newsletter that states, "Ultrafine particles... account for most of the particles in ambient air, though they contribute only a tiny fraction to mass... Concern has heightened recently, given evidence that UFP emissions might increase with greater use of gasoline direct-injection engines and other changes in fuels and technology." I warned Secretary Koh, "that unless fuel composition changes are synchronized with vehicle hardware advances, one of the president's signature achievements—significantly improved fuel efficiency—could inadvertently worsen urban air quality and substantially increase health costs as the light duty vehicle fleet turns over during the 2012 to 2025 period."

The secretary's subject matter experts from the Center for Disease Control on the conference call validated the information and my concerns. When I asked for the next steps on how we could collaborate on this critical mission, Secretary Koh told me, "We would love to help, but only EPA has jurisdiction over fuel quality." It was another long and disappointing cab ride to the airport and back to my *how to get around EPA drawing board.*"

DEPARTMENT OF JUSTICE
In 2018, Boyden Gray & Associates wrote to Douglas Rathbun, Competition Policy & Advocacy Section, Antitrust Division, of the Department of Justice, asking for support to help remove regulatory barriers created by EPA. The request outlined five actions EPA could take.

- Approve an alternative certification fuel with 25–30 percent ethanol.

- Fix the fuel economy formula to stop cheating ethanol blends.
- Reinterpret "substantially similar" to cover higher ethanol blends.
- Reinterpret the RVP waiver statute to apply to all fuel blends containing gasoline and at least 10 percent ethanol—not just E10.
- Adopt an updated lifecycle analysis of ethanol's greenhouse gas emissions.

The request focused on how, if the regulatory barriers were lifted, automakers could meet the goals of the national CAFE standards.

"Ford Motor Company, for example, "strongly recommend[ed] that EPA pursue regulations... to facilitate the introduction of higher-octane rating market fuels," noting that the "increased octane rating from increased ethanol content has the potential to allow for fuel economy, performance and emissions improvements through more efficient engine designs." Ford's recommendation was linked to EPA and DOT's greenhouse gas and fuel economy rules: "Progress on this issue will be a key parameter for consideration in [EPA and NHTSA's] ...mid-term evaluation of the light-duty CAFE Rule in 2017" (Boyden Gray & Associates 2018)."

BGA's letter to DOJ referenced "should" twenty-seven times, "would" forty-three times, and "could" sixteen times. And we hope by now you are not surprised to know that EPA didn't take any of those recommendations.

DEPARTMENT OF ENERGY

One of the primary reasons the RFS is under the jurisdiction of EPA and not DOE is that it is an amendment to the Clean Air Act. And the act has a greenhouse gas reduction and other environmental requirements. However, it is equally an energy issue. Unfortunately, DOE, through both Republican and Democratic administrations, is missing in action when it comes to helping address the problems and, importantly, reminding EPA of the many co-benefits of utilizing higher blends of ethanol to replace toxic aromatics/BTEX.

For example, DOE initiated a program to study how to improve fuels called the Co-Optimization of Fuels and Engines (Co-Optima Program), which we discussed in chapter 6. Their stated mission is "To explore how innovations in fuels and engines could boost fuel economy and vehicle performance while reducing emissions." The program has been in place for six years and involved nine of DOE's national laboratories and over forty industry partners. DOE brought together the brightest minds in the country. Among their findings, up to 30 percent in internal combustion engines could increase efficiency and reduce emissions from gasoline and diesel fuels (US Department of Energy 2022). Obviously, a higher ethanol blend would dilute and replace significant amounts of aromatic/BTEX compounds in gasoline.

When we met with DOE officials in 2020 to urge them to support our call for lower-carbon higher-octane fuel standards, DOE responded, saying, "We were not asked or invited to be part of the EPA fuel economy deliberations." Despite six years of great work at taxpayers' expense, no one at EPA or elsewhere talks about the Co-Optima Program.

TAKEAWAYS
- Meanwhile, in contrast to the tepid role our agencies to get out in front of and obvious beneficial development, India is wasting no time protecting their public health and economy. The Oil Ministry of India released a statement on June 3, 2021.

The Central Government hereby directs that the oil companies *shall* sell ethanol-blended petrol with a percentage of ethanol up to 20 percent as per the Bureau of Indian Standards specifications, in the whole of the States and union territories. This Notification shall come into force with effect from the 1st April 2023. (CNBC 2021).

WHAT'S NEXT?
- Who will outfox the fox and slay the fossil-fuel Hydra?

- Are electric vehicles (EVs) going to save the day?

- What options do consumers have to accelerate changes in the marketplace and the roles of our elected officials to protect our public health and the environment?

- What legislative or legal options can environmental, energy, public health, agriculture, and national security advocates leverage to help EPA out of the de facto gasoline aromatic/BTEX mandate ditch they are in?

- What can be done to build a brighter fuel future for the United States?

PART 3

We need a superhero that can protect our Energy, Environmental, Economic, Food, Health, and National Securities

The Many-Headed Fossil-Fueled Hydra

CHAPTER 13
Reality EV

The Gaslight Is On, but Nobody's Home

We have watched many alternative fuels audition for the world's largest gasoline market and fail. More than forty years of researching and advocating for alternative transportation fuels make it clear no single solution solves the United States' myriad of problems because of its reliance on crude oil. The nation does not have the silver bullets, magic beans, or taxpayer money to produce an all-electric, zero-emission, zero-internal-combustion-engine fleet in the near future. However, using current technology, a more realistic solution exists to achieve 100 to 372 miles per gallon of gasoline (MPGG).

REALITY IN DC
The Biden administration, driven by single-interest environmental organizations, is trying to ban internal combustion engines. The de facto electric vehicle (EV) mandate package is bundled with the promise of a bright all-EV future.

States are falling over one another to hang with the cool EV kids and are lining up to play the same all-EV game as outlined in Alex Brown's "Electric Vehicles Charge Ahead in Statehouses. Every State Is Involved" article. Brown quotes Marc Geller, a board member for the Electric Vehicle Association, "This is being taken seriously in a way it hasn't been before because the trajectory is evident." According to Brown, Dylan McDowell, deputy director of the National Caucus of Environmental Legislators, said, "We will see a lot more emphasis on electric vehicles in 2022 and 2023. This is the start of a really big turning point" (Brown 2022).

California leads the pack, and Oregon and Washington have joined them for a clean sweep of the "Left" Coast. According to Sarah Vogelsong's article in the *Virginia Mercury*, "Because of federal law establishing a two-year transition period, the California standards won't be effective in Virginia until early 2024, but once in force will bring Virginia in line with fourteen other states and Washington, DC, that have decided to follow the Golden State's path" (Vogelsong 2022). However, in an email obtained by the *Mercury*, Assistant Attorney General Michael Jagels concluded:

> "Virginia is bound by the California decision because the state chose to be statutorily and regulatorily aligned with California. Decoupling from California's path would require an amendment or repeal of the mandating legislation wrote. A senior Republican confirmed separately that attorneys with the state's legislative branch had reached the same conclusion. The ban, which if approved by the US Environmental Protection Agency wouldn't take effect for thirteen years, would not impact used car

sales or prohibit anyone from driving older-model vehicles with internal combustion engines (Vogelsong 2022)."

Voters and policy makers in states that made an EV commitment are now saying, "We did what?" Do reasonable people really think consumers driving a fleet of 284 million vehicles in 2022 can or will transform the whole buying and refueling game in little more than a decade? (Statistica 2022b).

The answer is no; we can't. Is there a role for EVs? Can EVs make a meaningful contribution to the goals of climate change and reduced petroleum use? Is it justifiable to provide start-up subsidies and assistance? Of course. But will this single-interest EV plan force the industry to produce what the government wants them to make? Is it sound public policy to forgo all other options and ignore the hundreds of billions of gallons of toxic aromatic/BTEX gasoline that will be needed for decades? No.

Several major hurdles need to be cleared to meet the nation's new goal of 50 percent EV sales by 2030 (White House 2021). The highest hurdle was the post-COVID-19 and Russian-Ukraine War inflationary economy. The second hurdle is federal and state budgets, and then full consumer acceptance to finish the race. However, federal and state governments, and their taxpayers, will need to have the conviction, courage, and budget necessary to maintain trillions of dollars in subsidies while incurring the wrath of established businesses literally being put out of business. The convenience store industry, for example, has tied its wagon to the sale of gasoline. The majority of 7-Elevens and the new breed of convenience stores across the country have significant investment in gasoline refueling. As this sector's customer base declines, it will experience stranded assets that will place a drag on the economy and burden on their customers.

Many key influencers in Congress, environmental organizations, and the media have been led to believe they need not worry about cleaning up gasoline or developing alternative liquid fuels. This thinking will influence the public to believe EVs will be the silver bullet to end decades of wars over crude oil and domestic battles to develop alternative fuels.

The sad but true reality is, regardless of the EV growth, billions of gallons of high carbon toxic gasoline will continue to be burned for decades. Any plan that includes the current level of aromatics/BTEX in gasoline is indefensible.

Consider another stark reality. If a ban on internal combustion engine (ICE) vehicles goes into effect in 2035, the date proposed in California, then an ICE sold on New Year's Eve 2034 will still need to burn gasoline for twelve to fifteen years (Schwartz, Hart. 2018). Under this plan, the influence of these vehicles on the environment will not begin its decline until 2050. Now consider the nearly one hundred million more ICE vehicles on the road since the passage of the Clean Air Act Amendments of 1990 (Statistica 2022a). The strategy of relying on a ban on ICEs will not provide the level of environmental protection needed.

Any new transportation fuel will have challenges and hurdles, whether it was ethanol in its infancy, methanol, natural gas, or now electricity for EVs. Practicality, cost, performance, emissions, and countless other issues need to be considered and resolved. Natural gas and methanol were once seen as the answer. Neither survived the consumer practicality or political endurance tests. Now, ethanol and biodiesel continue to work through their consumer acceptance and regulatory issues. If we could embrace ethanol today, we could begin improving our environmental impact immediately instead of waiting another thirty years for EVs to make a difference.

A fresh barrage of anti-ethanol articles usually surfaces when Congress considers legislation to solve a problem with ethanol. News headlines are a good barometer of what is going on in Congress and indicate the battles being waged to win public acceptance in the media's court of public opinion. News headlines are also an early indicator of the amount of money fossil fuel PR machines are pumping into opposing ethanol.

We categorized nearly one hundred EV-related articles before, during, and after the debates over the Inflation Reduction Act of 2022 that President Joe Biden signed into law on August 16, 2022 (Probasco 2022). The diversity of issues and voices foreshadows the numerous battles EV proponents will face in the coming election cycles. The following headlines should paint a picture worth a thousand words of EV stakeholder concerns.

- "Toyota Joins Tesla and GM in Losing Federal Electric Vehicle Tax Credits" *CNBC*. July 6, 2022 (Wayland 2022).

- "Automakers Say US Senate Bill Will Jeopardize 2030 EV Targets." *Reuters*. August 7, 2022 (Shepardson 2022).

- "Why Toyota—the World's Largest Automaker—Isn't All-in on Electric Vehicles." *CNBC*. September 13, 2022 (Wayland 2022).

- "Honda Exec: Lithium-Ion EVs Will Always Be More Expensive than Gas Cars." *Inside EVs*. September 18, 2022 (O'Hare 2022).

- "We Need More than Just Electric Vehicles." *The Institute of Electrical and Electronics* Engineers. August 20, 2022 (Maclean 2022).

- "Republicans Seek to Block State Gasoline Car Phaseouts." *E&E News*. September 8, 2022 (Forrest 2022).

- "Republicans Slam Biden Car Rule, Predict Higher Costs." *E&E News*. August 6, 2021 (Cama 2021).

- "Marco Rubio Says California Electric Car Plan 'Self-Defeating': People Will Be 'Charging Their Cars with Coal.'" *FOX Business*. September 18, 2022 (Blitzer 2022).

- "California Wants Everyone to Drive EVs. How Will Low-Income People Afford Them?" *The Guardian*. October 13, 2022 (Aoun 2022).

- "Electric-Vehicle Fires Have Burned Down Homes after Hurricane Ian Saltwater Damage. Florida Officials Want Answers." *Fortune*. October 15, 2022 (Mollman 2022).

REALITY IN THE DATA

According to the Massachusetts Institute of Technology's (MIT) "Insights into Future Mobility, Energy Initiative" study, the world's one billion passenger vehicles in 2015 consumed about 400 billion gallons of fuel. The study projects that in 2050, global oil consumption will be higher than in 2015 and only 25 percent less in their aggressive climate policy assumptions. Reinforcing our concern, the MIT study also noted that only one-fifth of that 25 percent is because of light-duty EVs, such as the average consumer might drive. The most significant contributors to the projected improvements in global oil consumption are improved fuel efficiency, fewer vehicle miles traveled, and reduced industrial use of oil (Massachusetts Institute of Technology 2019).

The MIT study cites more of our concerns. It references the need to upgrade and reinforce the power distribution system and the cost of refueling infrastructure and notes, "Our analysis does not account for these costs, nor does it tackle the question of who will pay for them." We clearly understand additional vehicle and recharging costs are not insignificant, and everyone will pay. What's worse is some will undoubtedly pay more than others.

For example, this MIT study estimates the average additional cost of an EV is about $10,000. In our interview with former Chrysler Director of Regulatory Affairs Reg Modlin, he points out, "Currently, EVs receive a federal tax credit of $7,500, and the Biden administration has proposed an additional $4,500 if the vehicle [was] made in the United States... the tax credit is capped for each automaker after a certain amount of vehicles. A consumer not within that cap would not get the credit."

Therefore, in many cases, federal EV incentives do not provide a full $7,500 dollar-for-dollar credit for everyone. It depends on the income of the buyer and the amount of credit available. Like any tax credit, one must have a tax liability to apply. Many Americans pay taxes out of their paychecks and do not owe taxes to apply for the credit against; therefore, those taxpayers cannot use the credit.

Like the "True Cost Gasoline" analysis in chapter 2, EV ownership costs also need to be considered; for example, Americans drive about fifteen thousand miles per year (US Federal Highway Administration). Assuming a generous twelve-year average fuel economy standard of twenty-five miles per gallon, the average driver buys six hundred gallons of gasoline annually. Over the five-year loan balance, those three thousand gallons of gasoline purchased divided by the $7,500 tax incentive equals a hidden subsidy of two dollars and fifty cents per gallon.

But driving on the nation's highways is not free either. The billions of dollars collected in federal and state excise taxes on gasoline and diesel fuel pay for the maintenance of our roads, bridges, and highways. If EV owners are not paying fuel excise taxes, they receive another hidden subsidy, but one the rest of the drivers will have to pay.

Not only that, but utility rebates, state and local tax incentives, reduced registration fees, and other subsidies are likely not sustainable. As Robert Walton cited in his article for

UtilityDrive, "Georgia electric vehicles sales dropped by 80 percent after the state tax credit was repealed." The Georgia state legislature repealed the incentive after it increased from $1 million in 2012 and it exceeded $14 million in 2013. Before that, Georgia was ranked second-most electric vehicles on the road (Walton 2017).

Using the MIT study as the baseline, if EVs reach 50 percent of the fleet by 2050 and receive the necessary $7,500 federal tax incentive to drive consumer demand—not including the "Made in USA" $4,500 credit—those 135 million EVs will cost taxpayers about $1 trillion. If we've learned anything from Georgia, we won't be able to keep up with that for long.

Our research of hundreds of articles and analyses of the nation's EV movement suggest the fears about charging and range are the primary concern of consumers before comparing costs. The idea that the US might develop a charging infrastructure as efficient and accessible as the current gasoline system is questioned by automakers and consumers alike.

Moreover, drivers still run out of gasoline in the United States despite 111,100 gasoline stations. In 2016, AAA helped thirty-two million stranded drivers, five hundred thousand of which ran out of gas (Grubs 2015). The EV refueling challenge worsens upon consideration that about 30 percent of Americans do not live in a single-family house, indicating that they may encounter issues owning or sharing a charging station. New EV owners with partially charged cars are sure to miscalculate how far they can drive, and the resulting congestion and safety issues from vehicles unable to move should be a significant concern.

Another concern is the cost of building said charging stations. There are about 750,000 gasoline dispensers in the United States. One Level 3 fast-charge electric vehicle supply equipment port can cost $50,000 (OhmHome 2022). Extrapolating these estimates, installing one recharging post per retail gasoline station would cost the nation $37 billion.

The meltdown of the Texas electrical grid in the winter of 2021, the years-long suspension of electrical power during California wildfires, and the complete loss of electricity in hurricane-ravaged Puerto Rico and Florida should raise more concerns about a complete reliance on EVs.

Even the Biden administration, as evidenced by recent statements by Energy Secretary Jennifer Granholm, are showing signs that they realize they may be overreaching in the race to electrify the transportation sector. As reported by Bloomberg News, in a meeting with oil industry executives in late December 14, 2022, concerning phasing out fossil fuels, she said, "Moving too fast could have unintended consequences that hurt people, cause backlash" (Natter 2022).

A review of recent headlines begs the question, is California just dreaming or waking up?

- "California Is Facing an Electricity Crisis. But It Has Also Mandated a Switchover to Electric Vehicles." *Forbes*, September 8, 2022 (Dolsak 2022).

- "Climate Change Overwhelming California Power Grid." *The Hill*, September 6, 2022 (Elbein 2022).

REALITY OF TOTAL SOCIETAL IMPACT

More questions are surfacing from the media and policy makers alike regarding the reality of "zero-emission vehicles." For example, most consumers would not think their battery-operated toothbrushes, toys, or appliances have zero environmental impact although they too appear to be zero emissions. We believe the term justifies EVs regardless of the total lifecycle impact. Just as ethanol was maligned when full lifecycle analysis was applied, albeit using flawed data, EVs must get their power from somewhere, and EPA's Lifecycle Carbon Analysis must be applied to understand their impact.

In our interview with Boyden Gray, he said, "It is absurd that EPA refuses to do a full lifecycle analysis on EV. Until you have a fair accounting for a [Lifecycle Carbon Analysis] for EVs, ethanol suffers."

What would a fair apples-to-apples analysis include? In addition to the apparent inclusion of the source of electricity, several other key factors should be considered. One of the most recent is the increased particulate matter pollution from roadways produced by the extra weight of the battery in the EV. The consequence results in a higher rate of tire deterioration because of the added weight, further exacerbating the well-documented health problems associated with particulates. These issues are often overlooked but can easily be researched.

We interviewed Marc Rauch, auto expert and co-publisher of The Auto Channel, which reaches about one million consumers and automobile enthusiasts worldwide every month. Marc discussed the research in his article "The Real Story on

Electric Vehicles" (Rauch 2021). Marc shared his concerns about consumer acceptance and the need to push or protect their elected officials who are spending a lot of tax dollars to develop the EV market.

"Prospective EV buyers worry about increasing electricity prices. The average cost of electricity in the US has increased from $0.050 per kilowatt hour in 1970 to $0.141 in 2021. Consumers worry about charging their vehicles during blackouts and brownouts from the antiquated electric grid system, downed power lines from storms, like in the Northeast, and the increasing number of wildfires in California. California accounts for about 40 percent of EV sales in the United States.

I read about consumers being worried about longer charging times than gasoline and possibly even longer when there is a line to recharge. Risks of fires from batteries overheating and exploding in vehicles, and enslaved person labor-like conditions involved in mining cobalt, an essential material used to make lithium batteries, are becoming more popular topics.

Like oil dependence and the Middle East, consumers are also concerned the US will trade being dependent on countries and regimes that also do not have its best interest at heart. For example, China is the world leader in lithium batteries and EV manufacturing. China makes over half of EVs and 65 percent of lithium batteries in the world. In 2022, the US Federal Bureau of Investigation reported China was the source of the most cyber-attacks on the US, more than all other nations combined.

That's a lot to digest over Thanksgiving dinner when your daughter announces she will buy an EV to help save the planet."

THE REALITY OF FULL PUBLIC ACCEPTANCE

Given these concerns, it is not unreasonable to suggest those believing in the EV 100 percent market penetration vision need to rethink mandating these vehicles at the expense of anything and everyone else. It's not even a smart play for the most diehard EV fan. EV mandates require sustaining policies that have unanswered questions and deny consumer choice. This has already led to more opposition, which is growing daily.

As noted previously, the public acceptance of ethanol over the past four decades has been turbulent. Our research shows EVs are beginning to experience a similar consumer acceptance roller coaster. We thought oil interests had been unusually quiet on EVs compared to the oil industry's disdain for ethanol. It was not until 2022 that pushback from the oil industry, automakers, policy makers, the media, and academia became obvious in the nation's headlines. Some companies and organizations may likely have been selling false hope of EVs' rapid success or had a clear understanding that the long uphill road to full public acceptance would protect gasoline's status quo.

Just like automaker's commitments are waiving, consumer commitment is equally as problematic. Here are some examples of recent EV consumer trust or bust headlines.

- "Toyota Exec Says Lack of Consumer Demand Makes US Goal of 50 percent Electric Vehicles by 2030 a Long Shot." *Forbes*. August 23, 2022 (Henry 2022)

- "Americans Support Incentives for Electric Vehicles but Are Divided over Buying One Themselves." *Pew Research Center*. August 2, 2022 (Carey 2022)

- "Gas Prices Are Falling. So Is Interest in Electric Cars." *CNN Business*. August 5, 2022 (Valdes-Dapena 2022).

- "Biden Talks up Electric Vehicle Revolution—but Is America Ready to Give up Gas?" *The Guardian*. September 17, 2022 (Perkins 2022).

Others in the media have shared our concerns. In *The Washington Post*, writer Charles Lane's article, "Why Electric Cars Still Don't Live Up to the Hype," states, "66 percent of the EVs registered are owned by people making more than $100K per year. Mass adoption of electric cars, however, cannot occur unless they can do everything gas-powered vehicles can do... at a comparable total cost of ownership. Otherwise, electric cars will be a niche product for upper-income folks... Government subsidies for [EVs] will be a regressive transfer of social resources in return for little climate benefit, given that the US power grid the cars draw from is 64 percent fueled by coal and gas" (Lane 2019).

According to Alex Kopestinsky's article "What Is the Average American Income in 2022?" he states, "Around 15.5 percent of Americans earned between $100,000 and $149,999 (Kopestinsky 2022). In business school terms, [EVs have] a relatively small 'total accessible market' of the 332.4 million people living in the United States that would be considered 'financially suitable targets' to purchase EVs" (US Department of Commerce 2022).

REALITY

The warning signs of EVs public acceptance roller-coaster ride appeared much sooner than the summer of 2022. Based on the threat EVs had on the world's largest gasoline market, we knew EVs were going to be increasingly scrutinized. EVs were going to be evaluated under the same critical microscope and with the same bias filters as ethanol. Because so many people were hearing about the positive benefits of EVs and the negative impacts of ethanol, we started compiling research to help balance the two and find ways to build a coalition of EV and biofuel advocates.

We first published *Reality EV* in 2020. Our research was in response to claims by environmental groups and policy makers that cleaning up gasoline or supporting biofuels was a waste of time and money. It was by no means an attempt to discourage federal and state government investment in EVs, but instead a plea that they first examine the facts.

Our concerns as expressed in *Reality EV* were echoed in an article authored by former Senator Tim Wirth (D-CO), chairman of the United Nations Foundation, and Senator Charles Grassley (R-IA) titled, "Environmental Advocates Should Take Another Look at Biofuels" (Wirth and Grassley 2019).

"There is a lot of talk about reducing greenhouse gas emissions, but what's needed are practical strategies to get there. Even a rapid transition to electric vehicles will leave hundreds of millions of conventional cars and trucks on US roads for the next thirty years."

This article is another example of how bipartisan priorities are achieved not by an immediate switch to EVS but by replacing carcinogenic octane additives in gasoline with cleaner, faster-to-market, and high-octane biofuels. How fast is fast? Thousands of consumers are already buying higher blends of ethanol for their cars even if they are not flexible-fuel vehicles, or FFVs, and the more common this becomes, the faster we improve our impact on the environment.

EV and biofuel advocates working together can achieve historic improvements in a new and improved CAFE, one which:

- contains low-carbon and higher-octane gasoline standards,

- forces EPA to comply with the technology-forcing and mobile source toxic provisions in Section 202 (l) of the CAAA, and

- incentivizes automakers to incorporate flexible-fuel vehicles (FFVs) and hybrid plug-in technology as standard public safety features on all vehicles. This new standard would be similar to the plug-in hybrid-electric vehicle (PHEV) technology General Motors (GM) unveiled in 2008 with the Chevy Volt (Groom 2008). The PHEV technology could be packaged with technology in the 22 million FFVs nearly every other automaker produced in the past two decades.

This potentially historic achievement to protect public health and the environment would give consumers *an immediate choice* to get nearly one hundred miles per gallon of gasoline. Initial CAFE standards needed to include a reduction in gasoline consumption, and with our recommendations above, they can. CAFE standards should also recognize the value of ethanol and support automakers in their effort to clean up gasoline emissions. A new CAFE gasoline standard must require minimal refueling infrastructure or auto manufacturing investment. Like the US lead phasedown programs, this initiative would make refiners accountable for participating in a technology-forcing aromatic/BETX phasedown. Compared to the nine years it took EPA to phase out lead additives from 1979 to 1988, a new CAFE-driven aromatic/BTEX phasedown would be cheaper—less expensive not inferior—better, faster, safer, and potentially face less consumer resistance.

This approach is achievable compared to other options because of a historical precedent. Mark Lewis was the assistant editor of the *EPA Journal* in 1985. In his article, "Lead Poisoning: A Historical Perspective," Lewis points out that while EPA's first lead phasedown regulation was issued in 1973, automakers started equipping cars with catalytic converters in 1975, making all-new vehicles capable of only running on unleaded. By 1985, leaded gasoline still accounted for 40 percent of gasoline sales, but "EPA estimated ambient lead levels dropped 64 percent between 1975 and 1982" (Lewis 1985). Imagine what would be possible today if our nation had industry leaders who lead instead of simply complying with regulations.

GM is an excellent example of what could be possible. GM started producing vehicles designed to run on unleaded gasoline in 1971. In 1990, we were at the historic meeting of the Congressional Automotive and Alcohol Fuel Caucuses when Ron Sykes, one of GM's senior Washington representatives, announced the company officially approved 10 percent ethanol blends in warranty statements. At that time, GM was the largest corporation in the US, Ford was second, and ExxonMobil was third (Fortune 500 1990). We watched other automakers quickly follow suit.

In 1999, GM started producing FFVs capable of using ethanol blends up to 85 percent. By 2004, GM made over 1 million FFVs (Auto.com 2022). In March 2006, Chrysler LLC, GM, and Ford Motor Company pledged to convert 50 percent of the company's fleet to FFVs by 2012 (Austin 2008).

By 2010, GM offered consumers seventeen models of FFVs. In a press release, GM's Vice President of Environment, Energy, and Safety Policy, Mike Robinson states, "We anticipate more than 8.5 million flex-fuel vehicles on the road by 2012, exceeding our pledge made in 2006 and the potential to reduce the CO_2 footprint of driving more than 6.8 million tons per year" (General Motors 2010).

That was the good news. Unfortunately, the environmental community fought for years to have Congress remove the FFV incentive for automakers because the incentive assumed that 85 percent ethanol would be used all the time and not actual gallons consumed. We supported the legislation because the intended outcome would stop the chicken versus egg battle of which should come first: the alternative fuel cars or the fuel. Somebody had to play rooster, and Congress did just that.

The loss of the FFV incentive for automakers was a causality of the disinformation wars waged by oil interests on Capitol Hill and in the media. The ethanol gaslight was on, and people were swarming to it like moths to a flame. We worked with automakers to fight back. They proposed innovative ways to account for E85 consumption at the pumps and in FFVs. But Congress succumbed to pressures from the oil lobby and environmentalists, and the credit was allowed to expire. They threw the baby out with the bath water.

The production of FFVs decreased. Now those vehicles will not be able to take advantage of the advancement of ethanol, which is proven to lower greenhouse gases by almost half while also lowering air toxics and particulate matter. We feel those key influencers got duped into believing all biofuels are bad.

Meanwhile, the good news is thousands of people are choosing higher blends of ethanol even if their vehicle is not an FFV. Per our interviews with Jim Seurer, CEO of Glacier Lakes Ethanol, Seth Harder, general manager of Husker Ag ethanol, and Dave and Steve Vander Griend of ICM Inc., in the past few years, thousands of happy consumers in Kansas, Nebraska, and South Dakota are choosing low-carbon, high-octane 30 percent ethanol blends in their vehicles. To date, those programs have not recorded any consumer complaints. The best news is that it is not too late to take advantage of lessons learned if automakers can achieve what Henry Ford did with the Model T, and if EPA will let them.

REALITY PHEV-FFV

In our interview with Dave Hallberg, he said,

"E40 represents the apex of ethanol's octane-boosting properties, thus optimizing vehicle fuel efficiency while reducing carbon and toxic emissions by maximizing the displacement of aromatics/BTEX. Ethanol leaders in Brazil indicated the country may prioritize using E40 hybrids, and most of South America and the Caribbean would likely follow suit. If the US policy makers did the same, automakers would be empowered to harmonize engine design platforms and thus reduce vehicle costs of manufacture to the consumer. Other outcomes include a reduction in battery capacity, reduced vehicle weight, tire and road wear, concerns about disposal, and there would be less demand for lithium and other precious metals, which put enormous strain on global supply chains and the environment. Furthermore, the electric grid and consumers would be less vulnerable to increasing demand spikes and disruptions from either physical or cyber-attacks. When given the option, why not take both?"

INTENDED OUTCOMES AND CONSEQUENCES
Higher Blends of Biofuels Empower Consumers to Get More Miles per Gallon of Gasoline

Percent of Ethanol	Miles Traveled per Year	50 Percent of Miles Traveled on Electricity	Average Miles per Gallon	Fuel Consumed	Gallons of Gasoline Consumed	Miles per Gallon of Gasoline
10	15,000	7,500	37.2	202	181	82.7
20	15,000	7,500	36.1	208	166	90.2
30	15,000	7,500	35	214	150	99.9
85	15,000	7,500	27.9	269	40	372

- US fuel economy standards have increased an average of one to two miles per gallon since 1978. (National Highway Traffic Safety Administration 2014) (National Highway Traffic Safety Administration 2022)

- Drivers average about thirty-five miles daily and commute to work in about twenty-five minutes (Hardesty 2022). More than half of all daily trips were less than three miles in 2021 (US Department of Energy 2022).

- Hybrid Electric Plug-ins, model years 2012 to 2019, average about 37.2 mpg (Fuel Economy.gov 2022).

The first CAFE standards legislated the reduction in gallons of gasoline consumed per mile. Now CAFE also measures carbon intensity per gallon. Therefore, we believe it would be good climate change and public health policy to include the 46 percent reduction from ethanol use and give automakers

CAFE credits to produce Plug-in Hybrid Electric Flexible-Fuel Vehicles (PHE-FFV). Why? Because it would stimulate the entrepreneurial spirit to build the better widget and market for cheaper (less expensive), better (more efficient), faster (to market than other alternatives), and (environmentally) safer ethanol blends—when compared to gasoline or aromatics/BTEX.

As discussed in chapter 3, the ten-year average of ethanol was twenty-six cents per gallon less than gasoline. The octane value of ethanol is about eighteen cents per gallon, and the carbon reduction is worth about sixty-five cents per gallon.

Therefore, just like incentives for automakers to produce EVs, We are sure you would agree it might be a better overall policy to incentivize automakers to make PHE-FFVs as a standard public health safety feature despite the added cost of about fifty dollars? All things considered, the total societal benefits would be more significant. Consumers' resistance to change and the price of refueling would be negligible.

Based on all that we know is true, we would guarantee that if ethanol is discounted by the equivalent two dollars and fifty cents EV per gallon subsidy, and if policy makers and consumers captured ethanol's value, the price is essentially better than free. Consumers would flock to free and run from their dependence on crude oil, gasoline, and aromatics/BTEX.

TAKEAWAYS
- Even a wildly successful EV program will be paired with hundreds of millions of internal combustion engines

consuming trillions of gallons of gasoline over the next decade.

- Like the battle to get lead out of gasoline, the environmental community, policy makers, and the public must recognize the realities of our transportation system and seek a balance to ensure we are using every tool at our disposal to achieve many public policy goals.

- Ethanol use and production is the sum of its parts, the multitude of synergistic benefits.

- Don't be duped by thinking the nation must wait for the perfect silver bullet replacement fuel. You can help end the political chicken or egg game that kicks the environmental and energy policy can down the oil-paved road for your children to solve.

WHAT'S NEXT?
- What can your elected officials do?

- In the face of legislative stalemates, what legal actions can be taken to protect public health and the environment and force government and industry to protect citizens by reducing mobile source air toxics to the maximum extent achievable?

CHAPTER 14
Moving Forward

To Follow Suit

Our editors felt we spent a *lot* of time validating the history of what oil companies, Congress, and the EPA did or did not do to support alternative transportation fuels. We made it a point to cover all the bases of the Greek tragedy that is our current bureaucratic fuel battle. So, let's move forward.

We now focus on what it will take for the United States to build a promising fuel future. Hopefully, the aromatic/BTEX phaseout can follow in the footsteps of other historic reforms like removing lead additives in gasoline or smoking and tobacco use. Examine the water contamination at the Marine Base of Camp Lejeune, a case from the 1950s in which members of the camp were routinely exposed to toxic water. Examine the forced recalls of sunscreens, after-sun lotions, antifungals, antiperspirants, and deodorants from several major consumer product makers, including Johnson & Johnson and Procter & Gamble, in which benzene was found. How can biofuel activists take advantage of the legal precedent set before us in the past?

Edward-Isaac Dovere of *Politico Magazine* has repeatedly interviewed former Governor of California, Arnold Schwarzenegger. We believe Schwarzenegger's remarks about his lawsuit against oil companies in Dovere's March 12, 2018, story captured the essence of the past and a glimpse into the future.

> "This is no different from the smoking issue. The tobacco industry knew for [...] decades that smoking would kill people [...] and were hiding that fact [...]. Then eventually they were taken to court and had to pay hundreds of millions of dollars because of that. The oil companies knew [...] that there would be global warming happening because of fossil fuels, and [...] that it would be risky for people's lives. [...] [I]t's absolutely irresponsible to know that your product is killing people and not have a warning label on it, like tobacco. Every gas station and car should have a warning label on it, every product that has fossil fuels should have a warning label on it. Next mission: taking oil companies to court for knowingly killing people all over the world (Dovere 2018)."

In this historic speech, Governor Schwarzenegger argues that, at the very least, his lawsuit would raise awareness about fossil fuels and encourage people to look to alternative fuels and clean cars. We hope he's back to help and reads *Gasolinegate*. If he does, the governor can easily connect the dots between the longer-term impacts of climate change and the much more direct and immediate public health threat from aromatics/BTEX in our cars, air, and bloodstreams. In the high-stakes poker game of politics versus industry versus the people, we believe aromatics/BTEX trumps climate change in terms of urgency, ease and cost to implement change, and possibility for immediate public benefits. The nation's reliance on aromatics/BTEX needs to end.

COURT OF LAST RESORT

EPA's criminal enforcement program investigates and assists in prosecuting known or negligent environmental violations. According to EPA, "[2017] cases resulted in a total of 153 years of incarceration for individual defendants, plus fines of $2,829,202,563 for individual and corporate defendants, with an additional $3,092,631 in court-ordered environmental projects and $147,520,585 in restitution" (US Environmental Protection Agency 2017b). Since the passage of the Clean Air Act Amendments of 1990 (CAAA), nearly a thousand civil cases and settlements have appeared on the EPA docket (US Environmental Protection Agency 2022a).

As noted earlier, Boyden Gray and others define purposeful legislative ambiguity as "agency capture." Consider agency capture in terms of the triangular conflict of fossil fuel interests influencing Congress and Congress influencing legislation and federal agencies. Both parties are searching for the absolute truth, a clear definition of the law in the face of Congressional legislative ambiguity.

In each of these cases, the courts will research and depose both parties to determine what the party knew, when they knew it, what they did about it, and what damage resulted from a lack of knowledge or action. From that point, the court moves forward to determine accountability and set the course for corrective actions. Like us, you must wonder why no one has sued EPA over aromatics/BTEX in gasoline, especially considering alternatives flooding the market and new technologies desperately trying to find a home (see "Chapter 16: Back to the Fuel Future").

Common sense does not prevail when comparing what we think are less-significant court cases below. We believe the root cause of inaction could be those who know but have conflicting business interests and those duped by misinformation who unknowingly continue to carry the fossil fuel gaslight. For example:

- The ethanol industry might hesitate to sue big oil, their biggest customer and adversary.

- The ethanol industry might be hesitant to sue EPA regarding toxics, fearing retaliation from a sector that can also be their other biggest ally or adversary.

- Insurance companies—health and property—might be hesitant to sue oil companies, which are also some of their biggest clients.

- EPA might be hesitant to support more biofuels and ethanol in fear of retaliation by Congress cutting their budget or not providing the political courage and conviction needed to take on big oil.

- Perhaps the environmental community and EPA simply got and continued to get pressured, duped, and gaslit by highly paid, highly skilled people conducting well-financed disinformation campaigns.

Like us, many clean fuel advocates remain perplexed as to why the environmental community has not seized on the need to reduce benzene and taken this issue to the courts. In our exchanges with Senator Daschle, he stated, "The environmental community should be ashamed of themselves for not supporting ethanol, demanding more reductions in aromatics in gasoline, or for that matter, both."

PRECEDENCE

Are you also wondering by now if the lack of progress in developing cleaner gasoline is negligence, collusion, ineptitude, or a financial conundrum? Our experience fighting for cheaper, better, safer alternative transportation fuels truly has been the definition of "insanity," and it drove us crazy. We finally resorted to a deep dive into how other movements and organizations made progress when they reached their wit's end.

The following examples of cases, headlines, and related stories give EPA, public health and environmental protection advocates, and consumers a precedent on which to act. They are all direct beneficiaries of the increased use of biofuels.

EXAMPLES OF THE PEOPLE VERSUS BIG OIL AND OTHER INDUSTRIES

Tobacco Master Settlement Agreement

In May 1994, Mississippi Attorney General Mike Moore launched a lawsuit against thirteen tobacco companies, eventually resulting in a $246 billion, fifty-state settlement.

The settlement created a trust fund to pay for medical costs resulting from tobacco addiction and ended similar lawsuits by states and individuals. The payment also prohibited class action lawsuits against tobacco companies in the future. However, the judgment lasts forever (Moore 1997).

Please watch the video of the Coalition of State Attorneys General Tobacco Industry Settlement Press Conference. The QR code below will take you to www.StateAG.org and a CNN video embedded in the announcement, or use the URL provided in the chapter appendix citation (Moore 1997).

At the Coalition of State Attorneys General Tobacco Industry Settlement Press Conference, Mike Moore said, "This is the most historic public health achievement in history. The case was the most contentious thing I have seen in my life." In his remarks, Moore thanked his army for the victory. He recognized the attorney generals, trial lawyers, and public health officials of America. He also thanked the US Surgeon General and the President of the United States. Moore said, "We didn't start the war," and recognized those who fought the battle for the previous fifty years. Moore went on to say,

> "We wanted to change how they did business, and we have done that. We wanted to make sure everyone, every single person in America and the entire world, knows the truth about what the tobacco industry has done to the people of this world for the last fifty years, and we have done that. We have a whistleblower provision that will protect everybody that helped us in the past now and in the future."

The settlement also dissolved the Tobacco Institute, Center for Indoor Air Research, and Council for Tobacco Research. At this point in *Gasolinegate*, we believe you will see the correlation between smoking, tobacco companies, and our fight for safer gasoline.

Video of the Press Conference of the Coalition of State Attorneys General announcing the Tobacco Industry Settlement (Moore 1997).

IS BIG OIL NEXT?

In 2020, Minnesota Attorney General Keith Ellison filed a climate liability lawsuit against Exxon Mobil Corp., the American Petroleum Institute, and three Koch entities. In a phone interview with *E&E News* writer Maxine Joselow, Ellison said, "The tobacco companies were deliberately lying about the harmful effects of cigarettes, and they had to pay for those false statements. With Exxon Mobil, Koch, and API, we will show that they, too, were deliberately misleading and lying to the public about how their products caused climate change so they could keep making billions of dollars" (Joselow 2021).

We have used the Dieselgate Volkswagen Clean Air Act Civil Settlement as an example of the EPA taking action to sue for not complying with the Clean Air Act, its Amendments, or other violations. Below is a small sampling of headlines illustrating the growing trend to make the industry legally and financially accountable. We paraphrased them slightly for readability and provided the citations for fact-checking.

- Local Governments Can Sue Oil Companies over Climate Change (Egelko 2022).

- Shell Loses Climate Case That May Set Precedent for Big Oil (Baazil 2021).

- California Attorney General Rob Bonta Opens an Investigation into "Decades-Long Plastics Deception Campaign, Perpetuating a Myth that Recycling Can Solve the Plastics Crisis" (Richardson 2022).

- US Supreme Court Takes No Action on Bayer's Bid to Nix Weedkiller Suits (Hurley 2022).

- Environmental Justice Law in New York Could Prevent New Pollution [from Industry] in Hard-Hit Neighborhoods (Kane 2022).

- US Attorney General Garland and EPA Launches Department of Justice Office Focused on Environmental Justice (Gregorian 2022).

THE PEOPLE VERSUS EPA

We think most people would be surprised by the number of lawsuits filed against EPA for violating the same laws for which they prosecute companies and individuals (e.g., Clean Air Act, Clean Water Act, Safe Drinking Water Act, Toxic Substances Control Act, Comprehensive Environmental Response, Compensation and Liability Act, Emergency Planning and Community Right-to-Know Act [EPCRA]).

Many environmental statutes that govern EPA contain provisions that allow citizens to sue the agency when it fails to perform an act or duty required by the law. Unlike provisions allowing citizens to challenge final agency actions, these suit provisions usually require a potential plaintiff to first provide the EPA with a "Notice of Intent to Sue" before filing the lawsuit. Not all such notices result in lawsuits filed (US Environmental Protection Agency 2017b).

Since 2013, EPA has received 468 "Notice of Intent to Sue" advance filings, and 315 have been for violating the CAA. These lawsuits hold EPA accountable for complying with legislation, and based on the Flint, Michigan, water case, they also hold EPA financially and personally liable.

- Represented by Earthjustice, the Center for Biological Diversity, Environmental Defense Fund, National Parks Conservation Association, and Sierra Club filed the lawsuit that "Would Compel the Environmental Protection Agency to Enforce Air Pollution Law" (Environmental Defense Fund 2022).

- Judge approves $626 million dollar settlement for Flint tainted-water lawsuit prompting several lawsuits and neglect charges against former Michigan Governor Rick Snyder (Fitz-Gibbon 2021).

- The Environmental Integrity Project, Chesapeake Climate Action Network, and Sierra Club filed their notice of intent to sue EPA under the Clean Air Act, for underestimating Greenhouse Gas Emissions from US landfills by at least 25 percent (Environmental Integrity Project 2021).

- Salt Lake City and other cities sue EPA for stronger ozone protections. Communities at issue include Baltimore, Maryland; Chicago, Illinois; Cleveland, Ohio; Dallas, San Antonio, and Houston, Texas; Denver, Colorado; Phoenix, Arizona; Salt Lake City, Utah; and Washington, DC (Fitzgerald 2022).

- The Natural Resources Defense Council, together with Sierra Club and the Environmental Integrity Project Groups sue EPA for stronger clean air protections (Sierra Club 2021).

- The Center for Biological Diversity and Center for Environmental Health initiated a lawsuit challenging EPA's failure to update air pollution emission standards (Center for Biological Diversity 2022).

- Several environmental groups sue EPA over failure to update inadequate, decades-old standards for controlling toxic emissions (Budryk 2022).

- Lawsuits against EPA by Louisiana residents could slash toxic emissions in America's "Cancer Alley" (Laughland 2022).

- Growth Energy sues EPA for failure to issue requirements under the Renewable Fuel Standard Program under section 304(a)(2) of the Clean Air Act (US Environmental Protection Agency 2021).

Growth Energy represents about half of the ethanol production facilities in the United States, and they do not mention aromatics/BTEX in their lawsuit (see "Chapter 15: Missing in Action").

TORT COURT

The Federal Tort Claims Act (FTCA) is federal legislation enacted in 1946. It provides a legal means for compensating individuals who have suffered a personal injury, death, or property loss or damage caused by a federal government employee's negligent or wrongful act or omission. It generally allows individuals to recover monetary damages from the United States under circumstances where the United States, if a private person, would be liable in accordance with the law of the place where the negligent or wrongful act or omission occurred.

We think the fight for clean fuel is relevant considering on August 4, 2017, then-EPA Administrator Scott Pruitt announced EPA would reconsider claims by businesses and individuals under the Federal Tort Claims Act. The previous EPA administration denied seventy-nine administrative claims filed by farmers, ranchers, homeowners, businesses, employees, state and local governments, and others seeking damages in connection with the Gold King Mine incident, an environmental disaster in which EPA personnel released toxic waste into the Animas River. Administrator Pruitt said,

> "EPA should be held to the same standard as those we regulate. When I was appointed EPA Administrator by President Trump, I committed to review the Gold King Mine decision made by the previous administration. A new review is paramount to ensure that those who have, in fact, suffered losses have a fair opportunity to have their claims heard (US Environmental Protection Agency 2017a)."

DÉJÀ VU ALL OVER AGAIN, AGAIN, AND AGAIN

Sean Reilly, writing for *E&E News* states in her June 2, 2022, article, "EPA Proposes Updating Gasoline Regs, Slashing Emissions,"

> "If the package is made final, EPA predicts that stricter standards and other control requirements would cut releases of hazardous pollutants, a category that includes cancer-causing benzene, from about 6,100 tons to 3,900 tons, a drop of 36 percent. About 9,500 facilities would be covered and minorities make up 59 percent of the people living within 3.1 miles of the 117 gasoline distribution facilities. The expected upfront compliance costs to industry add up to almost $67 million (Reilly 2022)."

Reilly also noted EPA responded by saying, "the added expenses are not expected to result in a significant market impact, regardless of whether they are passed on to the purchaser or absorbed by the firms" and for reasons not spelled out in the proposal, EPA predicted there will be modest increases in emissions of sulfur dioxide, carbon dioxide, and other pollutants.

According to Reilly, in assembling the proposal, EPA met with several trade groups "to collect data and discuss industry practices." One of those was the American Petroleum Institute, whose spokesperson, Scott Lauermann, said the trade group reviewed the proposal and looked forward to providing feedback during the sixty-day window for written comments. EPA said they would also hold a virtual public hearing *if requested*. Kathryn Clay, president of the International Liquid Terminals Association, said of the draft rule in the interview,

> "We think it's a win-win. It's achievable and a good step forward. However, the ten-milligrams threshold would impose significant economic costs that terminals would have no choice but to pass on to their customers and ultimately would be borne by consumers in the form of higher gas prices."

We are unaware of any new research that shows a safe threshold for benzene above *zero* as established in 1948 by the American Petroleum Institute and the Center for Disease Control.

What could drive EPA's new concern and sudden change of heart over benzene emissions? EPA is also undertaking the package above as part of a settlement to a federal lawsuit brought by Our Children's Earth Foundation filed on February 2, 2022 (US Environmental Protection Agency 2022c). In the case, the group alleged EPA was long past the Clean Air Act deadlines for conducting mandatory reviews of regulations dating back to 1983. Kudos to Sean Reilly for an amazing, all-inclusive article that captures what we believe is the essence of our problem and possible solution.

- A small nonprofit has legal standing simply by the fact they breathe air.

- The group believes EPA has failed to meet mandatory directives.

- EPA admits benzene is a carcinogen.

- EPA did not make progress on regulations established in 1983 and will settle the lawsuit.

Therefore, how can EPA not address the elephant of benzene in gasoline currently emanating from the nation's 287 million vehicles into everyone's living rooms?

FINAL PLEADINGS

The pleas to the world in videos by Dr. Perera, Mike More, and Reid Detchon are genuinely compassionate and based on an enormous amount of personal experience and evidence.

But is there enough evidence for the courts to help EPA protect public health and the environment?

Dave Hallberg, founder of the Renewable Fuels Association, has been researching this topic since 1988 when he worked closely with clean fuels advocates in Congress during the Congressional deliberations that created Section 202 (l) in the Clean Air Act Amendments of 1990. Here is a summary of Hallberg's findings, precedents, and why he thinks legal action can and should be taken to protect public health and the environment by controlling aromatics/BTEX:

- ☑ Over thirty years of documentation aligned with consistent leadership at EPA/OTAQ.
- ☑ History of missed opportunities for correction.
- ☑ Existing Congressional legislative endangerment finding.
- ☑ The precedent of Section 202 (l) of the Clean Air Act Amendments of 1990.
- ☑ Date certain requirements.
- ☑ The effort to repeal Section 202 (l) during the 2005 Energy Policy Act debates.
- ☑ Documented collaboration with oil interests MOVES Model manipulation.
- ☑ Use of the MOVES model to enforce state implementation plans.
- ☑ The impact of flawed Lifecycle Carbon Model on national transportation fuels policy.
- ☑ 2007 MSAT Rule SOA obligation is fifteen years overdue.
- ☑ EPA's 2011 report to Congress on Clean Air Act and costs & benefits ethanol.
- ☑ EPA's noncompliance with the mandatory Section 202(l) MSAT provision that would improve the nation's balance

sheet by trillions of dollars in reduced oil import and health cost savings.
- ☑ EPA's 2016 Mid-Term Evaluation of the CAFE Rule.
- ☑ Technology-Forcing legal precedents in the CAAA.
- ☑ Current technology forcing vehicle emissions controls are proven ineffective.
- ☑ UFPs are unrecognized, unregulated, and are a disproportionate health threat compared to other actions.
- ☑ EPA's MY2023 and later LDV GHG 2021 Final Rule data and statements.
- ☑ The precedent of current climate change litigation.
- ☑ The precedent of current and future environmental justice impact and enforcement
- ☑ New Supreme Court Major Questions Doctrine eviscerates the Chevron deference doctrine.
- ☑ EPA's track record on small refiner RFS waivers.
- ☑ EPA's current and likely future actions to modify the RFS.
- ☑ EPA's Final Safe 2 Rule is flawed.
    - All air pollution particles—regardless of size and composition—are not equal in terms of potency.
    - EPA's MOVES Model is defective and incapable of accurately predicting the most harmful tailpipe emissions.
    - EPA's final rule will not substantially reduce PM-bound toxics from the existing LDV fleet. Instead, GDI engines will dramatically increase emissions of the most harmful UFP-borne toxics.
- ☑ Rules Impact, the Federal Tort Claims Act (FTCA), and Qui Tam process, i.e., the whistleblower (National Whistleblowers Center 2022b).

- "Under the False Claims Act, qui tam allows persons and entities with evidence of fraud against federal programs or contracts to sue the wrongdoer on behalf of the United States Government. In qui tam actions, the government has the right to intervene and join the action. If the government declines, the private plaintiff may proceed on his or her own. Some states have passed similar laws concerning fraud in state government contracts" (National Whistleblowers Center 2022a).

TAKEAWAYS

- Why has an organization or individual not sued EPA for failing to comply with Section 202 (l) of the CAAA?

WHAT'S NEXT?

- Who will lead the battle cry to form the next army of attorneys generals, trial lawyers, and public health officials of America to fight "General Denial?"

- Will the US Surgeon General, the President of the United States, and environmental organizations enlist?

Wanted: Legislative superheroes to enforce protection of public health by reducing air pollution from motor vehicles, engines, and the fuels used to operate them.

Job Description: Enforce Section 202 (l) in the Clean Air Act to the greatest extent possible in order to regulate fuels and fuel additives for use in motor vehicle, motor vehicle engine, or non-road engine or nonroad vehicles if such fuel, fuel additive, or any emission products causes or contributes to air or water pollution that may endanger the public health or welfare. Must also address emission products of such fuel or fuel additives that may impair any emission control devices used on vehicles or engines to reduce harmful emissions.

CHAPTER 15

Missing in Action

Where Have All the Champions Gone?

Note to readers: We felt the next two closing chapters written in first person from our individual experiences would offer additional insights to our collective story.

By Doug Durante

As the preceding chapters have shown, *Gasolinegate* is a story of negligence, oversight, hypocrisy, greed, and ineptitude. But perhaps most of all, it is a story of missed opportunity. The opportunity to protect public health, strengthen our energy and national security, reduce greenhouse gas emissions and address climate change, enhance the rural economy, generate significant employment, and tax revenue to the treasury... The list goes on, and the opportunity presented itself time and time again.

I am sitting on an airplane in March 2022, bound for Detroit, Michigan, to meet with agriculture, auto, and ethanol stakeholders in an attempt to stitch together some strategy to capture those benefits. The sad reality is that after forty years of trying, we are chasing the same elusive *kumbaya* moment that would have allowed everyone to claim victory. Sure, we put some scores on the board over the years but not in the sustaining way that would have made this trip unnecessary. And when we did, negligence, oversight, hypocrisy, greed, and ineptitude chipped away at the fabric of those successes and often brought us back to our starting point. And the main culprits were EPA, the oil industry, and the environmental community.

But as I look out the window from thirty thousand feet, I recall those scattered victories and remain more convinced than ever that ethanol was a unique cog in the wheel and remains so. The first-time ethanol emerged as a player was in the Clean Air Act Amendments of 1990. As we discussed in detail, Title II of that bill addressed mobile source emissions and thanks to a cadre of knowledgeable senators from both sides of the isle, we were able to get lead out of gasoline and set the stage for ethanol to assume its highest value, which was as a source of octane, and clean octane devoid of the toxins, poisons, and carcinogens that were being used by refiners. As an oxygenate, ethanol increased combustion of fuels, reducing harmful tailpipe emissions, and as such addressed a number of criteria pollutants that prior to this bill had gone unchecked. At that time, there were nearly fifty cities in violation of carbon monoxide standards and dozens more had serious ozone and smog problems.

When we saw the interest in updating the 1970 Clean Air Act, we formed the Clean Fuels Development Coalition to overcome the hurdle to creating change. While we were ethanol advocates, in order to break the bunker mentality, we worked with automakers, agricultural groups, environmental organizations, chemical producers, some oil companies, consumer groups, government agencies, and Republicans *and* Democrats in Congress. Keep in mind, this was at a time when politics was not the blood sport it is today, and bipartisan approaches to problems were not considered heresy.

This diverse group found common ground and worked together to create historical change. Each one of them had a problem because Congress and the public were hot on their trail. Advancing ethanol was in everyone's interest at that time.

As noted, pollution was off the charts, our dependence on imported oil was going in the wrong direction, the US automakers were facing brutal competition from overseas, and American agriculture was struggling to cover the cost of production. Our coalition successfully made the argument that ethanol could be a lynchpin to addressing each of these challenges.

Washington is full of special interest groups. But that's likely the wrong title. From our perspective, they should be called one-interest groups. There is nothing "special" about their often money-motivated, myopic views. They become one trick pony shows with total disregard for the rest of the herd. It's rare that these one-interest groups, corporations, and politicians have come together for the good of their customer or country.

Is the ethanol industry a special interest? Sure, some would say so. But in a world of special, or single-interest, industries and companies, and the entire structure of Washington, DC, built around such efforts, ethanol has the ability to solve a multitude of issues at once.

The Clean Air Act Amendments of 1990 (CAAA) were a proving ground for such cooperative efforts and while the oil industry cried foul and ran expensive ads decrying "government gas," we were in the thick of the battle and eventually the very composition of gasoline in the US was altered to the benefit of anyone who breathes.

I am very honored to have been part of that. We were young and energetic and our crew of warriors on and off the hill outworked the powerful oil industry. With Senate heroes like Democrat Tom Daschle and Republican Bob Dole, we passed critical amendments. I personally went to Democrat Bill Richardson of New Mexico in the House to get him to offer a companion to the Senate bill, and he in turn got Republican Richard Madigan of Illinois to cosponsor with him. While Richardson had undoubtedly been briefed on the bill, I was nonetheless elated to sit with just he and I in his office and leave with his signature.

And guess what? We were right and they were wrong; cleaner gasoline formulas have effectively eliminated carbon monoxide violations in US cities and significantly reduced smog and ground level ozone. But getting to that point necessitated running the gauntlet that is EPA. As the agency charged with developing the rules and regulations governing the new fuels, they seemed to find every reason to keep ethanol out of the mix and deferred to oil companies on a majority of issues.

While it is rarely utilized, federal agencies are sometimes confronted with a law that is so broad and sweeping, and impacts so many different stakeholders that they have a regulatory negotiation, or an open process that is hybrid of a trial, a debate, a hearing, and an elementary school food fight. I was a member of that negotiating committee, and it was an educational, albeit less than fun, experience. In addition to the oil and ethanol industries, air quality officials, state government representatives, environmental and health groups, and automakers were all at the table. EPA was the arbiter and, despite what I believe was a resentment that Congress was telling them how to do their job, we got through it and the health of the public was the beneficiary.

As one of my advisors and good friends, Reg Modlin of Chrysler told us, "EPA is conflict adverse." I will always remember the feeling that EPA, rather than being an advocate for the public and our friend, was an adversary much more on the side of the status quo of oil than the big picture. And what is that big picture? It is looking beyond their own silo, as important as the environment and health is, to recognize energy security, American agriculture, support for the auto industry, and numerous other benefits could be woven into the program. Maximizing the use of domestic, renewable ethanol should have been a guiding principle.

Over the next decade, CFDC continued to be a melting pot for any non-petroleum fuel source and advocates for clean fuels. We were successful in getting cities across the US to adopt clean fuel programs and sponsored Environmental Inaugural Balls for incoming Presidents George Bush, Bill Clinton, George W. Bush, and Barack Obama that became the hottest ticket in town. Pollution was down, imported oil was reduced, ethanol plants were being built, and things were looking up.

Along the way, the next big test to see if anyone could agree on anything came when Tom Daschle introduced the Renewable Fuel Standard. The oxygen requirement in the clean fuels programs established in the 1990 Clean Air Act had the desired effect of kick-starting domestic ethanol production but the unintended consequence of unleashing the methanol-based fuel MTBE on the nation's water supply.

While a lot of things Congress does are answers to questions nobody asked, in this case the RFS was like a ray of sunshine bursting through the clouds. The water contamination issue from MTBE created widespread panic literally from coast to coast. California banned it, and many northeast states attempted to do the same. For many, the answer was to throw out the barrel, rather than the apple that was the contaminant. The oil industry saw this as a golden opportunity to eliminate the oxygen content which would free them up to concoct a pure hydrocarbon product.

Since serving as a catalyst to domestic ethanol production was one of the clear objectives of the 1990 programs, and that production was a result of ethanol's properties of oxygen and clean octane, a role for ethanol needed to be preserved. After fighting it initially, the oil industry did an about face and agreed to what was essentially a trade of the oxygen requirement in reformulated gasoline for a renewable requirement in all gasoline.

They did not do that because they were good guys; they did it thinking they could beat the system. The RFS established total requirements with trading, averaging, and credits. At a mere five billion gallons required in a market of 140 billion gallons of gasoline, they shrugged off the requirement knowing that much could easily be absorbed throughout the system, and they were marking it up anyway. EPA didn't like the RFS either but likely saw it the way the oils did: a minor inconvenience. We are watching the petroleum industry fight tooth and nail today against the RFS because it went from that minor inconvenience to a full-fledged threat.

In late 2005, Ed Murphy, senior vice president of the American Petroleum Institute, appeared on a radio program CFDC produced called *The Ethanol Minute*. In it, he stated how important it was to have ethanol in the fuel mix *to avoid tight supplies and price spikes.*

What the oil industry didn't count on was the ingenuity and determination of American agriculture and the associated engineering firms and financing institutions to respond to that call for more ethanol by blowing right past the five-billion-gallon mark in short order. So, from the oil company's perspective, ethanol was fine if it could be kept in its place of sitting at the kiddy table, but when it became clear that it could assume a much larger slice of the fuel pie, it became unacceptable. Barely two years after the first RFS, the program was expanded to a mind boggling thirty-six-billion-gallon target. It was to be a mix of corn and so-called advanced biomass feedstocks but either way, it was a brutal wake-up call to the oil industry that there was a new sheriff in town.

From that day on, the petroleum industry has discredited, maligned, and fought ethanol in a myriad of ways. Their army of state petroleum marketers and distributors launched renewed labeling requirements, often suggesting onerous warning labels be prominently affixed to pumps "warning" that this product contains ethanol. The "warning" labels are especially ironic given that their own product contained toxic carcinogens at alarming levels.

Backdoor funding of studies claiming there was a net energy loss, it was harmful to vehicles, it used too much water, it used too much fertilizer, it was endangering wildlife and upsetting the balance of land use, it really did not reduce pollution, it actually cost more because it had a slightly lower energy content, and of course the big one, it was using food for fuel.

Fuel testing is like a survey. Depending on how it is structured, the results can come out any way you would like. A group called the Coordinating Research Council is a cooperative effort between the oil and auto industries to test fuels. With oil company engineers and scientists leading the effort, the results were predictable. They often took high aromatic/toxic fuel, added ethanol, then concluded the ethanol was the culprit. EPA had several opportunities to step in and set the record straight but failed to do so.

During that period around the expansion of the RFS, many health and environmental groups were pushing EPA to reduce toxic compounds in gasoline, as required by the Clean Air Act as part of the original Daschle-Dole provisions in the 1990 amendments.

In a 2007 cost-benefit analysis of replacing those toxics with ethanol, EPA went as far as to concede ethanol had superior octane properties but, at the time, oil was nineteen dollars per barrel and the second phase of the RFS had not kicked in, so they argued there was not enough ethanol to justify a dramatic decrease in aromatics. They did lower benzene slightly but ignored the multitude of toxic emissions that remained linked to aromatics. In fifteen years since then, they have never conducted another cost-benefit analysis.

I can only imagine the office celebrations at API and the National Petroleum Refiners when that decision was made. Bring on aromatics, the new lead.

SO WHERE DOES THIS LEAVE US?
As hard as it is to imagine, the disconnect between improving fuel quality and meeting a host of public policy goals is worse today than ever. With few exceptions, the industry fights every drop of ethanol. The decade-long struggle to allow 15 percent ethanol blends in the fuel pool is a prime example. It's true that 10 percent ethanol increases the vapor pressure of gasoline when added to make a blend. Increased vapor pressure creates evaporative emissions. You may recall seeing vapors coming off your engine or from a gas pump on a hot day. And those emissions are indeed part of the smog

problem. But 10 percent ethanol blends more than make up for that extra vapor pressure because they improve tailpipe emissions dramatically. What's more, the increase in vapor pressure peaks at 10 percent and starts coming back down when more ethanol is added. So naturally, 15 percent blends present no danger and should be accorded the same treatment as the 10 percent blends.

Well, that would be how someone who really cared about having ethanol in the mix would think —and stop me if you have heard this before—*to avoid tight supplies and price spikes.* Instead, after a decision had finally been made to allow the 15 percent blends, the petroleum industry sued to overturn it. After it was reinstated a second time, they sued again.

Keep in mind there is no *requirement* to use 15 percent blends; it is simply *an option.* They have convinced boaters, small engine manufacturers and consumers, motorcyclists, and just about anyone who uses gasoline that ethanol is bad. The doublespeak arguments are laughable if anyone would consider that they offer E0—no ethanol—and charge a dollar more per gallon. It is self-defeating in many respects for the petroleum industry to fight. First, it pits them against the ethanol industry and American agriculture in a political and public relations fight that drains resources. It has proven to be a fight that puts elected officials in a very difficult position and results in resentment of both industries. Second, ethanol has historically been significantly less expensive than gasoline, resulting in the oil industry selling it at gasoline prices and enjoying a substantial mark up. Why would they want to deny themselves that option? Is leaving that money on the table with the hope of eventually wiping out ethanol altogether the cost of preserving market share?

As we go to print in early 2023, the American Petroleum Institute has pivoted on their opposition to E15 and now supports the vapor pressure waiver previously restricted to 10 percent blends to be applied to any amount of ethanol. Wow, you might say. They have come around! Unfortunately, API are not doing it for the good of the country or to help the economy. They are doing it because the alternative was a complex maneuver by eight governors who would have effectively required a special blendstock for ethanol that would not need the waiver. The result would have forced refiners to make a unique gasoline for just those states, which would present a host of challenges ranging from producing such a fuel to segregating storage to pricing. So, in this case, they couldn't beat 'em so they joined 'em! It is good news for anyone interested in clean fuels and ultimately, we think the petroleum industry will take advantage of this opportunity.

Even with ethanol in almost all the fuel in the country, and the fact that 10 to 15 percent blends are warranted for all cars since 2001, toxic aromatics producing fine particulates that are either benzene emissions or benzene derivatives remain in gasoline. Refiners will use these carcinogens until EPA stops them, and EPA has shown no inclination to do so. Gasoline is carbon intensive, and these benzene and aromatic additives are the most carbon intensive components in gasoline.

We remain dependent on foreign oil, despite the nonsense spewed by politicians and oil company execs that the US is energy independent. Right. We are so independent that the cutoff of Russian oil due to their war in the Ukraine sent our prices to record highs. If we were truly independent, how would that be possible?

How is it that we have a mandate, by virtue of regulations that hinder the use of higher blends of ethanol, to remain dependent on petroleum and breath fumes and emissions from carcinogenic gasoline? That is a de facto benzene and aromatic mandate.

It is time to call out the stakeholders and challenge everyone to defy these benefits that a national program using ethanol as a lynchpin can provide.

Can there be such a thing as an infinite win-win? We think so. The stakeholders have been asleep at the wheel in recent years, but it's not too late to wake up and avoid going into the ditch that has been fifty years in the making since the Iranian oil embargoes of the 1970s and now extending to worldwide pollution that is undeniably coming largely from the transportation sector. Despite having missed so many opportunities to get this right, opportunities are still there for every nongovernmental organization (NGO) to get involved.

- The oil industry, despite their long history of fighting ethanol, has an opportunity to improve the quality of their fuel and remain in play. The cry for electric vehicles has been primarily based on the assumption that the current slate of transportation fuels cannot reduce carbon. That is completely false. A higher concentration of ethanol such as a 30 percent blend would reduce the carbon footprint of gasoline significantly. In the decades it would take for EVs to make a meaningful contribution, this cleaner, lower-carbon gasoline would have been hard at work.

- The environmental community as a whole has been the most myopic, tunnel-vision interest group of them all, often refusing to accept new science and ignoring other public policy goals. They "let the perfect be the enemy of the good." They oppose ethanol for things like nitrogen run off and land use, yet the alternative is the continued devastation of oceans and land alike. Opposing ethanol prolongs the life of pure gasoline and all its ills. For those who want to protect our land and our seas, anything that reduces the dependence on oil should be a win for them. Embracing ethanol and taking the time to understand the reality of today's modern ethanol industry with its positive carbon footprint reduces the use of oil and meets their "special interest."

- With such an increase in awareness of personal health and well-being, the same groups that fight to get chemicals out of food might also fight to get the chemicals out of the gasoline emissions they are digesting every day. They can join in the fight for full disclosure by fighting for labels on gasoline pumps, which is just as important as labels on food.

- National security advocates have a huge role in this debate. The military is the world's largest consumer of energy, and they consume it fighting to protect OPECs dominance on oil. Some want a strong military. What could make it stronger than making oil less relevant? Some want peace. What could be more peaceful than stopping unfriendly oil-producing nations from weaponizing the supply and demand of oil?

- Select NGOs fight to stop starvation and keep food prices low for the vast majority of the planet in poverty. What better way to protect and grow food supplies than stopping farmers from going out of business and selling to developers? The modern ethanol industry converts one bushel of feed grain corn into almost three gallons of fuel *and* the coproduct of the equivalent of two bushels of protein, which becomes animal feed. Increased demand for corn to be used for ethanol brings with it incredible improvements in efficiency with more corn grown on less land than at any time in history. This model can be replicated across the globe and help lift impoverished countries.

- Automakers can provide highly efficient vehicles utilizing clean burning gasoline as they develop advanced technologies, EVs, and remain competitive in a global market. High-octane, low-carbon gasoline allows automakers to make minor compression adjustments that would yield significant increases in milage and performance. Unlike EVs, these improvements are available immediately in new and existing vehicles.

- Insurance companies—already under immense pressure because of health and property claims—know that study after study confirms that reducing pollution from mobile sources can save millions of lives and billions in healthcare costs. Whether it is the World Health Organization or the American Lung Association, health experts warn of the impending crisis from climate change to respiratory related illness and fatalities. Insurance companies can be a key beneficiary of fuel improvements.

- Technologists and entrepreneurs have taken their talents elsewhere. What bigger market disrupter could be more rewarding than the largest motor fuel market in the world. Elon Musk gets it. Where are the rest?

Who would be willing to support this type of broad legislation? Let me think… How about everybody! The public benefits from cleaner air, domestic refining and auto industries thrive, environmentalists and health groups can meet their mandates, politicians of any party can claim victory, the toll of a lifetime of dependence on oil can be reversed, and a future that includes clean fuels and clean air would be much brighter.

Last but not least, missing in action on so many of these issues has been the ethanol industry itself. That may seem odd given our unabashed support for ethanol. And our support is not to be mistaken for shilling for the ethanol industry, which we are not. But the term "ethanol industry" requires some clarification. The feedstock suppliers, namely corn growers, have the clear and transparent objective of increasing demand for their product. While self-serving, it is grounded in an understanding of the benefits ethanol provides and that more is better. Many ethanol producers have a different view of the world, and increasing ethanol supplies is not always in their interest.

Wait, what? Who wouldn't want more demand for the product they make? The answer is whoever makes that product already. Like kids in the treehouse pulling the rope up before anyone else can get in, ethanol producers don't want to share their slice of the pie. And that does not make them bad guys. Who would want another ethanol plant when it is difficult enough to move the ethanol we already have? Who would want to have to outbid your fellow producer for corn or reduce your coproduct prices to capture that market?

The creation of our Clean Fuels Development Coalition was because of the design and engineering firms who were ready, willing, and able to build ethanol plants; the advanced technology providers developing various ways to convert non corn feedstocks into ethanol; equipment and service companies; and rural states and communities looking for a lifeline. Very few ethanol producers had the vision to see that increasing demand based on value would translate to higher returns and greater profits. Our first chairman at the CFDC was Roger Burken of Chief Ethanol who had such foresight but was criticized by his fellow producers for not staying low profile and being content with a small share of the market. Some of that was because of the fact that the ethanol tax exemption was a minor blip on the federal budget in terms of cost. However, many large producers were concerned that as ethanol volumes increased, it could make that tax exemption a target for potential repealing. It was not in their interest to create more demand.

But it was for so many others. One of the tireless advocates we worked closely with was Bob Harris, the head of the Nebraska Energy Office for then-Governor Ben Nelson.

Bob would later do a tour of duty in Washington at the Department of Energy. With Nelson, Bob was point man for the Governors' Ethanol Coalition, which he and Nelson formed to bring together all the states with interest in ethanol. This was a formidable group, and working with us and others, they came up with several programs that would have increased ethanol demand significantly.

In our interview with Bob Harris, he expressed frustration with the Renewable Fuels Association (RFA), which, after Hallberg left, had become dominated by Archer Daniels Midland (ADM), the largest ethanol producer in the country. RFA was the trade association for the ethanol industry and showed little interest in some of the innovative policy proposals by the governors. Harris and his Deputy Larry Pearce led the charge for a renewable oxygen standard in 1992 that would have ensured a guaranteed market for domestic ethanol. In 1995, they designed a Fuels for the Heartland program that would have established a uniform fuel standard with ethanol for fifteen Midwestern states. In 1997, that effort continued with a spinoff Fuels for America program that also would have created a single national fuel standard to include ethanol.

As Harris recounts, and we were working directly with them and can attest, we got little help from the "industry." Despite bringing this to the attention at the highest levels of the White House, we were unable to bring ethanol to the finish line. He and I went door-to-door in the Executive Office Building and throughout the US Senate and House of Representatives, but they were not hearing it from "the industry."

Nearly forty years after the Clean Air Act Amendments opened the door for oxygenates like ethanol and required EPA to reduce toxics that ethanol could replace, the producers remain missing in action. With more than two hundred ethanol producers and two major trade associations with combined budgets of more than $30 million, they never, ever, call for the enforcement of the toxics provision. Senator Daschle continues to argue if that provision was enforced, the industry really wouldn't need to do anything else.

The ethanol producers, at least their position as put forward through their associations, have not seized that opportunity and prefer to tie themselves to the fifteen billion gallon "guaranteed" demand of the RFS. That demand is far from guaranteed as the RFS evolves. As Boyden Gray says, ethanol saves lives. What other industry would not make that their primary calling card?

This conundrum holds true today. It was first brought to light in an article, "Farmers over an Ethanol Barrel: We Aren't Going to Walk the Plank." Written by Doug Sombke of the Farmers Union Enterprises, it was published by The Auto Channel. Publishing the article created a buzz in the ethanol industry and some backlash for publisher Marc Rauch.

Sombke states in his article,

> "It's rare when an industry will voluntarily give up market share, lower prices in times of crisis, self-regulate, welcome new competition, or anything else that is not self-serving. While they do so in the name of their shareholders, it is always at the expense of its customers. Oil

companies did not volunteer to get rid of lead. It took regulators a hundred years to gradually phase it down. The first seatbelt was patented in 1885 and not required in cars until 1966. McDonalds and other fast-food manufacturers held on to trans fats as long as legally possible. Science and people change status quo, not industry. The US fuel ethanol industry is no different (Sombke 2019). "

We provided a QR code below, or you can use the URL in the appendix to access the complete article (Sombke 2022).

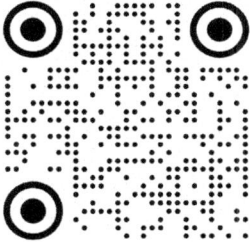

"Farmers over an Ethanol Barrel: We Aren't Going to Walk the Plank," Doug Sombke, National Farmers Union, *The Auto Channel*

TAKEAWAYS

- The list of key leaders, media influencers, and NGOs missing in action includes the many US presidents who have traveled to OPEC countries to also negotiate over a barrel of oil. Doug Sombke's message to the ethanol industry was also directed to the White House in his editorial "SDFU to President [Biden]: If You Want to

Increase Fuel Supplies Come See What We Are Doing Here" (Sombke 2022). Sombke states,

- "Today, ethanol displaces more than 400 million barrels of oil each year thanks to nationwide use of E10. Increasing blend levels to 30 percent, as is successfully being done in South Dakota, could replace more oil than we currently import from Saudi Arabia and Russia combined, providing more than $100 billion in savings to US consumers. The pathway to capture these benefits is simple: President Biden could direct his EPA Administrator to establish a nationwide E30 "clean octane" standard, which EPA has the statutory authority to do under the Clean Air Act. Ethanol's high octane will replace the toxic carcinogens currently used to increase octane and reduce the carbon emissions from today's gasoline [in every automobile]. It is a health, economic, and GHG and climate initiative rolled into one" (Sombke 2022).

WHAT'S NEXT
- Will the nation go to bat for more biofuels, or will its bat of opportunity be left on the shoulder once again to take another *called third strike*? Let's review some perspectives provided in chapter 1.

    1. "Corporations have neither bodies to be punished, nor souls to be condemned; they therefore do as they like" —Edward, Lord Thurlow 1731–1806, English jurist (Oxford 2016).
    2. Willful ignorance (uncountable) (idiomatic, law). Noun: A bad faith decision to avoid becoming

informed about something so as to avoid having to make undesirable decisions that such information might prompt. It may also be shown as for a person to have no clue in a decision but still goes ahead in their decision. Synonyms: (bad faith decision to remain ignorant): vincible ignorance (Lawyerment 2022).

3. *Merriam-Webster* defines gaslighting as psychological manipulation of a person usually over an extended period of time that causes the victim to question the validity of their own thoughts, perception of reality, or memories and typically leads to confusion, loss of confidence and self-esteem, uncertainty of one's emotional or mental stability, and a dependency on the perpetrator.

- Will consumers finally be given the chance to choose a higher blend of less expensive, cleaner, and safer biofuels? What fuel future will the nation leave to the next generation? Will the next generation inherit our wisdom or continued mistakes?

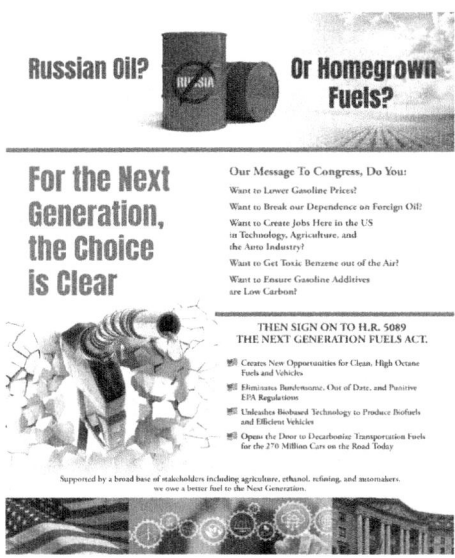

The Clean Fuels Development Coalition (CFDC) is part of a growing coalition that is finding common ground once again to asking Congress to use increased biofuels to enhance the nation's economic, environmental, energy, public health, and national securities (Durante, 2022).

CHAPTER 16

Back to the Fuel Future

Now You Know What We Know

BY BURL HAIGWOOD

If elected to a local, state, or federal legislative energy or environmental committee, how would you vote on issues related to ethanol and biofuels? Is cleaning up gasoline with more renewable fuels an unachievable radical request in pursuing perfection driven by single-interest thinking with complete disregard for practicality? Will my decision have an immediate or long-term positive impact on my family, country, or myself? Would you be a naysayer or a hell-yeah-sayer? What would your verdict be if called to be a juror in an environmental justice wrongdoing lawsuit?

Doug and I presented you with a lot of information about a shady past and a gloomy present. Now it is time for a glimpse into what can be a very bright fuel future if a successful legislative, regulatory, or legal resolution can stop the status quo in Congress and at your local gasoline station.

Do you recall how the movie *Back to the Future* ended? (Wachowski 1985).

Doc screeches into the driveway in his DeLorean time machine. He is frantic with a sense of urgency; he goes through the trash can pleading with Marty to go back to the future with him. Doc collects banana peels and an open Miller High Life beer.

Doc places the food remnants and beer into the Mr. Fusion Home Energy Reactor biomass fuel converter on the top of his DeLorean.

Marty says, "What are you talking about? What will happen to us in the future? Do we become a-holes or something?"

"No, no, no, no," Doc says. "Both you and Jennifer turn out fine. It's your kids, Marty. Something has gotta been done about your kids."

Because I had been living in my homegrown film version of *Gasolinegate* since 1977, this scene put a chill of excitement down my spine. Biomass and alcohol fuels finally hit the big screen! Doc must be talking about the impact of gasoline on the environment, economy, national security, and future of Marty's children. Were they going down new roads not littered with no alcohol in my gasoline signs, legislative potholes, or paved with detractors of cheaper—less expensive—better, safer biofuels?

To which a**holes was Marty referring? Were they the same ones I was fighting? Were the film's writers referencing Henry Ford's vision for fuel ethanol and the first Model T that could run on any combination of gasoline and ethanol? I could not wait for *Back to the Future Part 2* and *Part 3*. Just like on December 21, 2021, when our efforts to change the CAFE standards were ignored, I was sadly disappointed again. Don't worry. There is still hope.

You do not need a time machine to go into the "fuel future" to find out. Here are three comparisons on earth, at this exact time in history, which represent what I hope is our cheaper, safer fuel future. I think you will agree there appear to be three parallel realities as if we are characters in *The Matrix* (Wachowski 1999). Except it's a Fuel Matrix. So, let's jump in an PHEV FFV and go on tour.

FIRST STOP, BRAZIL

The best proof of our bright fuel future is Brazil's present. Same world, same time and reality, and inhabited by people just like us. People living in a country politically and publicly united on using ethanol for over four decades. Brazil and the United States started alternative fuel programs about the same time. Except Brazil's public-private-government partnership worked together and pounced on the opportunity to solve a crisis impacting everyone in their country. They built a transportation fuel system based on the need for economic development and job creation that also became a public health program. They knew investing in ethanol would fuel their economy and proved it.

I do need to travel back in time to make a point. In 1995, I had a chance of a lifetime to visit Brazil with Senator Ben Nelson from Nebraska when he was chair of the Governors' Ethanol Coalition (Knight-Rider Financial 1995).

I finally had the chance to meet Plinio Nastari, one of Brazil's ethanol revolution pioneers. Mr. Nastari began his speech by saying they did not pursue ethanol development to replace oil. I was puzzled. I must have messed up the translation button. Plinio went on to say,

> "Our primary concern and objective for our ethanol policy were to keep the rural economy strong by creating jobs and processing sugar cane into more valuable products to sustain the farmland. This program would reduce the migration of people to their already overpopulated cities that were also straining to maintain their infrastructure. As a bonus, every Brazilian would get cleaner air due to their commitment to use domestically produced renewable ethanol as a supplement to petroleum, not as a complete replacement."

Unlike my experience at home, Brazil armed its citizens with information. They let Brazilians know by using higher ethanol blends they would make their air cleaner and their economy more robust. I toured sugar cane mills and manufacturing plants making cars that could run on any combination of ethanol or gasoline. I even filled up a car with 50 percent ethanol at an Exxon station. Holy Mojito!

Brazilians live in a parallel reality to the United States, where every car can run on *at least* 27 percent ethanol and up to

100 percent if and when the driver chooses. Higher blends of ethanol were available at every fuel dispenser in Brazil. They were selling fuel the US EPA classifies as illegal. Brazilian refiners distributed ethanol through a countrywide pipeline, a feat the US oil industry said could not work. I witnessed thousands of Brazilians driving flexible-fuel vehicles and US automakers who stopped making FFVs because they lost a tax incentive for a component that cost about fifty dollars.

That short-sighted un-investment by Congress is becoming costly compared to other technology-forcing measures EPA requires of automakers. Not making FFV a standard safety feature also fuels EPAs rhetoric they cannot implement a new low-carbon, higher-octane standard because there are too many "legacy," or older model, vehicles. A legacy that will continue to place the economic burden on automakers to force new, higher priced emission reduction technologies on consumers. Technologies forced automakers to clean up the oil industry's dirty gasoline. Brazil is a firsthand lesson in relying on practicality instead of self-inflicted regulatory legality.

Brazilians live in a parallel reality where their ethanol consumption reduces the cost of their gasoline, health care, taxes, *and* mobile source air toxic pollution to the greatest extent possible. They do not even have a law that demands it, like Section 202 (l) in the CAAA. Brazilians are doing something that will help save themselves and their rainforest.

In our recent exchanges with Plinio, he told us, "The appeal of committing to increasing ethanol production was holistic. This public policy-driven strategy solved many problems policy makers faced because of pressure from their constituents. At the same time, this approach appealed to most of their constituents because it supported the rural and urban sectors and created a common ground for socially minded and corporate-minded politicians to agree."

Plinio said, "At some point, even based on the amount of research available in the 1970s, the debate over whether the country should proceed reached a point of ridiculousness, liability, or negligence if we did not take advantage of this window of opportunity. God blessed Brazil with the vast resources to be manufactured into value-added products to support all citizens."

It still confounds and angers me how so many people can protect fossil fuels based on economic stability and free market arguments yet not see those same principles apply to biofuels. Plinio did suggest they had a general, not a president or Congress, which made it easier to negotiate and make progress.

SECOND STOP, THE BRAVE NEW WORLD OF NEW TECHNOLOGY AND POSSIBILITY

You can use your computer or iPhone as a fuel matrix portal to take a virtual tour of the bright *Brave New World of New Technologies and Possibilities* at www.BiofuelsDigest.com. That is what I did on June 16–17, 2022, while conducting research for *Gasolinegate*. I read articles in *The Digest* about biobased projects and new products produced in Belgium, Kuwait, Sweden, Romania, Switzerland, and the United States. My virtual tour left me amazed and hopeful. I think you will agree Jim Lane, editor and publisher of *The Digest*, corralled the art-of-the-possible and presents what happens when the potential of the great minds of democracy and capitalism is unleashed (The Digest 2022).

While on *The Digest* website I reviewed the list of more than three hundred companies and organizations that attended 2022 Biofuel Digest's Advanced Bioeconomy Leadership Conference, I did not find EPA on the attendee list.

These individuals within organizations are pursuing the entrepreneurial dream to build the next cheaper, better, faster, and safer product. Suppose you read *The Digest* articles or attended one of their conferences. In that case, I hope you also felt a genuine sense of excitement, enthusiasm, and passion for technology and being in the room where the future happens.

LAST STOP, BACK TO REALITY DC
Compared to the advancement of so many other products, the United States has been living in a fuel matrix based on a history of disinformation and singular product dominance for over 160 years.

The birth of biofuels in the 1920s created the next generation of biofuels fuels of the 1980s. The biofuels of the 2000s will build the bridge to more efficient production, new feedstocks, new biobased products, and more innovation.

Congress and consumers should empower America's farmers to protect and value-add the resources that create jobs to sustain their families and protect our food supplies. If environmental organizations are afraid of developing new lands, help preserve the family farm. Do not force farmers to sell out to an urban developer based on the perception that cheap oil is somehow less harmful.

The emerging and thriving biotech companies on *Biofuel Digest's Advanced Bioeconomy Leadership Conference* attendee list are proof capitalism is working. New decentralized biorefineries deliver food, fiber, and safer chemicals in a diversified economy, offering consumers new choices so they won't be held hostage over a barrel on a rickety, leaking oil barge relying on an archaic navigation system directly into the Sea of Dumb-butts.

There are many routes but only one truth and moral compass to guide us. The holistic benefits of a biofuel future should unite the majority in Congress and the White House, federal agencies, environmental and public health advocates, the hawks and the doves, physicians, and a new league of environmental justice fighters.

This powerful coalition can bring safer gasoline to market for every car with infrastructure already delivering fuel to every gas station in the United States at virtually no extra cost. Who is not for that?

The United States' reliance on crude oil connects almost every news story. Most products are transported to the market or are in other ways connected to the world price of crude oil. Therefore, I believe most would agree—and are learning the hard way—the price of crude oil impacts everything in our lives daily. The biofuel revolution is like the American Revolutionary War. A revolution sparked by people angry about double taxation without proper representation.

- Consumers are taxed on their gasoline at the federal and state level to pay for roads,

- They pay more taxes to provide health care to those sickened from air pollution,

- They pay more taxes for our military to protect the world's oil supply in the Middle East and now from Russia.

- They pay more taxes because of the lost economic opportunity from not being able to choose the better option.

When considering,

- Before Russia invaded Ukraine, gasoline was two dollars and fifty-eight cents per gallon and surpassed five dollars per gallon in just six months.

- In 2021, the US imported *8 percent of its petroleum products from Russia. OPEC's share of US total petroleum imports was about 11 percent*, and its share of US crude oil imports was 13 percent. *Saudi Arabia, the largest OPEC petroleum exporter to the United States*, was the source of 5 percent of US total petroleum imports and 6 percent of US crude oil imports. Saudi Arabia is also the largest source of US petroleum imports from Persian Gulf countries (Energy Information Administration 2022).

- OPEC and Saudi Arabia defied pleas from President Biden to increase supplies to help with the world's economic downturn.

Why would anyone choose to buy products controlled by so few that negatively impact the lives of so many?

Would you buy your coffee drinks from a store owned by OPEC or a Russian autocrat? Or would you go to Starbucks?

Maybe it is time for another metaphorical Boston Tea Party.

LAST STOP, THE INTERSECTION OF TODAY AND OUR FUEL FUTURE
People often say I have too much faith in the public because they don't care. My response has always been, "they just don't know what we know—yet." I am confident that at this point in your cleaner gasoline research journey, you will comprehend the 2022 White Paper *The Real Cost of Gasoline… Is to Our Health: Time for a Cleaner, More Efficient Fuel* (Detchon and Modlin 2022).

I think it is essential to understand the background and connections of the two authors.

Reid Detchon is the senior advisor for Climate Solutions and former vice president for Energy and Climate Strategy at the United Nations Foundation. He was also the former executive director of the Energy Future Coalition and principal deputy assistant secretary for Conservation and Renewable Energy at the US Department of Energy.

Reg Modlin is a veteran of over forty years in regulatory affairs and environmental planning for the automotive industry. He was the former director of regulatory affairs for Chrysler Corporation. In that role, Modlin was responsible for all aspects of environmental compliance and policy development, trade, vehicle emissions, safety, and fuel economy standards.

Most would likely consider these two at odds and bump heads in the halls of Congress on these issues. However, they are both members of the Clean Fuels Development Coalition Advisory Committee, and they would assure you it is not for the money. They also agree that cleaning up gasoline and addressing the issues you have learned about should be a priority of the EPA, and the goal for improvement is achievable *today*.

Their white paper will take about ten minutes to read. You can read it in its entirety with the QR code provided below.

Here are some highlights with emphasis noted in italics:

- "*The problem is getting worse, not better.* Thanks to technological advances, our cars are cleaner now than they used to be—except in one area, where the problem is not the engine but the fuel it burns and the particulate matter it produces. Fine-particle pollution is one of the deadliest forms of air pollution, and where recent trends have us moving backward, not forward.

- "Almost all of the fine particles from cars and light trucks—*nearly 96 percent—come from a blend of toxic chemicals called aromatic hydrocarbons*, used by oil refiners to increase gasoline octane and enhance engine efficiency and vehicle performance. They amount to 20 percent of every gallon of gasoline and have a disproportionate effect on public health—not just our hearts and lungs, but also on child development.

- "Ultrafine particles combine in the air to form dangerous pollutants (known collectively as secondary organic aerosols) that can last longer and travel farther than previously thought by EPA—*an effect not captured in EPA air quality models*. These secondary aerosols are a much bigger health threat compared to the primary emissions. According to EPA's 2011 National Air Toxics Assessment, *secondary formation is the largest single contributor to cancer risks in the US, accounting for 47 percent of the total risk nationwide.*

- "Among the worst ultrafine particles are carcinogenic PAHs (polycyclic aromatic hydrocarbons), whose harm to young children includes reduced IQ—just like the tetraethyl lead that was added to gasoline for octane until it was phased out decades ago. *Aromatics are the only source of PAHs from cars and light trucks.* Fetal exposure to extremely low levels of PAHs—levels found in high-traffic urban areas—has been associated with developmental delay at age three years and reduced IQ at age five years.

- "This combination of benefits—the lower carbon impact of ethanol, plus the increased efficiency of cars that use it—means that widespread use of E30 would reduce

greenhouse gas emissions by just as much as EPA's recent rulemaking. In other words, *EPA has missed an opportunity to double its reductions of greenhouse gases* by not including improved fuels in the new regulations.
- "Blending more ethanol into gasoline will improve public health, combat climate change, reduce gas prices, and increase our energy security at no extra cost. And new legislation is not required—EPA has all the authority it needs to advance these climate, public health, and environmental justice goals. *It's time for EPA to seize the moment and act*" (Detchon and Modlin 2022).

The Real Cost of Gasoline... Is to Our Health: Time for a Cleaner, More Efficient Fuel (Detchon and Modlin 2022).

THE WORLD AND ETHANOL ARE NO LONGER FLAT

I feel privileged to live in a braver new world where sailors navigate around the globe because the world is no longer flat. I've witnessed people walking away from car accidents that would have killed them years ago and devastated families. I've seen people coming home from the hospital cured of diseases that would have killed them less than a decade ago.

I've driven my cars safely down the road on cleaner, safer, renewable biofuels over one hundred thousand miles over four decades. It still saddens me to drive through rusted rural economies held hostage over a barrel of oil, only to be tossed overboard because humans are not on the top of the most endangered species list.

Each of us can play a role in creating this new fuel future. Together, we can stand firm on common ground to accept the truth based on science—not politics or paychecks. A common ground for Americans to fight for their life, liberty, and the pursuit of happiness.

Democracy and truth have endured many tests and prevailed through more challenging times. We have presented you with the next opportunity that will empower us to continue to evolve as a country, as individuals, and as one humanity. All are connected by the single bond that things can and will get better if progress is not obstructed and laws are not circumvented.

We need to see beyond our current day struggles, knowing there is a brighter future if, individually and collectively, we take action now. The United States of America has a proven track record of fighting to right wrongs, but only when united by science and truth. I hope every time you put your hand on that gasoline pump to fill up your car, you now see the holistic "magical connection" of these issues you are concerned about every day.

Whether you are a Republican, Democrat, Independent, Libertarian, or Socialist, cheaper, cleaner, safer gasoline today should provide a path to something you value and want in the future. You are empowered to take action to protect yourself and your family. If you choose to do nothing, you support status quo, and what biofuels detractors count on, which is that you are too confused and consumed in the fear they created to cause inaction and fuel the disinformation gaslight. "Doing the same thing and expecting different results" is the, albeit slang, definition of insanity. Choosing to use status quo aromatics/BTEX over biofuels supports the diagnosis.

For decades, the public has been waiting on their government to decide if the chicken (legislation) or egg (consumer demand) should come first. Be the rooster. Buy and support biofuels. Lord knows we have enough political chickens and rotten eggs for one lifetime.

Like browsing Netflix, we have connected our issue to familiar messages in *The Cigarette Papers*, *The Poison Squad*, *The Ethanol Papers*, *The Matrix*, *Back to the Future*, and videos of *Jack the Fuel Test Dummy*. You have heard pleas from environmental, public health, and legal experts. Armed with *Gasolinegate* and the path to more research, you can make a more informed decision.

Here are a dozen actions you can take today to flex your consumer power and be the change you want to see in the world.

1. Don't get duped by taking the disinformation bait of false hope that promises to deliver a blank silver bullet solution at some undefined time in the future.

2. When you read an article or listen to an interview that is obviously presenting misinformation—by the sin of omission or commission—help them by commenting and leaving a #Gasolinegate to guide them to the truth, and they become accountable.

3. When your state or federal elective officials actively get in the way of cleaner, safer gasoline progress through action or inaction, send them a #Gasolinegate note or a *Gasolinegate* eBook.

4. If you are presented with a choice to buy E0, don't be duped. Don't be afraid to join the millions of people using higher blends of renewable biofuels worldwide.

5. If you have the luxury of buying your milk, bread, and coffee, while refueling your car, please let the person at the counter know you prefer cleaner gasoline. Contact the company via their website or their Twitter account and ask them to install at least one pump with higher blends of cleaner gasoline with less benzene.

6. Patronize and invest in companies listed in the *Biofuels Digest*. By their actions, companies like Valero prove they invested in ethanol, biofuels, and bio-based products they brought to market.

7. Contemplate selling a few shares of your fossil fuel stocks. Diversify your portfolio and hedge your bet and funds with companies building your bright fuel future. Let us all hope your investment will be the next Google or

Amazon stock your children inherit as evidence you did not get duped.

8. Join an activist group that supports environmental protection, economic stimulation, advocates for public health, or supports our veterans who have fought many of the nation's wars over protecting crude oil supplies. Encourage the organization to be part of a growing coalition that is demanding immediate actions that will result in a brighter fuel future. Engage in their discussions and podcasts so you can share your knowledge.

9. If you can afford an EV, please buy one. You will reduce the cost of safer gasoline for the ones that cannot afford an EV. If you cannot afford an EV, consider a hybrid plug-in that empowers you to use electricity *and* higher ethanol blends. This powerful combination of technologies enables you to get more miles per gallon of gasoline.

10. If you are buying a used car, consider a flexible fuel vehicle (FFV). There are twenty-one million to choose from. FFVs are today's version of Doc's bio-fueled DeLorean. This technology will empower you to blend the amount of ethanol that matches your courage and conviction not to support the oil industry's disinformation campaign to protect aromatics/BTEX and our nation's reliance on crude oil. There are 4,185 E85 stations in the United States. You can find one using the US Department of Energy's Alternative Fuel Data Center, which I helped start up, website at afdc.Energy.gov/fuels/ethanol_locations.html#/find/nearest?fuel=E85.

11. If you belong to a faith group, please ask them to support our coalition by holding local, state, and federal elected officials accountable for speaking the truth about ethanol, renewable energy, and dirty gasoline.

12. Please stay informed by staying in touch.

    - Now that you have read *Gasolinegate*, if you have a better idea of how to solve the problems we have presented or have feedback and suggestions, please let us know at gasolinegate@gmail.com.
    - Follow me on Twitter @burl_haigwood. Please consider using #Gasolinegate in your social media to support our mission when appropriate.
    - Support our safe gasoline education and awareness campaign by joining our *Gasolinegate* Facebook page at www.Facebook.com/profile.php?id=100084183754428.
    - Stay up to date on research, issues, and interviews with subject matter experts on our *Gasolinegate* website at www.gasolinegate.com

Because you read *Gasolinegate*, you've already done something to help. Pay your knowledge forward by giving your copy of *Gasolinegate* to a friend or family member and having a conversation afterward.

Now, every time you buy gasoline, you can choose if you will be a duped naysayer or be a hell-yeah-sayer to renewable fuels. I hope you are now emboldened with the knowledge of choice – Burl's Bolden Rule of Consumerism – be bold enough to do unto those companies that have done unto you.

You can choose your storyline. How will your Back to the Fuel Future chapter end?

Are you, by inaction, protecting the aromatics/BTEX in our gasoline that is killing us, or will you jump on the biofuels bandwagon?

Let's work together to *"Save the Humans."*

Thank you for reading *Gasolinegate*.

AFTERWORD
Why I Say Yes to Renewable Fuels

BY JIM LANE
I have long been an optimist on the future of renewable fuels in the US and around the world. For an equally long time, there have been the naysayers. Many of them come from outside of the industry, but not all.

Some were for corn ethanol until there was cellulosic ethanol, and they were for that until algae came along. They were for algae until there were renewable chemicals, and they were for that until there was fracked natural gas. Then they were for vegan foods, then cannabis. Many of those trend-surfers have moved along to crypto or EVs. Some have come back to fuels because of the evident success of renewable diesel and the burgeoning demand for sustainable aviation fuel.

AFFORDABLE OR UNAFFORDABLE
Some have been against corn ethanol in particular because they are naysayers. As former Navy Secretary Ray Mabus

told me on a number of occasions, "there are always naysayers, and they are always wrong. They said that shifting from sail to coal was crazy, that changing from coal to oil was dangerous, that nuclear would never work on something as small as a submarine, and that biofuels would never be affordable for the Navy."

The naysayers waved the "unaffordable" card in 2014 when the Navy bought a small amount of renewable fuel for demonstration purposes and paid twenty-five dollars a gallon. There was less talk about the costs when, in 2016, the Navy began purchasing biofuels at scale and the cost plummeted to two dollars and twelve cents a gallon. A lot of people today would like to have two dollars and twelve cents fuel, biofuels or not. The point is, the "affordability" debate has always been hooey. When carbon is properly accounted and paid for, and the fuels are purchased at scale, biofuels win every time. That's why there are more than fourteen billion gallons of announced renewable diesel and sustainable aviation fuels that are in development, under construction, or being commissioned around the world right now.

Think about that for a second. Fourteen billion new gallons, on top of some eleven billion gallons of existing capacity, and thirty billion gallons of ethanol capacity. Putting everything on an ethanol-equivalent basis to account for energy density, seventy billion gallons of ethanol-equivalent renewable fuels capacity is available or on the way. Forty-one billion of that in the USA, if we add, in renewable natural gas and CNG vehicles.

Some of these projects will come online later in the decade, and some might not be built. But you can see that Congress wasn't crazy when it established the Renewable Fuel Standard with a target of thirty-six billion gallons by 2022.

THE NAYSAYERS AND THE NAY THEY SAY

If you were to Google the topic of renewable fuels, you'd see articles like, "Next-Gen Biofuel Dreams Fade; Developers Blame EPA" in Agri-Pulse and "Cellulosic Ethanol Falling Far Short of the Hype" in *Forbes*, and you might be pardoned for thinking that the whole journey toward renewable fuels is a failure. It's certainly written that way by the naysayers.

As Secretary Mabus says, the naysayers are always wrong. In this case, why is the perception in such contrast with the reality?

For one, there's an epic fight for market share between fossil fuels and renewables, and obviously the other guys are going to try and send the industry to the devil. As Red Sox owner, John Henry opined in *Moneyball*,

> "What it's threatening is their livelihoods, it's threatening their jobs, it's threatening the way that they do things. And every time that happens, whether it's the government or a way of doing business or whatever it is, the people are holding the reins, have their hands on the switch, they go batshit crazy (Miller 2011)."

Second, a lot of people want biofuels to fail because they don't like large-scale production agriculture, preferring to think that America should become a network of smaller, possibly organic, farms. They think that adding fuels makes it harder to produce food. Not so. The Achilles heel of agriculture is not land competition but commodity market instability. Agriculture is risky. The sun won't shine, the rain won't fall, the market goes up and down like a yo-yo. Not much we can do about drought, but agricultural markets can be stabilized in two ways: one path is paved with bailouts for farmers, crop subsidies, cheap loans, payments for crops not planted, and so forth. The other path is to diversify the product portfolio—same as most families do with their IRAs—and that means getting beyond food and feed and breaking into fuels. Ethanol is a market that can absorb the kind of tonnage that farms produce.

It's a playbook that John D. Rockefeller understood. The petroleum industry began in the power sector, expanded to lubricants and solvents, then to fuels, then to polymer chemistry and the world of materials and packaging, even to food and pharma. Today, power companies are expanding into transportation—EVs—and they have begun expansion into chemicals and materials too, and one day, I reckon they'll chase vegan foods with waste CO_2 and water-split hydrogen. Agriculture and farmers use the same playbook everyone else does. It's catch-as-catch-can.

FOOD VERSUS FUELS

Because oil companies want a monopoly on gasoline engines and food marketers want farmers to be their serfs, the two sectors play the "food versus fuel" card whenever they can. Inadvertently serving their ends, even environmentalists argue that biofuels divert virgin land to industrial production, and that we can "save the rainforest and the orangutans" by banning palm oil.

Actually, zoning laws and lack of enforcement are responsible for the diversion of virgin land, in the Amazon and the American suburbs alike. Urban planners bemoaned the expansion of suburbs and the resulting traffic and smog and death of downtown districts until they simply found better ways to zone for mixed-use residential living in the downtown districts. Cities like Miami have enjoyed an urban revival and a big expansion in population during the pandemic did not result in people moving into the Everglades to find housing, grow food, or capture timber. The zoning laws worked. Good fences make good neighbors.

We are protected by more than zoning laws. We are protected by the "Law of Land Intensification," which is a term I just made up. It states that when demand surges, real estate supply changes vertically, not horizontally, to meet it. As I mentioned earlier, in Miami, developers do not respond to surges in demand by building single-family homes in the Everglades. They built high-rises. In the same way, when farm product prices rise, land prices rise. Farmers do not respond by buying more land. They plant more on the land they have.

If you look back and compare a hundred years ago to now, food prices are 3.5 times higher and production is up four times, but we are using less acres to do it. That can be good news for buyers because more yield means more supply, which can lead to lower prices. But this can only happen if the risks to agriculture are kept low enough that financing is cheap. The lack of alternative markets is the road to risk, risk is the road to high interest rates, and usurious interest is the road to high food prices. It's in everyone's interests to have diversified agricultural markets.

MORE OPPORTUNITIES IN THE COUNTRYSIDE

The importance of diversity, at the end of the day, is why I am optimistic about the future of renewable fuels and the bioeconomy. I see that sophisticated market options will bring new skills to the farm, and more rural-based, well-paying jobs in science, processing technology, risk finance, and distribution. An ossified product set leads to rural depopulation, meaning fewer skills are needed close to the farm.

Ossification also diverts money. Today, you might pay five dollars for a box of cornflakes and yet only fifteen cents or so is in the actual corn. After paying for the mortgage, farm equipment, and seed, maybe four cents is retained in the community. The rest is globalized and made opaque. No one really knows how the food is made, where fuel comes from, or what it takes to make an iPhone, and most of that is because manufacturing is separated from the people. When people stop caring about anything except price, injustice reigns. The bioeconomy can change that. New products bring investment and demand new skills to towns like Ames, Iowa, or Corvallis, Oregon. Plus, better-paying jobs right on the farm supports farmers.

PICKING WINNERS

I am optimistic about renewable fuels not because of this product or that product, this molecule or that. It's foolish to predict what demands the future might have. If we had to make decisions twenty years out about supply and demand based on what we knew from science at that instant, we never would have built smartphones, the internet, automobiles, streamed entertainment, organic foods, electric lights, or just about anything worth having. Great ideas may take a long time in the coming, but deployment is quick. Netflix grew like a weed. So did iPhones and web browsers. Nylon expanded rapidly after it was available at scale. As did cars, talking motion pictures, and television. We have to be flexible. Technology brings new options, and the future brings new needs.

Thankfully, we don't have to predict whether New Coke or Coke Classic is the product of the future. Companies take that risk, and sometimes, like Blockbuster, they choose unwisely and fail. All we have to do is decide that "entertainment will be needed" or "beverages will be needed" and let markets and companies work out the best way to supply that need. To accelerate progress, we might intervene to provide incentives or buy down the costs of risk financing. If we say "in the future, we'll need better diagnostics in health care," we are on the right track. If we say "in the future, we need Theranos," we are asking for trouble.

I don't know what the future of ethanol is. I know it has been around for a long time, it's easy to make, and there are a lot of applications. It seems safe to suggest that "we'll need more ethanol." Will it continue to be used in a blend with gasoline?

Will it become an intermediate used to make sustainable aviation fuel? Will it be used at 100 percent strength in E100 cars like we see in Brazil? Who knows? I sure don't. But we know how to make ethanol cheaply, it provides a low-carbon alternative to gasoline, and the world is transitioning to lower-carbon fuels—fast. So, if I had to bet, I'd bet on a big future for a little molecule: ethanol.

LOOK WHAT HAPPENED AFTER ETHANOL WAS BORN

Just think if we hadn't invested in ethanol in the 1990s and early 2000s and brought forward the first Renewable Fuel Standard in 2005 in the United States. Capital markets that dove into biobased technology in the later 2000s would not have had the catalyst. Would RNA technologies have been explored as fast and intensively as they were by well-backed venture firms who saw applications in agriculture as well as pharma? I doubt it. We might have had mRNA vaccines, but maybe not by 2021. Biobased health and beauty products, vegan foods, sustainable materials, renewable chemicals, and the advent of heavy-duty fuels. All of these owe a great debt to the excitement over ethanol as the first biobased molecule to be manufactured in billions of gallons per year. The fortunes made in ethanol investment in the 2000s made it easier to raise funds for industrial biotechnology as a whole in the years since.

Today, there are more than ten thousand biobased products certified by the US Department of Agriculture, a revolution has taken place in the past twenty years, and the impacts are just beginning to be felt. I read once that Amyris ingredients are used in products that have 250 million consumer buyers, yet only a handful on them would have heard of Amyris. I anticipate a similarly impactful future for ethanol.

More companies, more applications of technology, and more researchers are joining the field. This revolution began with perhaps one feedstock, one product, and one market. Now, there are five hundred different vegan food companies and thousands of biobased projects around the world. As an optimist, I believe this is only the beginning.

We're healthier, happier, and stronger as a society when we make the renewable choice. Because every country can produce renewables, no longer will the future belong only to those countries who win the fossil fuels lottery and discover vital raw materials below the earth's surface.

BECOMING ENERGY SECURE
Around the world, we speak of energy independence, but I have never believed that it brings safety or good times. The United States was energy independent in 1941, and that did not prevent World War II. Our energy independence in 2018–19 did not eliminate the problems of terrorism, ease the trade rivalry with China, or simmer down the Russian interest in aggression.

What we need is energy security. All of us, everywhere, need to have replete resources to meet our national aspirations with the resources we each have at hand. That's security, and the path to peace. Only renewables can take us along that path because only renewables are everywhere. Regrettably, the future will take time to create. Rome was not built in a day, but students of the hard data will see lots of good signs, including the expansion of solar, wind, biofuels, electrification of the fleet, and the pursuit of renewables and not just energy.

BEYOND FLEX-FUELS, FLEX-EVERYTHING

I hope as an optimist that we will heed Napoleon's maxim that the "cardinal sin of a commander in the field is to 'form a picture.'" That is, never make assumptions about how a battle will unfold. Flexibility wins and balance is the goal. This is a path to happiness.

Acknowledgments

AUTHOR COMMUNITY

We acknowledge and appreciate those in our author community who supported and inspired us with beta reading, feedback, and contributing to our community funding campaign, which helped bring our book to fruition.

Federal Legislative Superhero: Doug Sombke, President, South Dakota Farmers Union. A copy of *Gasolinegate* will be distributed to each U.S. Congressional Office and the White House.

State Legislative Superhero: Seth Harder, General Manager, Husker Ag. Copies of *Gasolinegate* will be distributed to key state legislators who are seeking ways to increase the use of low-carbon, cleaner-burning gasoline and renewable transportation fuels.

Berit Mansour
Buddy and Kathy DePhillip
Carmen Bettis
Chris and Sharon Miller

Claire Haigwood
Dave Vander Griend
Eric Koester
Francine Ryan

Glenda Crawford
Grecia Haigwood
Heidi Bumpers
Hilary Durante
Howard Marks
Jack McNulty
Jackie Stepan
Jan O'Neill
Jill Hamilton
Karen Snyder
Ken and Mary Swindell
Lisa Blake
Lisa Jacobson
Lucia Cuomo
Mark Bathrick
Mark and Bunny Matheny
Mark Early
Marty Bates
Matthew Haigwood

Michelle Potter
Mimi Devitt
Neal and Alicia Murphy
Nelda and John Cusic
Norma and Eric Leavitt
Patricia Haigwood
Pete and Sue Herdic
Ralph and Tish Wahlberg
Richard and Judy Cady
Rod and Gwen Haigwood
Roger Burken
Roger and Collet Mitchell
Shelly Hedrick
Terry A. Ruse
Tim and Sheri Lausin
Todd C. Sneller
Tony DePhillip
William and Missy Barkdoll

MISSION SUPPORT TEAM

We also recognize and appreciate those who worked closely with the Clean Fuels Development Coalition to bring you more renewable and alternative transportation fuels.

Aaron Whitesel, Former Senior Policy Advisor, US Senator Richard Lugar

Amory Lovins, Co-Founder and Chairman Emeritus, Rocky Mountain Institute

Arnie Klann, President, BlueFire Renewables, Inc.

Ben Henneke, President, Clean Air Action Corporation, Former Chairman, Clean Fuels Development Coalition

Bib Swain, Former President, Delta-T

Coleman Jones, Former Technical Fellow, Fuels / Biofuel Implementation Manager, General Motors

Dave Loos, Director of Biofuels Research, Illinois Corn Growers Association

Eve Fay-Glen, Office Administrator, Information Resources, Inc.

Gary Herwick, Former Director of Transportation Fuels, General Motors

Grecia Haigwood, Teacher, Former Office Administrator, Information Resources, Inc.

Greg Dierkers, Supervisor, US Department of Energy, Energy Technology Program Specialist, State Energy Program, and Former Clean Fuels Coordinator, Information Resources Inc.

Greg Krissek, Chief Executive Officer, Kansas Corn Growers Association

Howard Marks, President and CEO, K Street Alternative Energy Strategies, Former Policy Advisor, US Senator Charles Percy

Jan Hartke, Former Co-Chair, Environmental Inaugural Ball

Jeff Burnam, Former Legislative Assistant, US Senator Richard Lugar

Jill Hamilton, President, Sustainable Energy Strategies, Former Co-Director, Alternative Fuels Division, Information Resources, Inc.

Jim Woolsey, Former Director of Central Intelligence Agency, Co-Founder United States Energy Security Council, Founding Member, Set America Free Coalition, Former Board of Advisors, Clean Fuels Foundation

Jonathan W. Coppess, former Lead Policy Advisor, Senator Ben Nelson (NE)

Kevin Adler, Former Editor, *Octane Week*, Information Resources, Inc.

Larry Pearce, Director Nebraska Energy Office, Executive Director Governors Biofuel Coalition

Lee Butler (General, USAF Ret.), Former Chairman, Clean Fuels Foundation

Lee Reeve, President and CEO, Reeve Agri-Energy

Linda Bluestein, Former Editor, *Oxy-Fuel News* and Director of the National Alternative Fuels Hotline, Information Resources, Inc.

Maureen Lorenzetti, Former Editor, *Oxy-Fuel News*, *Alcohol Update*, Information Resources, Inc.

Ray Durante, former Clean Fuels Development Advisor

Roger Burken, former General Manager, Chief Ethanol

Sheri Lausin, Former Editor and Special Events Director, Information Resources, Inc. and Clean Fuels Foundation

The QR code below will take you to a collection of photos from Burl Haigwood and Doug Durante's personal photo collection. Photos include special events, conferences and many of the people listed in the Dedication, Special Thanks, and Acknowledgments sections.

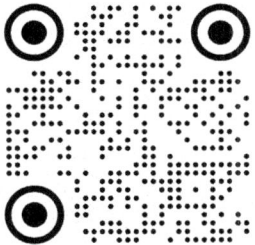

Appendix

FOREWORD

Farhi, Paul. 2022. "Semafor Hired a Climate Writer. Then Chevron Ran Ads on His Stories." *The Washington Post*. December 15, 2022. https://www.washingtonpost.com/media/2022/12/15/semafor-bill-spindle-chevron/.

CHAPTER 1

American Petroleum Institute. 1948. "API Toxicological Review." Hobson Law. Accessed September 22, 2022. http://web.archive.org/web/20030310145140/http://hobsonlaw.com/benzene_pages/pdffile.pdf.

Clean Fuels Development Coalition. 2019. "Ethanol Fact Book." Clean Fuels Development Coalition. Accessed December 28, 2022. http://cleanfuelsdc.org/wp-content/uploads/2018/05/CFDC-2010-Ethanol-Fact-Book.pdf.

Congressional Research Service. 2022. "The Renewable Fuel Standard (RFS): An Overview." Congressional Research

Service. Accessed October 4, 2022. https://crsreports.congress.gov/product/pdf/R/R43325.

C-SPAN. 1990. "Clean Air Act Signing Ceremony." C-SPAN. November 15, 1990. 15:27. https://www.c-span.org/video/?15006-1/clean-air-act-signing-ceremony.

Durante, Doug, and Burl Haigwood. 2019. "What's in Our Gasoline Is Killing Us: Mobile Source Air Toxics and the Threat to Public Health." Clean Fuels Development Coalition. Accessed September 11, 2022. https://cleanfuelsdc.org/wp-content/uploads/2019/05/MSAT-Fact-Book_042919.pdf.

Epstein, Samuel. 1989. "Health Requires That We Replace Gasoline." *Los Angeles Times*. March 17, 1989. Accessed December 28, 2022. https://www.latimes.com/archives/la-xpm-1989-03-17-me-1472-story.html.

Fann, Neal, A.D. Lamson, S.C. Anenberg, K. Wesson, D. Risley, and B. J. Hubbell. 2012. "Estimating the National Public Health Burden Associated with Exposure to Ambient $PM_{2.5}$ and ozone." *Risk Analysis* 32, no. 1 (May): 81–95. https://doi.org/10.1111/j.1539-6924.2011.01630.x.

Hallberg, David 2014. "Killing Them Softly: Oil Companies and the Public Health Threat of Gasoline Emissions in Urban Areas." Clean Fuels Development Coalition. Accessed December 28, 2022. https://cleanfuelsdc.org/wp-content/uploads/2018/05/CFDCHallbergWP.pdf.

Karavalakis, Georgios, Daniel Short, Diep Vu, et al. 2015. "Evaluating the Effects of Aromatics Content in Gasoline on

Gaseous and Particulate Matter Emissions from SI-PFI and SIDI Vehicles." *Environmental Science & Technology* 49, no. 11 (May): 7021–7031. https://doi.org/10.1021/es5061726.

Kitman, Jamie. 2016. "The War against Ethanol: A History of the Fuel, Part 2." *Motortrend.* September 26, 2016. https://www.motortrend.com/features/war-against-ethanol-part-ii-history/.

Kovarik, William. 1994. "The Ethyl Controversy: How the News Media Set the Agenda for a Public Health Controversy over Leaded Gasoline 1924–1926." PhD Dissertation. University of Maryland. https://billkovarik.com/wp-content/uploads/2016/12/Ethyl3.pdf.

Minnesota Biofuels Association. 2016. "Ethanol and Octane for Beginners." *Minnesota Biofuels Association* (blog). May 17, 2016. https://mnbiofuels.org/media-mba/blog/item/1511-octane-and-ethanol-for-beginners.

Morris, David, and Irshad Ahmed. 1992. "The Carbohydrate Economy: Making Chemicals and Industrial Materials from Plant Matter." Institute for Local Self Reliance. September 11, 2022. https://ilsr.org/wp-content/uploads/2013/12/the-carbohydrate-economy.pdf.

Morris, David. 1992. "Hydrocarbons versus Carbohydrates: The Continuing Battle in the United States." Feasta. Accessed September 11, 2022. http://www.feasta.org/documents/wells/contents.html?six/morris.html.

Ophardt, Charles. 2003. "Gasoline Compounds." Virtual Chembook. Assessed September 22, 2022. http://chemistry.elmhurst.edu/vchembook/515gasolinefs.html.

Rauch, Marc. 2017. "Uncovering and Unmasking the GAS ROOTS of Modern Ethanol Opposition – 3 Part Series." The Auto Channel. Accessed September 11, 2022. https://www.theautochannel.com/news/2022/05/21/1146076-uncovering-and-unmasking-gas-roots-ethanol-opposition-3-part-series.html.

Stolark, Jessie. 2016. "A Brief History of Octane in Gasoline: From Lead to Ethanol." Energy and Environmental Institute. Accessed September 11, 2022. https://www.eesi.org/papers/view/fact-sheet-a-brief-history-of-octane.

Tzu, Sun. 210. *The Art of War*. Mankato, Minnesota: Capstone Publishing.

US Center for Disease Control. 2022. "Toxicological Profile for Benzene." Agency for Toxic Substances and Disease Registry, Department of Health and Human Services. Accessed September 21, 2022. https://wwwn.cdc.gov/TSP/PHS/PHS.aspx?phsid=37&toxid=14.

US Department of Energy. 2021. "Gasoline Explained: History of Gasoline." US Energy Information Administration. Accessed September 22, 2022. https://www.eia.gov/energyexplained/gasoline/history-of-gasoline.php.

US Environmental Protection Agency. 2022. "Renewable Fuel Standard Program." US Environmental Protection Agency.

Accessed October 4, 2022. https://www.epa.gov/renewable-fuel-standard-program.

von Stackelberg K, J. Buonocore, P.V. Bhave, and J.A. Schwartz. 2013. "Public Health Impacts of Secondary Particulate Formation from Aromatic Hydrocarbons in Gasoline." *Environmental Health* 12, no. 19 (February). https://doi.org/10.1186/1476-069x-12-19.

CHAPTER 2

Clean Fuels Development Coalition. 2019. "Ethanol Fact Book." Clean Fuels Development Coalition. Accessed December 28, 2022. http://cleanfuelsdc.org/wp-content/uploads/2018/05/CFDC-2010-Ethanol-Fact-Book.pdf.

Clendaniel, Morgan. 2011. "The True Price of Gas: What It Should Really Cost to Fill Up." *Fast Company* (blog). June 23, 2011. https://www.fastcompany.com/1762661/true-price-gas-what-it-should-really-cost-fill.

Cobb, Loren. 2006. "Oil Addiction: The External Costs of Petroleum Use." *The Quaker Economist* 6, no. 142 (February). https://quaker.org/legacy/clq/2006/TQE142-EN-OilAddiction.html.

International Monetary Fund. 2015. "IMF Survey: Counting the Cost of Energy Subsidies." International Monetary Fund. Accessed September 23, 2022. https://www.imf.org/en/News/Articles/2015/09/28/04/53/sonew070215a.

Lockwood. Alan. 2012. "How the Clean Air Act Has Saved $22 Trillion in Health-Care Costs." *The Atlantic*, September 2012. https://www.theatlantic.com/health/archive/2012/09/how-the-clean-air-act-has-saved-22-trillion-in-health-care-costs/262071/.

National Defense Council Foundation. 2003. "The Hidden Cost of Imported Oil." National Defense Council Foundation. Accessed September 24, 2022. http://www.ndcf.org/energy/NDCF_Hidden_Costs_of_Imported_Oil.pdf.

National Renewable Energy Laboratory. 2008. "The Impact of Ethanol Blending on US Gasoline Prices." November 2008. National Renewable Energy Laboratory. Accessed September 27, 2022. https://www.nrel.gov/docs/fy09osti/44517.pdf.

Natural Resources Defense Council. 2011. "United Nations Declares Victory in Global Eradication of Leaded Gasoline." Natural Resources Defense Council. Accessed September 30, 2024. https://www.nrdc.org/media/2011/111027.

Taft, Nathan. 2017. "How Much Does a Gallon of Gas Actually Cost?" Fuel Freedom Foundation. Accessed September 22, 2022. https://www.fuelfreedom.org/gallon-gas-actual-cost/.

Tamminen, Terry. 2008. *Lives Per Gallon: The True Cost of Our Oil Addition*. Washington, DC: Island Press.

US Department of Justice. 2022. "Mobile Sources: Clean Air Act Mobile Source Cases." Environment and Natural Resources Division. Accessed September 24, 2022. https://www.justice.gov/enrd/mobile-sources.

US Department of Justice. 2016. "Volkswagen to Spend Up to $14.7 Billion to Settle Allegations of Cheating Emissions Tests and Deceiving Customers on 2.0 Liter Diesel Vehicles." Accessed September 30, 2022. https://www.justice.gov/opa/pr/volkswagen-spend-147-billion-settle-allegations-cheating-emissions-tests-and-deceiving.

US Department of State. 2022. "Oil Embargo, 1973–1974." US Department of State Office of the Historian. Accessed September 30, 2022. https://history.state.gov/milestones/1969-1976/oil-embargo.

US Environmental Protection Agency. 2011. "Benefits and Costs of the Clean Air Act 1990–2020, the Second Prospective Study." US Environmental Protection Agency. Accessed September 21, 2022. https://www.epa.gov/clean-air-act-overview/benefits-and-costs-clean-air-act-1990-2020-second-prospective-study.

US Environmental Protection Agency. 2011. "Report to Congress on the Benefits and Costs of Federal Regulations and Unfunded Mandates on State, Local, and Tribal Entities." US Environmental Protection Agency. Accessed September 24, 2022. https://www.epa.gov/transportation-air-pollution-and-climate-change/history-reducing-air-pollution-transportation.

US Environmental Protection Agency. 2022. "Fast Facts on Transportation Greenhouse Gas Emissions." US Environmental Protection Agency. Accessed September 24, 2022. https://www.epa.gov/greenvehicles/fast-facts-transportation-greenhouse-gas-emissions.

US Office of Management and Budget. 2007. "Report to Congress on the Benefits and Costs of Federal Regulations and Unfunded Mandates on State, Local, and Tribal Entities." White House. Accessed September 24, 2024. https://www.whitehouse.gov/wp-content/uploads/legacy_drupal_files/omb/assets/OMB/inforeg/2007_cb/2007_cb_final_report.pdf.

US Senate Committee on Finance. 2007. "Hearings on Grains, Cane and Automobiles: Tax Incentives for Alternative Fuels and Vehicles." US Senate Committee on Finance. Accessed on September 30, 2022. https://www.finance.senate.gov/imo/media/doc/041907testjw.pdf.

Useem, Jerry. 2003. "The Devil's Excrement." *Fortune Magazine*. February 2003. https://archive.fortune.com/magazines/fortune/fortune_archive/2003/02/03/336434/index.htm.

World Bank. 2016. "The Cost of Air Pollution: Strengthening the Economic Case for Action." The World Bank. Accessed September 24, 2022. https://www.worldbank.org/en/news/press-release/2016/09/08/air-pollution-deaths-cost-global-economy-225-billion.

World Health Organization. 2015. "Economic Cost of the Health Impact of Air Pollution in Europe." World Health Organization. Accessed September 24, 2022. https://www.euro.who.int/__data/assets/pdf_file/0004/276772/Economic-cost-health-impact-air-pollution-en.pdf.

CHAPTER 3

Clean Fuels Development Coalition. 2019. "You Don't Know Jack about What's in Your Gasoline." June 18, 2019. Video, 10:21. https://youtu.be/VK5RoVW6hhs.

Fueling American Jobs Coalition. 2022. "Nationwide, Bipartisan Support to Fix the RFS." Fueling American Jobs Coalition. Accessed December 28, 2022. https://www.fuelingusjobs.com/.

Gamberini, Sarah. 2020. "Social Media Weaponization: The Biohazard of Russian Disinformation Campaigns." *Joint Force Quarterly 99* (blog). November 19, 2020. https://ndupress.ndu.edu/Media/News/News-Article-View/Article/2420792/social-media-weaponization-the-biohazard-of-russian-disinformation-campaigns/.

Gelles, David. 2022. "The Texas Group Waging a National Crusade Against Climate Action" *The New York Times*. December 4, 2022. https://www.nytimes.com/2022/12/04/climate/texas-public-policy-foundation-climate-change.html.

Glantz, Stanton, John Slade, Lisa A. Bero, Peter Hanauer, and Deborah E. Barnes, editors. 1996. *The Cigarette Papers*. Berkeley, California: University of California Press.

Grassley, Chuck. 2008. "Grassley Urges Iowans to Push Back against DC-Hatched Smear Campaign against Ethanol." Senator Chuck Grassley. Accessed September 27, 2022. https://www.grassley.senate.gov/news/news-releases/grassley-urges-iowans-push-back-against-dc-hatched-smear-campaign-against-ethanol.

Lawyerment Legal Dictionary. 2022. Lawyerment. Accessed October 4, 2022. https://dictionary.lawyerment.com/topic/willful_ignorance/.

Madson, Philip W. 2012 "Generation 1.5 Ethanol: The Bridge to Cellulosic Biofuels." Clean Fuels Development Coalition. Accessed December 18, 2022. https://cleanfuelsdc.org/wp-content/uploads/2018/05/CFDCKatzenWP_0912_LR.pdf.

Merriam-Webster Dictionary. 2022. "Gaslighting." Merriam-Webster. Accessed December 28, 2022. https://www.merriam-webster.com/dictionary/gaslighting.

Morris, Susan, and Crystal Raypole. 2021. "How to Recognize Gaslighting and Get Help." *Healthline* (blog). November 24, 2021. https://www.healthline.com/health/mental-health/negging#takeaway.

Oxford Essential Quotations. 2016. "Oxford Reference." Oxford University Press. Accessed October 4, 2022. https://www.oxfordreference.com/view/10.1093/acref/9780191826719.001.0001/q-oro-ed4-00010943?msclkid=d7ce848aaedc11ec82ea4797ed5987d1.

Quote Investigator. 2015. "A Lie Can Travel Halfway around the World While the Truth Is Putting on Its Shoes." Quote Investigator. Accessed October 4, 2022. https://quoteinvestigator.com/2014/07/13/truth/.

Sakai, Jill. 2022. "At Bioenergy Crossroads, Should Corn Ethanol Be Left in the Rearview Mirror?" *University of Wisconsin-Madison* (blog). February 14, 2022. https://news.wisc.edu/

at-bioenergy-crossroads-should-corn-ethanol-be-left-in-the-rearview-mirror/.

Sobczyk, Nick. 2022. "Hearings Set to Attack Fossil Fuel Industry and Its Backers." *E&E Daily* (blog). *E&E News*. September 12, 2022 https://www.eenews.net/articles/hearings-set-to-attack-fossil-fuel-industry-and-its-backers/.

CHAPTER 4

Legal Information Institute. "15 US Code § 26a - Restrictions on the Purchase of Gasohol and Synthetic Motor Fuel." Cornell Law School. Accessed October 3, 2022. https://www.law.cornell.edu/uscode/text/15/26a.

Ruse, Terry. 2022. "A Journey of a Thousand Steps." Clean Fuels Development Coalition. Accessed October 10, 2022. https://qr1.be/PR4M.

Sneller, Todd. 2019. "Ethanol Development in Nebraska: 1969–2019." Clean Fuels Development Coalition. Accessed October 10, 2022. https://qr1.be/NVIX.

CHAPTER 5

The Auto Channel. 2018. "Bob Hope Texaco Ethanol TV Spot." The Auto Channel YouTube Channel. August 20, 2018. 0:0:29. https://www.youtube.com/watch?v=Szee4Cwo5ks.

Clean Fuels Development Coalition. 2019. "Ethanol Fact Book." Clean Fuels Development Coalition. Accessed December 28,

2022. http://cleanfuelsdc.org/wp-content/uploads/2018/05/CFDC-2010-Ethanol-Fact-Book.pdf.

Coleman, Clayton, and Emma Dietz. 2019. "Fact Sheet | Fossil Fuel Subsidies: A Closer Look at Tax Breaks and Societal Costs." Environmental Energy Study Institute. Accessed September 27, 2022. https://www.eesi.org/papers/view/fact-sheet-fossil-fuel-subsidies-a-closer-look-at-tax-breaks-and-societal-costs#1.

Congressional Research Service. 2012. "US Oil Imports and Exports." Congressional Research Service. Accessed December 28, 2022. https://crsreports.congress.gov/product/pdf/R/R42465.

Durante, Doug, and Burl Haigwood. 2019. "What's in Our Gasoline Is Killing Us: Mobile Source Air Toxics and the Threat to Public Health." Clean Fuels Development Coalition. Accessed September 11, 2022. https://cleanfuelsdc.org/wp-content/uploads/2019/05/MSAT-Fact-Book_042919.pdf.

Energy Information Administration. 2021. "International Energy Outlook." US Energy Information Administration. Accessed September 25, 2022. https://www.eia.gov/outlooks/ieo/.

Hanley, Steve. 2022. "Ethanol Burns Clean but Creates More Emissions than Gasoline." *CleanTecnica* (blog). September 13, 2022. https://cleantechnica.com/2022/09/13/ethanol-burns-clean-but-creates-more-emissions-than-gasoline/.

Harrje, Evan. 1998. "The Real Price of Gasoline." November 1998. Friends of the Earth. Accessed September 27, 2022. https://www.fdnearth.org/files/2013/11/The-Real-Price-of-Gas.pdf.

Madson, Philip W. 2012. "Generation 1.5 Ethanol: The Bridge to Cellulosic Biofuels." Clean Fuels Development Coalition. Accessed December 18, 2022. https://cleanfuelsdc.org/wp-content/uploads/2018/05/CFDCKatzenWP_0912_LR.pdf.

Nastari, Plinio. 1998. "Proceedings of the Second International Conference on Alternative Aviation Fuels, November 6–8, 1997." US Federal Aviation Administration. Accessed October 4, 2022. http://www.tc.faa.gov/its/worldpac/techrpt/ar98-73.pdf.

Rauch, Marc. 2022a. "Battling Anti-Ethanol Snake Oil Myths." *The Auto Channel* (blog). Accessed October 4, 2022. https://www.theautochannel.com/news/2022/03/24/1122493-battling-redundancy-and-excessive-cost-anti-ethanol-snake-oil.html.

Rauch, Marc. 2022b. "It's Time for Ethanol Honesty." *The Auto Channel* (blog). Accessed October 4, 2022. https://www.theautochannel.com/news/2022/04/25/1134232-it-s-time-for-ethanol-honesty.html.

Rauch, Marc. 2019. *The Ethanol Papers*. United States: Dialog Press. https://www.theautochannel.com/news/2018/10/12/632678-ethanol-papers-massive-book-provides-whole-story-ethanol-fuel-free.html

Reuters. 2022. "Special Report: ADVISORY-Story on US Ethanol Plant Emissions Is Withdrawn." Reuters. September 23, 2022.

https://www.reuters.com/business/sustainable-business/how-us-regulators-allow-ethanol-plants-pollute-more-than-oil-refineries-2022-09-08/.

Rosentrater, Kurt, Kenneth Kalscheuer, Kenneth Garcia, et al. 2008. "The South Dakota Fuel Ethanol Industry." Open Prairie South Dakota State University. Accessed October 14, 2022. http://openprairie.sdstate.edu/extension_fact/144.

Schroeder, Joanna. 2016. "Car Clinic's Bobby Likis Talks #Ethanol & Mechanics." *Agwired* (blog). November 21, 2016. https://energy.agwired.com/2016/11/21/car-clinics-bobby-likis-talks-ethanol-mechanics/.

Stromeyer, Roman. 2016. "Dr. Maxwell Shauck a–d Grazia Zanin - Transatlantic Ethanol Fuel Flight." YouTube. February 15, 2002. 9:28. Accessed October 4, 2022. https://www.youtube.com/watch?v=96XnJh98LqQ.

Taheripour, Farzad, S. Mueller, H. Kwon, et al. May 2022. "Response to Comments from Lark et al. Regarding Taheripour et al. March 2022 Comments." May 25, 2022. Argonne, Illinois: Argonne National Laboratory. Accessed September 27, 2022. file:///C:/Users/Owner/Downloads/Response%20to%20Lark%20et%20al_b%20May%202022.pdf.

Texaco. 2022. "Trust Your Car 1960–1980." Texaco. Accessed November 25, 2022. https://www.texaco.com/en_us/home/about-texaco.html.

Urbanchuk, John. 2022. "Contribution of the Ethanol Industry to the Economy of the United States." Renewable Fuels

Association. Accessed October 3, 2022. https://d35t1syewk4d42.cloudfront.net/file/2141/RFA%202021%20Economic%20Impact%20Report%20Final.pdf.

Urban Air Initiative. 2018. "New Studies Show Ethanol Reduces Emissions and Improves Air Quality." Urban Air Initiative. Accessed on October 4, 2024. https://fixourfuel.com/2018/04/11/new-studies-show-ethanol-reduces-emissions-and-improves-air-quality/.

US Department of Energy. 2022. "Co-Optimization of Fuels & Engines." US Department of Energy, Office of Energy Efficiency & Renewable Energy. Accessed November 11, 2022. https://www.energy.gov/eere/bioenergy/co-optimization-fuels-engines.

US Department of Energy. 2008. "US Department of Energy: Biofuels & Greenhouse Gas Emissions: Myths versus Facts." US Department of Energy. Accessed October 4, 2008. https://www.energy.gov/sites/default/files/edg/news/archives/documents/Myths_and_Facts.pdf.

White House. 2007. "President Bush Participates in Panel on Cellulosic Ethanol." White House. Accessed October 4, 2022. https://georgewbush-whitehouse.archives.gov/news/releases/2007/02/20070222-5.html.

CHAPTER 6

AgUnited for South Dakota. 2022. "Key Facts." *AgUnited for South Dakota* (blog). https://agunited.org/about-us/key-facts.

Berry, John. 1984. "Cost-Benefit Foes Surprised." *The Washington Post*. April 1, 1984. https://www.washingtonpost.com/archive/business/1984/04/01/cost-benefit-foes-surprised/ca65d1a9-aa94-461f-a882-10853c1f375a/.

Burroughs, Davis. 2015. "Growing Chorus of Complaints on Chemicals in Gasoline." *Morning Consult* (blog). April 22, 2015. https://morningconsult.com/2015/04/22/growing-chorus-of-complaints-on-chemicals-in-gasoline/.

Clean Fuels Development Coalition. 2015. "Improving Air Quality through Transportation Fuels." Clean Fuels Development Coalition. Accessed October 5, 2022. https://cleanfuelsdc.org/wp-content/uploads/2018/05/CFDC-Issue-Brief-0311.pdf.

Clean Fuels Development Coalition. 1995. "Oxygenates Fact Book." Clean Fuels Development Coalition. Accessed October 5, 2022. http://cleanfuelsdc.org/wp-content/uploads/2018/05/oxyfactbook.pdf.

Congressional Record. 1990. "Senate-Thursday, March 29, 1990." GovInfo. Accessed December 28, 2022. https://www.govinfo.gov/content/pkg/GPO-CRECB-1990-pt4/pdf/GPO-CRECB-1990-pt4-7-1.pdf.

Daniels, Lee. 1985. "Prices of Leaded Gasoline Rising as New E.P.A. Curbs Take Effect." *New York Times*. June 29, 1985. https://www.nytimes.com/1985/06/29/business/prices-of-leaded-gasoline-rising-as-new-epa-curbs-take-effect.html.

Federal Register. 2010. "Part II Environmental Protection Agency 40 CFR Part 80 Regulation of Fuels and Fuel Additives:

Changes to Renewable Fuel Standard Program; Final Rule." Washington, DC: Government Printing Office. https://www.govinfo.gov/content/pkg/FR-2010-03-26/pdf/2010-3851.pdf.

Hallberg, David. 2014. "Killing Them Softly: Oil Companies and the Public Health Threat of Gasoline Emissions in Urban Areas." Clean Fuels Development Coalition. Accessed October 5, 2022. https://www.cleanfuelsdc.org/wp-content/uploads/2018/05/CFDCHallbergWP.pdf.

National Service Center for Environmental Publications. 2005. "Toward a Cleaner Future Office of Transportation and Air Quality Progress Report 2005." Washington, DC: US Environmental Protection. https://permanent.fdlp.gov/lps71726/420r05011.pdf.

National Service Center for Environmental Publications. 1990. "The Clean Air Act Amendments of 1990." Washington. DC: US Environmental Protection Agency. https://bit.ly/3Grhz7u.

Neal, Jeff. 2019. "The Oath of Office and What It Means." *Federal News Network* (blog). October 24, 2019. https://federalnewsnetwork.com/commentary/2019/10/the-oath-of-office-and-what-it-means/.

US Code of Regulations. 2022. "Part 80 Regulations of Fuels and Additives." Washington, DC: US National Archives. https://www.ecfr.gov/current/title-40/chapter-I/subchapter-C/part-80.

US Department of Energy. 2022. "Co-Optimization of Fuels & Engines." Washington, DC: US Department of Energy, Office of Energy Efficiency & Renewable Energy. https://www.energy.gov/eere/bioenergy/co-optimization-fuels-engines.

US Energy Information Administration. 2022. "South Dakota State Energy Profile." Washington, DC: US Energy Information Administration. https://www.eia.gov/state/print.php?sid=SD#:~:text=In%202021%2C%20the%20state%20ranked,at%201.4%20billion%20gallons%20annually.

US Environmental Protection Agency. 2022a. "Federal Gasoline Regulations." Washington, DC: US Environmental Protection Agency. https://www.epa.gov/gasoline-standards/federal-gasoline-regulations.

US Environmental Protection Agency. 2022b. "Gasoline Mobile Source Air Toxics." Washington, DC: US Environmental Protection Agency. https://www.epa.gov/gasoline-standards/gasoline-mobile-source-air-toxics.

US Environmental Protection Agency. 2022c. "Our Mission and What We Do." Washington, DC: US Environmental Protection Agency. https://www.epa.gov/aboutepa/our-mission-and-what-we-do.

US Environmental Protection Agency. 2022d. "Reformulated Gasoline." Washington, DC: US Environmental Protection Agency. https://www.epa.gov/gasoline-standards/reformulated-gasoline.

US Environmental Protection Agency. 2022e. "State Winter Oxygenates Guidance and Background Documents." Washington, DC: US Environmental Protection Agency.

https://www.epa.gov/gasoline-standards/state-winter-oxygenates-guidance-and-background-documents.

US Environmental Protection Agency. 2022f. "Summary of the Clean Air Act." US Washington, DC: US Environmental Protection Agency. https://www.epa.gov/laws-regulations/summary-clean-air-act.

US Environmental Protection Agency. 2009. "Report to Congress on Public Health, Air Quality, and Water Resource Impacts of Fuel Additive Substitutes for MTBE." Washington, DC: US Environmental Protection Agency. https://nepis.epa.gov/Exe/ZyPDF.cgi/P100KJ10.PDF?Dockey=P100KJ10.PDF.

US Environmental Protection Agency. 1990. "The Clean Air Act – Highlights of the 1990 Amendments." Washington, DC: US Environmental Protection Agency. https://www.epa.gov/sites/default/files/2015-11/documents/the_clean_air_act_-_highlights_of_the_1990_amendments.pdf.

US Environmental Protection Agency. 1984. "Executive Summary: Cost and Benefits of Reducing Lead in Gasoline." Washington, DC: US Environmental Protection Agency. https://bit.ly/3Q3utvy.

CHAPTER 7

Anderson, J, T. Wallington, R. Stein, and W. Studzinski. 2014. "Issues with T50 and T90 as Match Criteria for Ethanol-Gasoline Blends," *SAE Int. J. Fuels Lubr.* 7, no. 3 (November): 1027-1040. https://doi.org/10.4271/2014-01-9080.

California Proposition 65. 2016. "Service Stations." California Proposition 65. Accessed December 12, 2022. https://www.p65warnings.ca.gov/places/service-stations.

Clean Fuels Development Coalition. 2018. "Clean Fuels Development Coalition et al, Comments on the Proposed Safer Affordable Fuel-Efficient (SAFE) Vehicles Rule for Model Years 2021-2026 Passenger Cars and Light Trucks." Accessed October 8, 2022. https://cleanfuelsdc.org/wp-content/uploads/2022/10/SAFE-Rule-EPA-Docket-Comments-CFDC-10-26-18.pdf.

Clean Fuels Development Coalition. 2017. "Request for Comment on Reconsideration of the Final Determination of the Midterm Evaluation of Greenhouse Gas Emissions Standards for Model Year 2022-2025 Light-duty Vehicles; Request for Comment on Model Year 2021 Greenhouse Gas Emissions Standards, Docket EPA-HQ-OAR-2015-0827." October 5, 2017. https://cleanfuelsdc.org/wp-content/uploads/2022/10/EPAS-CFDC-MTE-Comments-10052017.pdf.

Clean Fuels Development Coalition. 2012. "Comments of Clean Fuels Development Coalition Comments: HTSA-2010-0131 and EPA–HQ–OAR–2010– 0799, Proposed Rule, 2017 and Later Model Year Light Duty Vehicle Greenhouse Gas Emissions and Corporate Average Fuel Economy." Accessed October 23.2022 https://cleanfuelsdc.org/wp-content/uploads/2022/10/2012-CFDC-GHG-CAFE-Comments-EPA-HQ-OAR-2010-0799-9574.pdf.

Detchon, Reid. 2020. "Defining the Problem." Safe Gasoline Campaign YouTube Channel. February 6, 2020. 1:43. https://

www.youtube.com/watch?v=B-JFeiHHWWs&list=PLCCY-PGWoIert-wyppDamV_11A7ucZRhS&index=9 and.

Detchon, Reid. 2020. "The Smoking Gun." Safe Gasoline Campaign YouTube Channel. February 6, 2020. 0:2:25. https://www.youtube.com/watch?v=TJ3f9djZExY&list=PLCCY-PGWoIert-wyppDamV_11A7ucZRhS&index=1.

Energy Futures Coalition, Urban Air Initiative, and the Governors' Biofuel Coalition. 2016. "Request for Correction of Information, Lifecycle Analysis of Ethanol and Gasoline under the Renewable Fuel Standard." Clean Fuels Development Coalition. Accessed October 5, 2022. https://cleanfuelsdc.org/wp-content/uploads/2022/10/EPAS-EFC-Comments-on-the-EPAs-Tier-3-Rule.pdf.

Environmental and Energy Study Institute. 2020. "National Clean Fuels Technology & Health Effects Leadership Forum." Environmental and Energy Study Institute. Accessed October 23, 2022. https://www.eesi.org/files/020620slides.pdf.

Google Patents. 2022. "High Efficiency Alcohol Fuel Engine" Google Patents Search. Accessed October 23. 2022. https://patents.google.com/patent/US20080230041A1/en.

Govinfo.gov. 2020. "Final Rule: The Safer Affordable Fuel-Efficient (SAFE) Vehicles Rule for Model Years 2021–2026 Passenger Cars and Light Trucks." Govinfo.gov. Accessed October 23, 2022. https://www.govinfo.gov/content/pkg/FR-2020-04-30/pdf/2020-06967.pdf.

Lambert, Fred. 2022. "Donald Trump Goes on Nonsensical Rant about Electric Cars: 'We Need to Get Rid of Them.'" *Electrek* (blog). September 5, 2022. https://electrek.co/2022/09/05/donald-trump-nonsensical-rant-electric-cars/.

Leach, F., E. Chapman, J. Jetter, L. Rubino, et al., "A Review and Perspective on Particulate Matter Indices Linking Fuel Composition to Particulate Emissions from Gasoline Engines." *SAE Int. J. Fuels Lubr.* 15, no. 1 (October). https://www.nrel.gov/docs/fy22osti/78722.pdf.

Regulations.gov. 2008. "PM2.5 NSR Implementation Final Rule. Revised Draft Federal Register Notice Transmitted to Office of Management and Budget (OMB) for Review August 27, 2007." Regulations.gov. Accessed October 23, 2022. https://www.regulations.gov/document/EPA-HQ-OAR-2003-0062-0271.

Rothschild, Edwin. 1989. *Cancer at the Pump*. Indianapolis, Indiana: Citizens Action.

Stanfield, Sky. 2004. "The Mobile Source Air Toxics Rule: How Does the Greatest Reduction Become No Reduction?" *Ecology Law Quarterly* 31, no. 3: 563–87. http://www.jstor.org/stable/24114227.

Union of Concerned Scientists. 2013. "The EPA's Tier 3 Fuel and Vehicle Standards Drastically Reduced Air Pollution and Improved Public Health." Union of Concerned Scientists. Accessed October 5, 2022. https://www.ucsusa.org/resources/epas-tier-3-standards.

Urgun-Demirtas, Meltem. 2019. "GREET: The Greenhouse Gases, Regulated Emissions, and Energy Use in Transportation Model." *Bioprose* (blog), *US Department of Energy*. May 16, 2019. https://www.energy.gov/eere/bioenergy/articles/greet-greenhouse-gases-regulated-emissions-and-energy-use-transportation.

US Environmental Protection Agency. 2007. "Control of Hazardous Air Pollutants from Mobile Sources Regulatory Impact Analysis: Assessment and Standards Division Office of Transportation and Air Quality US Environmental Protection Agency." Washington, DC: US Environmental Protection Agency. https://nepis.epa.gov/Exe/ZyPdf.cgi?Dockey=P1004LNN.PDF.

CHAPTER 8

Anderson, J, T. Wallington, R. Stein, and W. Studzinski. 2014. "Issues with T50 and T90 as Match Criteria for Ethanol-Gasoline Blends," *SAE Int. J. Fuels Lubr.* 7, no. 3 (November): 1027-1040. https://doi.org/10.4271/2014-01-9080.

Blum, Deborah. 2018. *The Poison Squad: One Chemist's Single-Minded Crusade for Food Safety at the Turn of the Twentieth Century*. New York, New York: Penguin Publishing.

Boyden Gray & Associates. 2017. "BG&A Files Request for Correction on Behalf of Kansas and Nebraska, Calling on EPA to Fix Flawed Emissions Model." Boyden Gray & Associates. Accessed October 8, 2022. https://boydengrayassociates.com/bga-files-request-for-correction-on-behalf-of-kansas-and-nebraska-calling-on-epa-to-correct-its-erroneous-emissions-factors/.

Boyden Gray & Associates. 2017. "EPAct/V2/E-89 and Motor Vehicle Emissions Simulator Model (MOVES2014) (Jan. 19, 2017)." Boyden Gray & Associates. Accessed October 8, 2022. https://boydengrayassociates.com/request-for-correction-of-information-concerning-epas-epactv2e-89-and-motor-vehicle-emissions-simulator-model-moves2014-jan-19-2017/.

Boyden Gray & Associates. 2016. "EPA Emails Show the Agency Relied on the Oil Industry to Design Anti-Ethanol Fuel Effects Study." Clean Fuels Development Coalition. Accessed July 2019. http://cleanfuelsdc.org/wp-content/uploads/2019/04/BGA-FOIA-EPA-EPact-Emails-Nov-4-2016.pdf.

California Proposition 65. 2016. "Service Stations." California Proposition 65. Accessed December 12, 2022. https://www.p65warnings.ca.gov/places/service-stations.

Lacombe, Romain. 2015. "Global Pandemic - Air Pollution." TedTalks YouTube Channel. April 30, 2015. 19:06. https://www.youtube.com/watch?v=FKBVwX8dVhI.

Public Broadcasting System. 2020. "The Poison Squad." Public Broadcasting System. January 28, 2022. 1:51:02 https://www.pbs.org/video/the-poison-squad-5sf93j/.

Sinclair, Upton. 1984. *The Jungle.* Cutchogue, New York: Buccaneer Books.

Thrasher, James, Amira Osman, and Dien Anshari. 2013 "Images in Cigarette Warning Labels: How Should They Warn?" *Virtual Mentor* 15, no. 8 (August): 704–712. https://journalofethics.ama-assn.org/article/images-cigarette-warning-labels-how-should-they-warn/2013-08.

US Environmental Protection Agency. 2022. "Latest Version of Motor Vehicle Emission Simulator (MOVES)." US Environmental Protection Agency. Accessed December 28, 2022. https://www.epa.gov/moves/latest-version-motor-vehicle-emission-simulator-moves.

US House of Representatives. 2022. "Historical Highlights the Pure Food and Drug Act." US House of Representatives. Accessed October 20, 2022. https://history.house.gov/Historical-Highlights/1901-1950/Pure-Food-and-Drug-Act/.

CHAPTER 9

Clean Fuels Development Coalition. 2018. "Clean Fuels Development Coalition et al, Comments on the Proposed Safer Affordable Fuel-Efficient (SAFE) Vehicles Rule for Model Years 2021–2026 Passenger Cars and Light Trucks." Clean Fuels Development Coalition. Accessed October 8, 2022. https://cleanfuelsdc.org/wp-content/uploads/2022/10/SAFE-Rule-EPA-Docket-Comments-CFDC-10-26-18.pdf.

Farmers Union Enterprises. 2019. "Gasolinegate: A Report from the Farmers Union Enterprises." Clean Fuels Development Coalition. Accessed November 11, 2022. https://cleanfuelsdc.org/wp-content/uploads/2021/12/CFDC-GasolinegateReport.pdf.

Major League Baseball. 2021. "Yogi Berra's Most Memorable Sayings." Major League Baseball. Accessed November 10, 2022. https://www.mlb.com/news/yogisms-best-yogi-berra-sayings.

National Highway and Transportation Safety Administration. 2021. "Corporate Average Fuel Economy." National Highway and Transportation Safety Administration. Accessed October 9, 2022. https://www.nhtsa.gov/laws-regulations/corporate-average-fuel-economy.

CHAPTER 10

Appelbaum, Binyamin. 2022. "Enough about Climate Change. Air Pollution Is Killing Us Now." *The New York Times.* April 19, 2022. https://www.nytimes.com/2022/04/19/opinion/air-pollution-fossil-fuels.html.

Fuller, Richard, Philip Landrigan, Kalpana Balakrishnan, Glynda Bathan, et al. 2017. "Pollution and Health: A Progress Update." *The Lancet Planetary Health* 6, no. 6 (May): E535–E547. https://doi.org/10.1016/S2542-5196(22)00090-0.

Jacobs, Hillary. 2015. "Environmental Justice in Maryland." *University of Maryland Environmental Law Clinic* (blog). *Beveridge & Diamond.* September 2015 (missing full date). Accessed October 31, 2022. https://www.bdlaw.com/publications/environmental-justice-in-maryland/.

Lieser, Ethen. 2020. "Study: Air Pollution Linked to 15% of All Coronavirus Deaths." *The National Interest.* October 2020. https://nationalinterest.org/blog/coronavirus/study-air-pollution-linked-15-all-coronavirus-deaths-171497.

National Aeronautics and Space Administration. 2020. "NASA Model Reveals How Much COVID-Related Pollution Levels Deviated from the Norm." NASA. November 17, 2020. https://www.nasa.gov/feature/goddard/2020/nasa-model-reveals-how-much-covid-related-pollution-levels-deviated-from-the-norm.

Perls, Hannah. 2020. "EPA Undermines Its Own Environmental Justice Programs." *Energy & Environmental Law Program* (blog). *Harvard Environmental Law School*. November 12, 2020. https://eelp.law.harvard.edu/2020/11/epa-undermines-its-own-environmental-justice-programs/.

Sullivan, Will. 2022. "EPA Creates National Office for Environmental Justice and Civil Rights." *Smithsonian Magazine*. September 2022. https://www.smithsonianmag.com/smart-news/epa-creates-national-office-for-environmental-justice-and-civil-rights-180980846/.

US Council on Environmental Quality. 2022. "Climate and Economic Justice Screening Tool." US Council on Environmental Quality. Accessed October 31, 2022. https://screeningtool.geoplatform.gov/en/#3/33.47/-97.5.

US Energy Information Administration. 2022. "Frequently Asked Questions: How Much Gasoline Does the United States Consume? And Diesel Fuel Explained: Use of Diesel." US Energy Information Administration. Accessed October 31, 2022. https://www.eia.gov/tools/faqs/faq.php?id=23&t=10.

US Energy Information Administration. 2020. "Crude Oil Prices Briefly Traded below $0 in Spring 2020 but Have since

Been Mostly Flat." US Energy Information Administration. Accessed November 11, 2020. https://www.eia.gov/todayinenergy/detail.php?id=46336.

US Environmental Protection Agency. 2022. "EPA Administrator Regan Announces Bold Actions to Protect Communities Following the Journey to Justice Tour." US EPA. https://www.epa.gov/newsreleases/epa-administrator-regan-announces-bold-actions-protect-communities-following-journey

US Environmental Protection Agency. 2017. "About the Office of Environmental Justice." US Environmental Protection Agency. October 31, 2022. https://www.epa.gov/sites/default/files/2017-09/documents/epa_office_of_environmental_justice_factsheet.pdf.

White House. 2021. "White House Announces Environmental Justice Advisory Council Members." White House. Accessed October 31, 2022. https://www.whitehouse.gov/ceq/news-updates/2021/03/29/white-house-announces-environmental-justice-advisory-council-members.

World Health Organization. 2022. Fact Sheet: "Ambient (Outdoor) Air Pollution." World Health Organization. Accessed October 22, 2022. https://www.who.int/news-room/fact-sheets/detail/ambient-(outdoor)-air-quality-and-health.

Wu, X., Nethery, R. C., Sabath, M. B., Braun, D. and Dominici, F., 2020. "Air Pollution and COVID-19 Mortality in the United States: Strengths and Limitations of an Ecological Regression Analysis." *Science Advances*, 6(45), p.eabd4049. https://projects.iq.harvard.edu/covid-pm.

CHAPTER 11

American Association for the Advancement of Science. 2016. "Press Release: Fossil Fuel Combustion Endangers Children's Health in Two Significant Ways: A Scientist Reviews the Evidence Children Are Vulnerable to Toxic Air Pollution and the Stressors of Climate Change." June 21, 2016. https://www.eurekalert.org/news-releases/655512.

American Lung Association. 2022. "State of the Air." American Lung Association. Accessed October 22, 2022. https://www.lung.org/research/sota/key-findings.

Caiazzo, Fabio, Akshay Ashok, Ian A. Waitz, Steve H.L. Yim, and Steven R.H. Barrett. 2013. "Air Pollution and Early Deaths in the United States. Part I: Quantifying the Impact of Major Sectors in 2005." *Atmospheric Environment* 79 (November): 198–208. https://doi.org/10.1016/j.atmosenv.2013.05.081.

Chu, Jennifer. 2013. "Study: Air Pollution Causes 200,000 Early Deaths Each Year in the US" *MIT News*. Massachusetts Institute of Technology. August 29, 2013. https://news.mit.edu/2013/study-air-pollution-causes-200000-early-deaths-each-year-in-the-us-0829.

Clean Fuels Development Coalition. 2019. "What's in Our Gasoline Is Killing Us: Mobile Source Air Toxics and the Threat to Public Health." Clean Fuels Development Coalition. Accessed September 11, 2022. https://cleanfuelsdc.org/wp-content/uploads/2019/05/MSAT-Fact-Book_042919.pdf.

Environmental and Energy Study Institute. 2015. "Comments on the Proposed Updates to the Air Quality Standards for Ground

Level Ozone, Docket ID No. EPA-HQ-OAR-2008-0699." Environmental and Energy Study Institute. Accessed October 22, 2022. https://www.eesi.org/files/EESI_Ozone_Regs_Comments_3.17.15.pdf.

Gramlich, John. "What the Data Says about Gun Deaths in the US." Pew Research Center (blog). February 3, 2022. https://www.pewresearch.org/fact-tank/2022/02/03/what-the-data-says-about-gun-deaths-in-the-u-s/.

National Institute of Health 2010. "Testimony Birnbaum February 4, 2010." Accessed May 20, 2019. https://www.niehs.nih.gov/about/assets/docs/testimonybirnbaumfeb042010_508.pdf.

National Institute of Health Sciences. 2022. "Past Directors and Nobel Laureate." National Institute of Health Sciences. Accessed October 23, 2022. https://www.niehs.nih.gov/about/history/pastdirectors/lindabirnbaum/index.cfm.

Nichols, Hannah. 2019. "What Are the Leading Causes of Death in the US?" *Medical News Today* (blog). July 4, 2019. https://www.medicalnewstoday.com/articles/282929.

Pennsylvania Department of Environmental Protection. 2022. "Toxic Pollutant Source Categories." Pennsylvania Department of Environmental Protection. Accessed October 22, 2022. https://www.dep.pa.gov/Business/Air/BAQ/MonitoringTopics/ToxicPollutants/Pages/Source-Categories.aspx#.

Perera, Frederica, and Kari Nadeau. 2022. "Climate Change, Fossil-Fuel Pollution, and Children's Health." *New England*

Journal of Medicine 386, no. 24 (June). https://www.nejm.org/doi/10.1056/NEJMra2117706.

Perera, Frederica. 2016. "Fossil Fuels Threaten Children's Health." Columbia University's Mailman School of Public Health. Columbia University's Mailman School of Public Health. June 21, 2016. 7:58. https://www.eurekalert.org/multimedia/635906.

Posnera, Laura N., and Spyros N. Pandisab. 2015. "Sources of Ultrafine Particles in the Eastern United States." *Atmospheric Environment*, Volume 111, (June 2015): Pages 103–112. https://www.sciencedirect.com/science/article/pii/S1352231015002575?via%3Dihub.

US Energy Information Administration. 2021. "Use of Energy Explained: Energy Use for Transportation." US Energy Information Administration. Accessed October 22, 2022. https://www.eia.gov/energyexplained/use-of-energy/transportation.php.

US Environmental Protection Agency. 2022a. "Climate Change Indicators: Heat-Related Deaths Data." US Environmental Protection Agency. Accessed October 31, 2022. https://www.epa.gov/climate-indicators/climate-change-indicators-heat-related-deaths.

US Environmental Protection Agency. 2022b. "How Mobile Source Pollution Affects Your Health." US Environmental Protection Agency. Accessed October 22, 2022. https://www.epa.gov/mobile-source-pollution/how-mobile-source-pollution-affects-your-health#near-roadway.

US Environmental Protection Agency. 2011. "Benefits and Costs of the Clean Air Act 1990–2020, the Second Prospective Study." US Environmental Protection Agency. Accessed October 22, 2022. https://www.epa.gov/clean-air-act-overview/benefits-and-costs-clean-air-act-1990-2020-second-prospective-study.

CHAPTER 12

Blas, Javier. 2022. "The Saudi-Russian Oil Axis Snubs Biden with Production Cuts." *The Washington Post*. October 5, 2022. https://www.washingtonpost.com/business/energy/the-saudi-russian-oil-axis-snubs-biden-with-production-cuts/2022/10/05/59397aa0-44d8-11ed-be17-89cbe6b8c0a5_story.html.

Britannica. Editors of Encyclopaedia. 2022. "Lobbying." Encyclopedia Britannica. Accessed November 11, 2022. https://www.britannica.com/topic/lobbying.

Boyden Gray & Associates. 2022. "E&E News Points to Boyden Gray & Associates as Leader on Major Questions Doctrine, Apr. 11, 2022." Boyden Gray & Associates. April 13, 2022. https://boydengrayassociates.com/ee-news-points-to-boyden-gray-associates-as-leader-on-major-questions-doctrine-apr-11-2022/.

Boyden Gray & Associates. 2018. "Comments on Roundtable on Anticompetitive Regulations: Removing Regulatory Barriers to Nonpetroleum-Based Fuels Such as Midlevel Ethanol Blends." Department of Justice. May 30, 2018. https://www.justice.gov/atr/page/file/1067206/download.

CNBCTV18. 2021. "India Brings Forward Target of 20% Ethanol-Blending in Petrol to 2023." June 3, 2021. https://www.cnbctv18.com/market/commodities/india-brings-forward-target-of-20-ethanol-blending-in-petrol-to-2023-9527571.htm.

Congressional Record. 1990. "Senate-Thursday, March 29, 1990." GovInfo. Accessed December 28, 2022. https://www.govinfo.gov/content/pkg/GPO-CRECB-1990-pt4/pdf/GPO-CRECB-1990-pt4-7-1.pdf.

Eggen, Dan, and Kimberly Kindy. 2010. "Three of Every Four Oil and Gas Lobbyists Worked for Federal Government." *The Washington Post*. July 22, 2010. https://www.washingtonpost.com/wp-dyn/content/article/2010/07/21/AR2010072106468.html.

Giorno, Taylor. 2022. "Federal Lobbying Topped $3 Billion through Third Quarter for the First Time Ever." OpenSecrets. October 26, 2022. https://www.opensecrets.org/news/2022/10/federal-lobbying-topped-3-billion-through-third-quarter-for-the-first-time-ever.

Grandoni, Dino. 2018. "The Energy 202: Some Senate Republicans Are Skewering Scott Pruitt. And Not Because of Chick-fil-A." *The Washington Post*. June 6, 2018. https://www.washingtonpost.com/news/powerpost/paloma/the-energy-202/2018/06/06/the-energy-202-some-senate-republicans-are-skewering-scott-pruitt-and-not-because-of-chick-fil-a/5b16a0751b326b08e883914c/.

Henry, John 2021. "Committee for the Republic Interview with C. Boyden Gray." Committee for the Republic YouTube

Channel. November 18, 202. 11:30:13. https://www.youtube.com/watch?v=won13ZEndLI.

Hydrocarbon Processing. 2012. "NPRA Finalizes Name Change, Becomes American Fuel & Petrochemical Manufacturers." *Hydrocarbon Processing Magazine.* January 25, 2012. https://www.hydrocarbonprocessing.com/news/2012/01/npra-finalizes-name-change-becomes-american-fuel-petrochemical-manufacturers.

National Geographic. 2019. "Environment/Explainer." *National Geographic.* May 3, 2019. https://www.nationalgeographic.com/science/article/how-trump-is-changing-science-environment.

Needleman, Herbert L. 2000. "The Removal of Lead from Gasoline: Historical and Personal Reflections." *Environmental Research* 84, no. 1 (September): 20-35. https://doi.org/10.1006/enrs.2000.4069.

Nelson, E. Benjamin, Trent Lott, and Joseph Lieberman. 2021. *Death of the Senate: My Front Row Seat to the Demise of the World's Greatest Deliberative Body.* Lincoln, NE: University of Nebraska Press.

OpenSecrets. n.d. "About." OpenSecrets. Accessed November 11, 2022. https://www.opensecrets.org/about.

OpenSecrets. 2022. "Revolving Door: Search Results Agency Search: Environmental Protection Agency Number of Records Found: 210." OpenSecrets. Accessed October 29, 2022. https://www.opensecrets.org/revolving/search_result.php?agency=Environmental+Protection+Agency&id=EIEPA.

OpenSecrets. 2021. "Industry Profile: Oil & Gas (Summary, Lobbyists, Background)." OpenSecrets. Accessed October 29, 2022. https://www.opensecrets.org/federal-lobbying/industries/summary?cycle=2021&id=E01.

OpenSecrets. 2020. "Top Contributors, 2019–202c." OpenSecrets. Accessed October 29, 2022. https://www.opensecrets.org/industries/indus.php?ind=E01&cycle=2020.

US Department of Energy. 2022. "Co-Optimization of Fuels & Engines: Findings and Impact." US Department of Energy. Accessed October 31, 2022. https://www.energy.gov/sites/default/files/2022-06/beto-co-optima-findings-factsheet.pdf.

US Environmental Protection Agency. 2018. "The Senate Does Its Duty." Twitter, April 13, 2018, 9:00 a.m. https://twitter.com/EPA/status/984778229356605443.

Vogelsong, Sarah. 2022. "Wheeler to Remain in Youngkin Administration as Senior Adviser." *Virginia Mercury*. March 14, 2022. https://www.virginiamercury.com/blog-va/wheeler-to-remain-in-youngkin-administration-as-senior-adviser/.

CHAPTER 13

Aoun, Gabriela. 2022. "California Wants Everyone to Drive EVs. How Will Low-Income People Afford Them?" *The Guardian*. October 13, 2022. https://www.theguardian.com/us-news/2022/oct/13/electric-vehicles-evs-california-low-income.

Austin, Anna. 2008. "The Road Ahead for FFVs." Ethanol Producer Magazine. *Ethanol Producer Magazine,* November

5, 2022. https://ethanolproducer.com/articles/5010/the-road-ahead-for-ffvs.

Auto.com. 2022. "More Flex-Fuel Vehicles Coming from General Motors." Auto.com (blog). Accessed November 5, 2022. https://www.auto123.com/en/news/more-flex-fuel-vehicles-coming-from-general-motors/46610/.

Blitzer, Ronn. 2022. "Marco Rubio Says California Electric Car Plan 'Self-Defeating': People Will Be 'Charging Their Cars with Coal." *Fox Business*. September 18, 2022. https://www.foxbusiness.com/politics/marco-rubio-says-california-electric-car-plan-self-defeating-people-will-be-charging-cars-coal.

Brown, Alex. 2022. "Electric Vehicles Charge Ahead in Statehouses." *Stateline Magazine*, January 24, 2022. https://www.pewtrusts.org/en/research-and-analysis/blogs/stateline/2022/01/24/electric-vehicles-charge-ahead-in-statehouses

Cama, Timothy. 2021. "Republicans Slam Biden Car Rule, Predict Higher Costs." *E&E Daily* (blog). *E&E News*. August 6, 2021. https://www.eenews.net/articles/republicans-slam-biden-car-rule-predict-higher-costs/.

Carey, Isabel. 2022. "Americans Support Incentives for Electric Vehicles but Are Divided over Buying One Themselves." Pew Research Center. August 1, 2022. https://www.pewresearch.org/fact-tank/2022/08/01/americans-support-incentives-for-electric-vehicles-but-are-divided-over-buying-one-themselves/.

Dolsak, Nives, and Aseem Prakash. 2022. "California Is Facing an Electricity Crisis. But It Has Also Mandated a Switchover to Electric Vehicles." *Forbes*, September 8, 2022. https://www.forbes.com/sites/prakashdolsak/2022/09/08/california-is-facing-an-electricity-crisis-but-it-has-also-mandated-a-switchover-to-electric-vehicles/?sh=7f9f38865671.

Elbein, Saul. 2022. "Climate Change Overwhelming California Power Grid." *The Hill*. September 6, 2022. https://thehill.com/policy/equilibrium-sustainability/3631118-climate-change-overwhelming-california-power-grid/.

Fuel Economy.gov. 2022. "Fuel Economy Ratings." US Department of Energy. Accessed November 11, 2022. http://bit.ly/3GruoAe.

Forrest, Jack. 2022. "Republicans Seek to Block State Gasoline Car Phaseouts." *Governors' Wind & Solar Energy Coalition* (blog). September 8, 2022. https://governorswindenergycoalition.org/republicans-seek-to-block-state-gasoline-car-phaseouts/.

Fortune. 1990. "A Database of 50 Years of FORTUNE's List of America's Largest Corporations." *Fortune*. Accessed December 12, 2022. https://archive.fortune.com/magazines/fortune/fortune500_archive/full/1990/.

General Motors. 2010. "General Motors Statement on Flex-Fuel Vehicle Pledge." General Motors. Accessed November 5, 2022. https://news.gm.com/newsroom.detail.html/Pages/news/us/en/2010/May/0505_flexfuel.html.

Groom, Nichola, and Nick Carey. 2008. "GM Unveils Electric Volt." *Reuters*. November 5, 2022. https://www.reuters.com/article/us-gm-volt-idUSN1637715120080916

Grubs, Alex. 2015. "AAA Rescued Record 32 Million Drivers in 2015; Blames New Technology for Breakdowns." *CNSNews*. July 22, 2018. https://www.cnsnews.com/news/article/alex-grubbs/aaa-rescued-record-32-million-drivers-2015-blames-new-technology-breakdowns.

Hardesty, Chris. 2022. "Average Miles Driven per Year: Why It Is Important." *Kelly Blue Book*. September 8, 2022. https://www.kbb.com/car-advice/average-miles-driven-per-year/.

Henry, Jim. 2022. "Toyota Exec Says Lack of Consumer Demand Makes US Goal of 50% Electric Vehicles by 2030 a Long Shot." *Forbes*. August 23, 2022. https://www.forbes.com/sites/jimhenry/2022/08/23/toyota-exec-says-lack-of-consumer-demand-makes-us-goal-of-50-electric-vehicles-by-2030-a-long-shot/?sh=41a90225b830.

Kopestinsky, Alex. 2022. "What Is the Average American Income in 2022?" *PolicyAdvice*. October 25, 2022. https://policyadvice.net/insurance/insights/average-american-income/.

Lane, Charles. 2021. "Why Electric Cars Still Don't Live Up to the Hype." The Washington Post. December 30, 2019. https://www.washingtonpost.com/opinions/why-electric-cars-still-dont-live-up-to-the-hype/2019/12/30/242ce200-2b29-11ea-bcd4-24597950008f_story.html.

Lewis, Jack. 1985. "Lead Poisoning: A Historical Perspective." US Environmental Protection Agency. Accessed November 5, 2022. https://archive.epa.gov/epa/aboutepa/lead-poisoning-historical-perspective.html.

Maclean, Heather, Alexandre Milovanoff, and Daniel Posen. "We Need More Than Just Electric Vehicles." *The Institute of Electrical and Electronics Engineers.* August 20, 2022. https://spectrum.ieee.org/electric-cars-2657880896.

MIT Energy Initiative. 2019. Insights into Future Mobility. Cambridge, MA: MIT Energy Initiative. http://energy.mit.edu/insightsintofuturemobility.

Mollman, Steve. 2022. "Electric-Vehicle Fires Have Burned Down Homes after Hurricane Ian Saltwater Damage. Florida Officials Want Answers." *Fortune.* October 15, 2022. https://fortune.com/2022/10/15/electric-vehicle-fires-homes-burned-hurricane-ian-saltwater-flooding-ev-batteries/.

National Highway Traffic Safety Administration. 2022. "CAFE Light Duty Program Reports." National Highway Traffic Safety Administration. Accessed November 11, 2022. https://one.nhtsa.cafécafe_pic/home/ldreports.

National Highway Traffic Safety Administration. 2014. "Summary of Fuel Economy Performance." National Highway Transportation. Accessed November 11, 2022. https://www.nhtsa.gov/staticfiles/rulemakcafépdf/cafe/Performance-summary-report-12152014-v2.pdf.

Natter, Ari, 2022. "US Energy Secretary Offers Olive Branch to Oil and Gas Industry." *Bloomberg*. December 14, 2022. https://www.bloomberg.com/news/articles/2022-12-14/us-energy-secretary-offers-olive-branch-to-oil-and-gas-industry.

O'Hare, Ben. 2022. "Honda Exec: Lithium-Ion EVs Will Always Be More Expensive than Gas Cars." *InsideEVs*. September 18, 2022. https://insideevs.com/news/610961/honda-exec-lithium-ion-expensive/.

OhmHome. 2022. "EV Charging Station Cost." OhmHome. Accessed October 2, 2022. https://www.ohmhomenow.com/electric-vehicles/ev-charging-station-cost/.

Perkins, Tom. 2022. "Biden Talks up Electric Vehicle Revolution – But Is America Ready to Give up Gas?" *The Guardian*. September 17, 2022. https://www.theguardian.com/business/2022/sep/17/biden-electric-vehicle-revolution-detroit-auto-show.

Probasco, Jim. 2022. "Biden Signs Inflation Reduction Act into Law." *Investopedia*. August 16, 2022. https://www.investopedia.com/biden-signs-inflation-reduction-act-6452601.

Rauch, Marc. 2021. "The Real Story on Electric Vehicles." *The Auto Channel* (blog). Accessed December 28, 2022. https://www.theautochannel.com/news/2021/12/03/1078802-real-story-viability-electric-vehicles.html.

Schwartz, Hart. 2018. "America's Aging Vehicles Delay Rate of Fleet Turnover" *The Fuse* (blog), *SAFE*. January 23, 2018.

http://energyfuse.org/americas-aging-vehicles-delay-rate-fleet-turnover/.

Shepardson, David. 2022. "Automakers Say US Senate Bill Will Jeopardize 2030 EV Targets." *Reuters*. January 23, 2018 https://www.reuters.com/business/autos-transportation/automakers-say-us-senate-bill-will-jeopardize-2030-ev-targets-2022-08-07.

Statistica. 2022a. "Number of Motor Vehicles Registered in the United States from 1990 to 2020." Statistica. Accessed November 5, 2022. https://www.statista.com/statistics/183505/number-of-vehicles-in-the-united-states-since-1990/.

Statistica. 2022b. "Number of Vehicles in Operation in the United States between 1st Quarter 2018 and 2nd Quarter 2022." Statistica. Accessed November 1, 2022. https://www.statista.com/statistics/859950/vehicles-in-operation-by-quarter-united-states/.

US Department of Commerce. 2022. "US Population Estimated at 332,403,650 on Jan. 1, 2022." *Blog, US Department of Commerce*. January 6, 2022. https://www.commerce.gov/news/blog/2022/01/us-population-estimated-332403650-jan-1-2022.

US Department of Energy. 2022. "More than Half of All Daily Trips Were Less than Three Miles in 2021." Office of Energy Efficiency & Renewable Energy. March 21, 2022. https://www.energy.gov/eere/vehicles/articles/fotw-1230-march-21-2022-more-half-all-daily-trips-were-less-three-miles-2021.

Valdes-Dapena, Peter. 2022. "Gas Prices Are Falling. So Is Interest in Electric Cars." *CNN Business*. August 5, 2022. https://www.

cnn.com/2022/08/05/business/ev-hybrid-shopping-gas-prices/index.html.

Vogelsong. 2022. "California's 2035 Ban on New Gas-Powered Cars Set to Apply to Virginia." *Virginia Mercury*. August 26, 2022. https://www.virginiamercury.com/2022/08/26/californias-2035-ban-on-new-gas-powered-cars-set-to-apply-to-virginia/.

Walton, Robert. 2017. "Georgia Electric Vehicle Sales Shrink 80% in Wake of Tax Credit Repeal." UtilityDrive. Accessed November 5, 2022. https://www.utilitydive.com/news/georgia-electric-vehicle-sales-shrink-80-in-wake-of-tax-credit-repeal/434092/.

Wayland, Michael. 2022. "Toyota Hits Electric-Vehicle Sales Milestone, Joins Tesla and GM in Triggering Phaseout of Tax Incentives for Buyers." *CNBC*. July 6, 2022. https://www.cnbc.com/2022/07/06/toyota-joins-tesla-and-gm-in-losing-federal-ev-tax-credits.html.

Wayland, Michael. 2022. "Why Toyota – the World's Largest Automaker – Isn't All-in on Electric Vehicles." *CNBC*. September 13, 2022. https://www.cnbc.com/2022/09/13/why-toyota-the-worlds-largest-automaker-isnt-all-in-on-evs.html.

White House. 2021. "Fact Sheet: The Biden-Harris Electric Vehicle Charging Action Plan." White House. December 13, 2021. https://www.whitehouse.gov/briefing-room/statements-releases/2021/12/13/fact-sheet-the-biden-harris-electric-vehicle-charging-action-plan/.

Wirth, Tim, and Charles Grassley. 2019. "Environmental Advocates Should Take Another Look at Biofuels." *The Digest*. August 15, 2019. https://www.biofuelsdigest.com/bdigest/2019/08/15/environmental-advocates-should-take-another-look-at-biofuels/.

CHAPTER 14

Baazil, Diederik, Hugo Miller, and Laura Hurst. 2021. "Shell Loses Climate Case That May Set Precedent for Big Oil." *Bloomberg*, May 26, 2021. https://www.bloomberg.com/news/articles/2021-05-26/shell-loses-climate-case-that-may-set-precedent-for-oil-industry?leadSource=uverify%20wall.

Budryk, Zack. 2022. "Environmental Groups Sue EPA over State Air Pollution Plans." *The Hill*. April 14, 2022. https://thehill.com/policy/energy-environment/3267908-environmental-groups-sue-epa-over-state-air-pollution-plans/.

Center for Biological Diversity. 2022. "Lawsuit Launched Challenging EPA's Failure to Update Air Pollution Emission Standards." Center for Biological Diversity. February 2, 2022. https://biologicaldiversity.org/w/news/press-releases/lawsuit-launched-challenging-epas-failure-to-update-air-pollution-emission-standards-for-soot-sulfur-nitrogen-2022-02-02/.

Dovere, Edward-Isacc. 2018. "Schwarzenegger to Sue Big Oil for 'First Degree Murder.'" *Politico*, March 12, 2018. https://www.politico.com/magazine/story/2018/03/12/arnold-schwarzenegger-sxsw-trump-big-oil-me-too-217345/.

Egelko, Bob. 2022. "S.F., Oakland Can Sue Oil Companies over Climate Change in State." *San Francisco Chronicle*, April 20, 2022. https://www.sfchronicle.com/bayarea/article/S-F-Oakland-can-sue-oil-companies-over-climate-17531944.php.

Environmental Defense Fund. 2022. "Lawsuit Would Compel the Environmental Protection Agency to Enforce Air Pollution Law." Environmental Defense Fund. April 13, 2022. https://www.edf.org/media/lawsuit-would-compel-environmental-protection-agency-enforce-air-pollution-law.

Environmental Integrity Project. 2021. "EPA Underestimates Greenhouse Gas Emissions from US Landfills by at Least 25 Percent." Environmental Integrity Project. December 9, 2021. https://environmentalintegrity.org/news/epa-underestimates-greenhouse-gas-emissions-from-u-s-landfills-by-at-least-25-percent/.

Fitz-Gibbon, Jorge. 2021. "Judge Approves $626M Settlement for Flint Tainted-Water Lawsuit." New York Post, November 10, 2021. https://nypost.com/2021/11/10/judge-approves-626m-settlement-for-flint-tainted-water-lawsuit/.

Fitzgerald, Erin. 2022. "Groups Sue EPA for Stronger Ozone Protections." Earthjustice. June 7, 2022. https://earthjustice.org/news/press/2022/groups-sue-epa-for-stronger-ozone-protections.

Gregorian, Dareh. 2022. "Attorney General Garland Launches Office Focused on Environmental Justice." *NBC News*. May 5, 2022. https://www.nbcnews.com/politics/justice-department/justice-department-launches-new-office-focused-environmental-justice-rcna27556.

Hurley, Lawrence. 2022. "US Supreme Court Takes No Action on Bayer Bid to Nix Weedkiller Suits." *Reuters*. June 13, 2022. https://www.reuters.com/business/us-supreme-court-takes-no-action-bayer-bid-nix-weedkiller-suits-2022-06-13/.

Joselow, Maxine. 2021. "Big Tobacco Had to Pay $206B. Is Big Oil Next?" *E&E Daily* (blog). *E&E News*. March 10, 2021. https://www.eenews.net/articles/big-tobacco-had-to-pay-206b-is-big-oil-next/.

Kane, Julia. 2022. "Environmental Justice Law in New York Could Prevent New Pollution in Hard-Hit Neighborhoods." *Grist*. May 9, 2022. https://grist.org/accountability/new-york-ambitious-environmental-justice-law/.

Laughland, Oliver. 2022. "Proposed Deal Between Residents and EPA Could Slash Toxic Emissions in America's Cancer Alley." *The Guardian*. June 8, 2022. https://www.theguardian.com/environment/2022/jun/08/cancer-alley-louisiana-denka-pollution-consent-decree?CMP=oth_b-aplnews_d-1.

Martin, Marisa, James Landman. 2020. "Standing: Who Can Sue to Protect the Environment?" American Bar Association. October 9, 2020. https://www.americanbar.org/groups/public_education/publications/insights-on-law-and-society/volume-19/insights-vol--19---issue-1/standing--who-can-sue-to-protect-the-environment-/.

Moore, Mike. 1997. "Coalition of State Attorneys General Tobacco Industry Settlement Press Conference." StateAG.org. June 20, 1997. 56:23. https://www.stateag.org/initiatives/the-tobacco-settlement#presser.

National Whistleblower Association. 2022a. "What Does Qui Tam Mean?" National Whistleblower Association. Accessed December 18, 2022. https://www.whistleblowers.org/faq/false-claims-act-qui-tam/.

National Whistleblower Association. 2022b. "Whistleblower Handbook." National Whistleblower Association. Accessed December 18, 2022. https://www.whistleblowers.org/faq/false-claims-act-qui-tam/.

Reilly, Sean. 2022. "EPA Proposes Updating Gasoline Regs, Slashing Emissions." *E&E Daily* (blog). *E&E News*. June 2, 2022. https://www.eenews.net/articles/epa-proposes-updating-gasoline-regs-slashing-emissions/.

Richardson, Mark. 2022. "Salt Lake City, Others Sue EPA for Stronger Ozone Protections." *Grist*, June 13, 2022. https://www.upr.org/utah-news/2022-06-13/salt-lake-city-others-sue-epa-for-stronger-ozone-protections.

Sierra Club. 2021. "Groups Sue EPA for Stronger Clean Air Protections." Sierra Club. Accessed September 9, 2021. https://www.sierraclub.org/press-releases/2021/09/groups-sue-epa-for-stronger-clean-air-protections.

US Environmental Protection Agency. 2022a. "Civil Cases and Settlements by Date." US Environmental Protection

Agency. Accessed November 23, 2022. https://cfpub.epa.gov/enforcement/cases/index.cfm?templatePage=3.

US Environmental Protection Agency 2022b. "Notices of Intent to Sue the US Environmental Protection Agency (EPA)." US Environmental Protection Agency. Accessed November 28, 2022. https://www.epa.gov/ogc/notices-intent-sue-us-environmental-protection-agency-epa.

US Environmental Protection Agency. 2022c. "Our Children's Earth Foundation v. Regan, No. 3:22-cv-00695-WHA (N.D. CA)." US Environmental Protection Agency Proposed Consent Decrees and Draft Settlement Agreements. Accessed November 12, 2022. https://www.epa.gov/ogc/proposed-consent-decrees-and-draft-settlement-agreements#cbdvr227.

US Environmental Protection Agency. 2021. "Notice of Intent to Sue for Failure to Issue Requirements under Renewable Fuel Standard Program. Growth Energy Hereby Provides Notice of Its Intent to Sue the Environmental Protection Agency." US Environmental Protection Agency. Accessed November 12, 2022. https://www.epa.gov/system/files/documents/2021-11/growth-energy-notice-of-intent-to-sue-re-2c22-rvos-and-set.pdf.

US Environmental Protection Agency. 2017a. "Administrator Pruitt Visits Gold King Mine on Anniversary of Spill." US Environmental Protection Agency. August 4, 2017. https://www.epa.gov/archive/epa/newsreleases/administrator-pruitt-visits-gold-king-mine-anniversary-spill.html.

US Environmental Protection Agency. 2017b. "2017 Major Criminal Cases." US Environmental Protection Agency. Accessed November 28, 2022. https://www.epa.gov/enforcement/2017-major-criminal-cases.

CHAPTER 15

Sombke, Doug. 2022. "Editorial: SDFU to President: If You Want to Increase Fuel Supplies Come See What We Are Doing Here." *Morning AgClips* (blog). July 20, 2022. https://www.morningagclips.com/sdfu-to-president-if-you-want-to-increase-fuel-supplies-come-see-what-we-are-doing-here/.

Sombke, Doug. 2022. "Farmers over an Ethanol Barrel: We Aren't Going to Walk the Plank." The Auto Channel. Accessed December 1, 2022. https://www.theautochannel.com/news/2019/10/01/712461-farmers-over-ethanol-barrel-we-arent-going-to-walk-plank.html.

CHAPTER 16

The Digest. 2022. "The Digest." *The Digest*. Accessed November 13, 2022. https://www.biofuelsdigest.com/.

Detchon, Reid, and Reg Modlin. "The Real Cost of Gasoline… Is to Our Health Time for a Cleaner, More Efficient Fuel." Clean Fuels Development Coalition. June 1, 2022. https://cleanfuelsdc.org/wp-content/uploads/2022/05/CFDC-Detchon-ModlinWP.pdf.

Knight-Rider Financial. 1995. "Ethanol Mission Set for Brazil." *Journal of Commerce Online.* August 31, 1995. https://www.joc.com/ethanol-mission-set-brazil_19950831.html.

Somasekhar, Arathy. 2022. "US Gasoline Prices Fall to Pre-Ukraine Invasion Levels." Reuters. August 31, 2022. https://www.reuters.com/business/energy/us-gasoline-futures-settle-lowest-since-before-ukraine-crisis-2022-08-30/.

US Energy Information Administration. 2022. "Oil and Petroleum Products Explained." US Energy Administration. Accessed December 28, 2022. https://www.eia.gov/energyexplained/oil-and-petroleum-products/imports-and-exports.php.

Wachowski, Lana, and Lilly Wachowski. 1999. *The Matrix.* Warner Bros. 1 hr., 36 min.

Zemeckis, Robert. 1985. *Back to the Future.* Universal Pictures. 1 hr., 56 min.

AFTERWORD

Miller, Bennett. 2011. *Moneyball.* Columbia Pictures. 1 hr., 33 min.